Live Life Unleashed

WELCOME TO

Lumpy Gravy

By
John
Long

Workman Publishing · New York

Special Abridged Edition for Scholastic Book Fairs

For more information about Lumpy Gravy and its licensed products, please contact
M. C. E. Media Syndicate, Chicago, IL.

Library of Congress Cataloging-in-Publication Data

Long, John, 1950–
Welcome to Lumpy Gravy / John Long p. cm.
ISBN 0-7611-0735-5 (pbk.)
1. American wit and humor.
Pictorial. I. Title.
NC1429.L566A4 1997
97-9722
741.5'973—dc21 CIP

Workman Publishing Co., Inc.
708 Broadway,
New York, NY
10003-9555

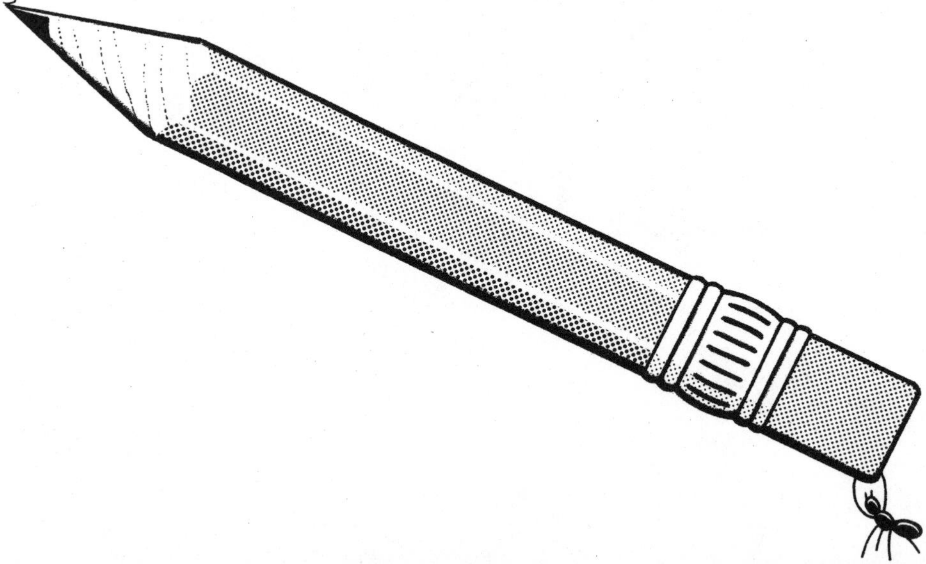

This book exists with the
help of many people
and I thank them all.

I'd especially like to
thank my mom, because
whatever I am today,
it's mostly due to
her guidance,
encouragement
and love.

Also
my wife, Janet, for
saving my life and
feeding my soul.

And,
John Woldenberg for
his hard work, creative
advice and his
never-ending chore of
keeping me focused.

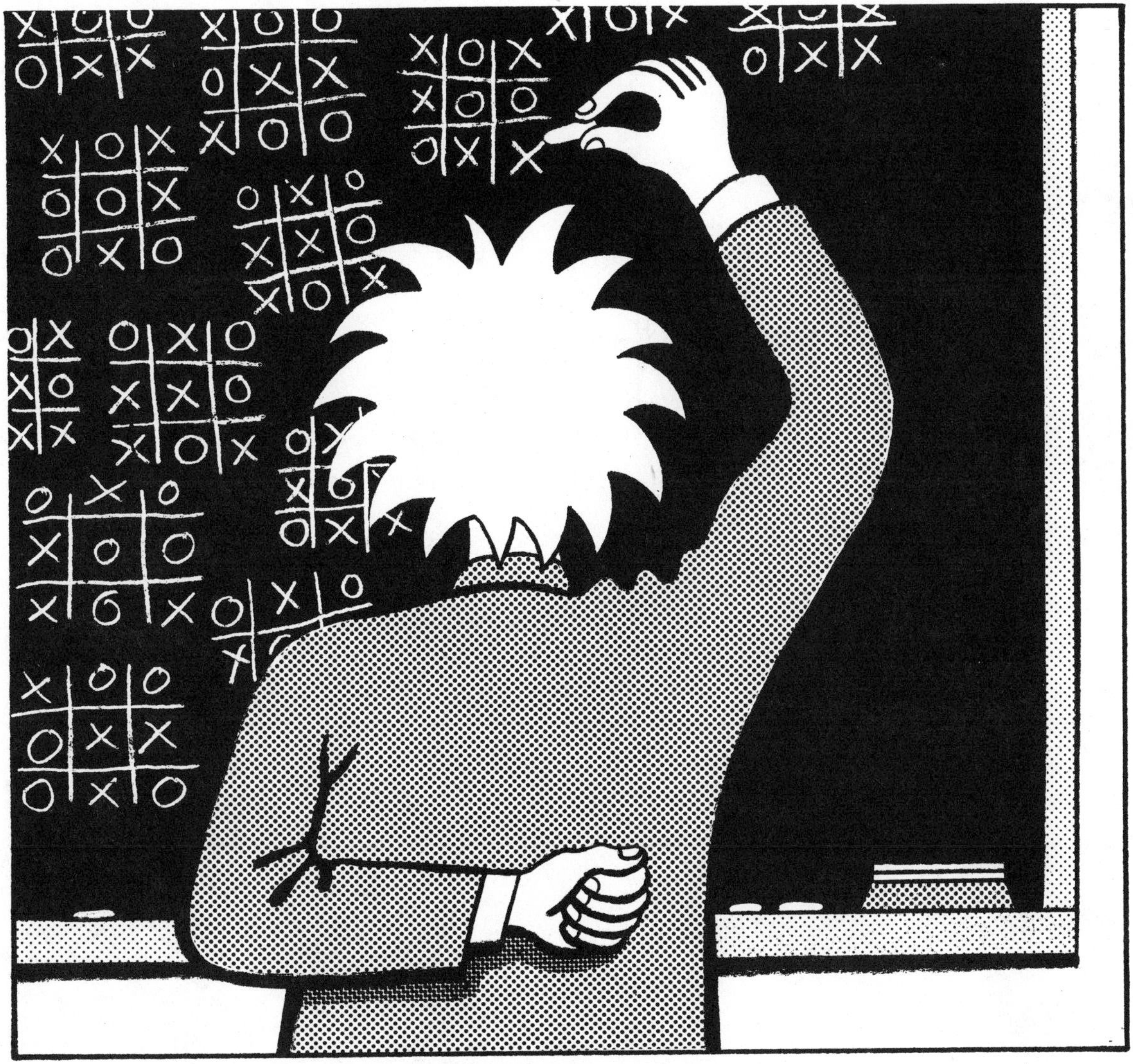

Einstein warming up

Family Life

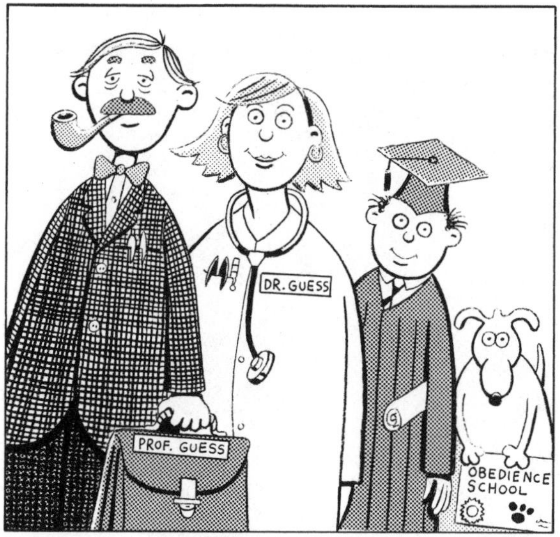
DR. GUESS
PROF. GUESS
OBEDIENCE SCHOOL

Educated Guesses

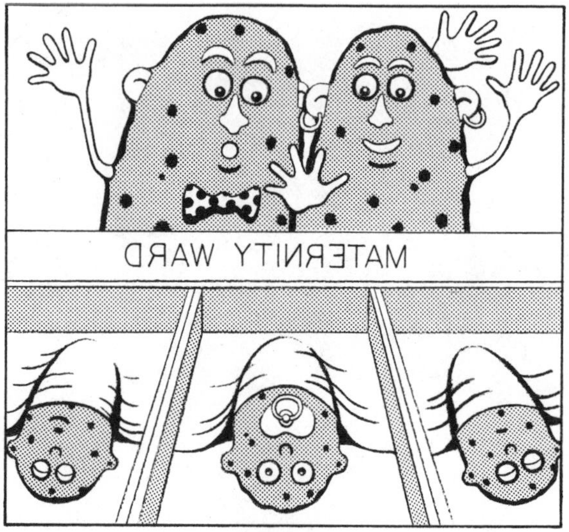
MATERNITY WARD

Tater tots

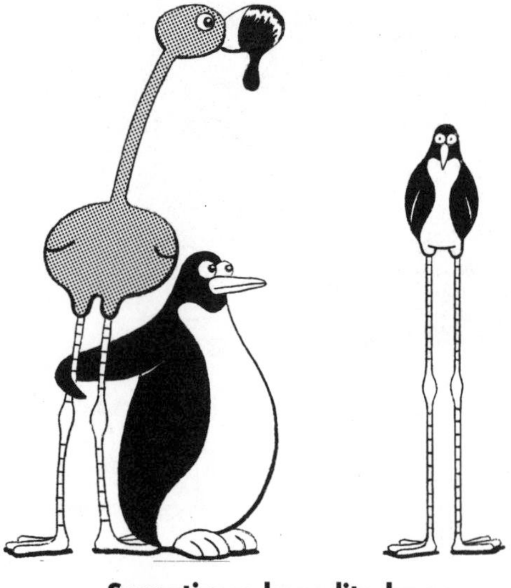

Sometimes heredity has a cruel sense of humor

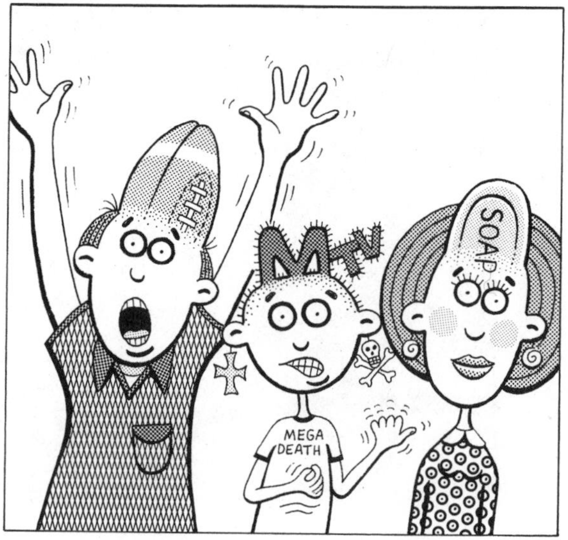
SOAP
MEGA DEATH

You are what you watch

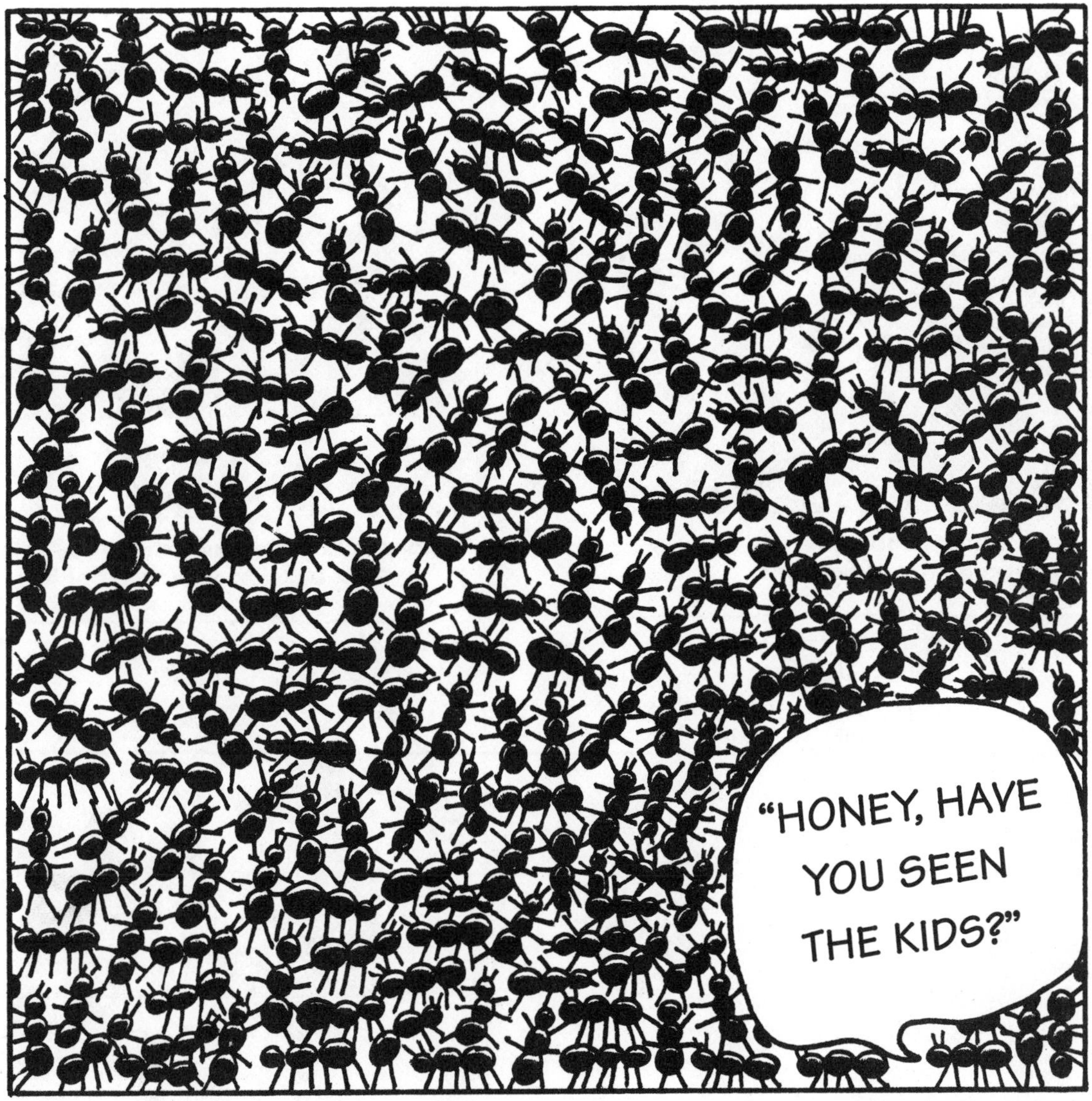
"HONEY, HAVE YOU SEEN THE KIDS?"

New Arrivals

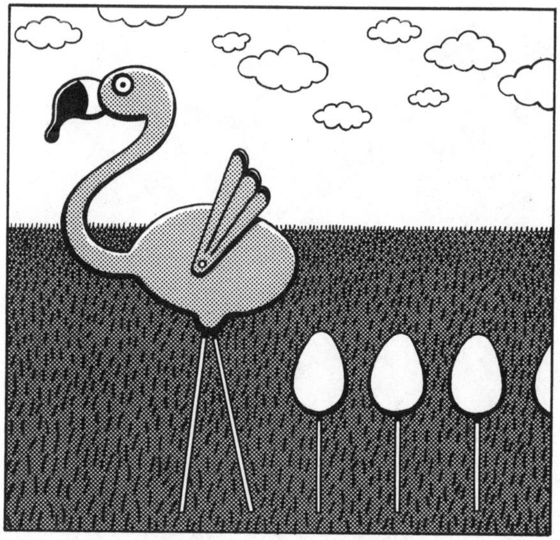

Where baby lawn ornaments come from

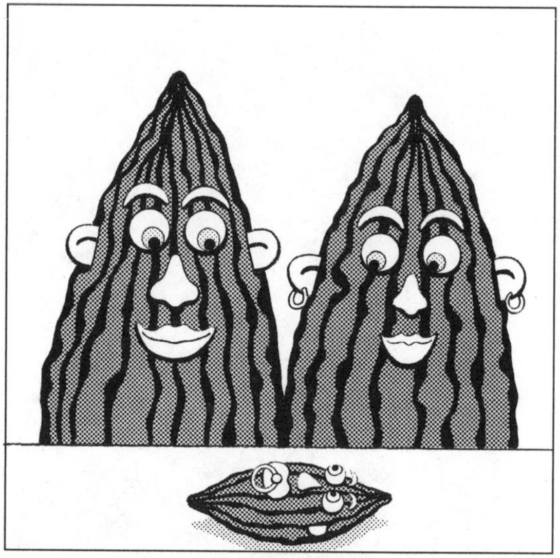

Mr. and Mrs. Raisin affectionately refer to their baby as a new wrinkle

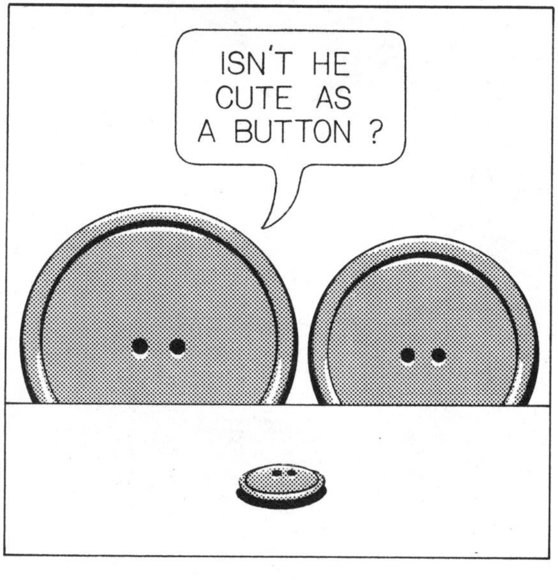
ISN'T HE CUTE AS A BUTTON ?

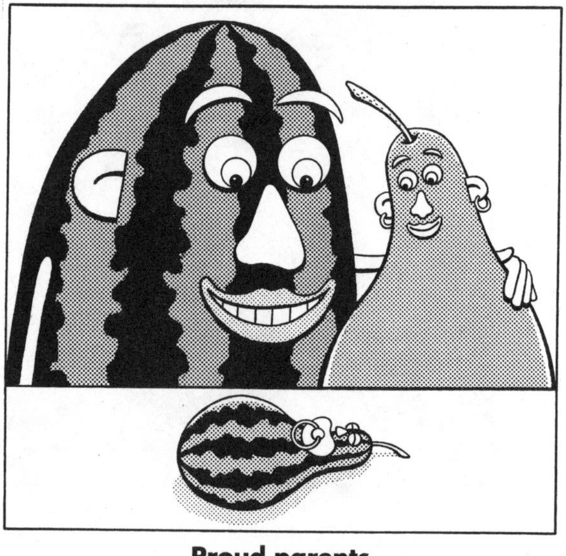

Proud parents

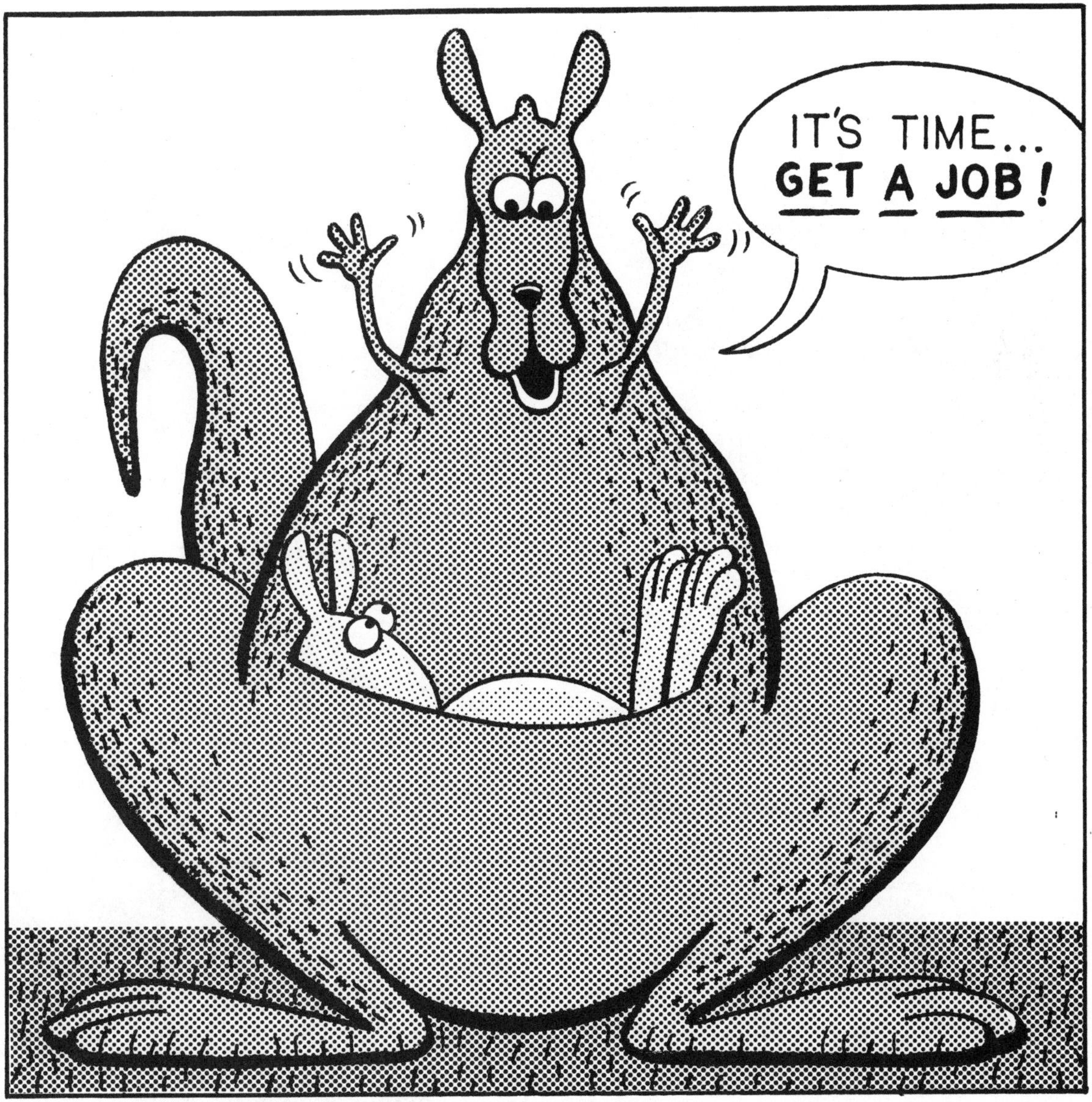
IT'S TIME...
GET A JOB!

Kids Will Be Kids

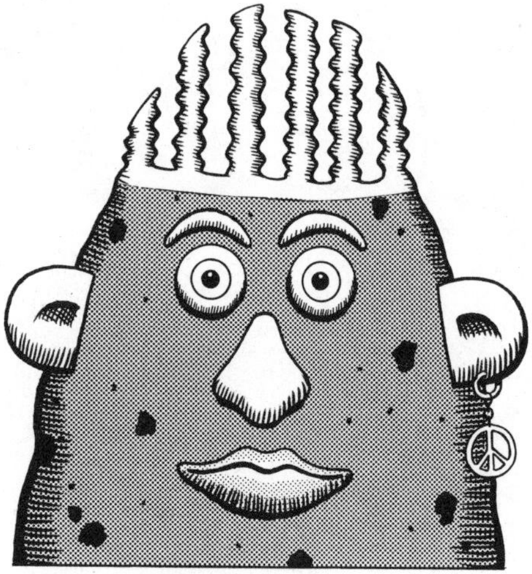

Junior Potato Head decided to get a julienne cut

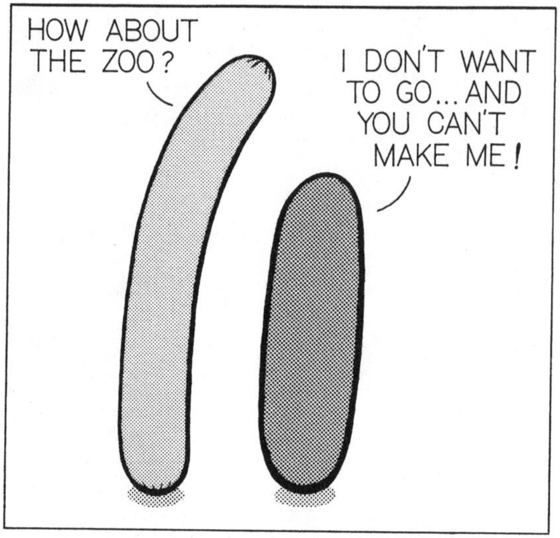
HOW ABOUT THE ZOO?
I DON'T WANT TO GO... AND YOU CAN'T MAKE ME!

Hot dog with a brat

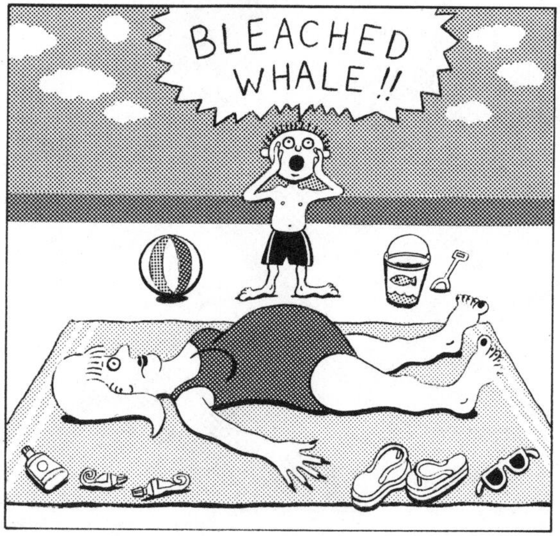
BLEACHED WHALE!!

Beach brat

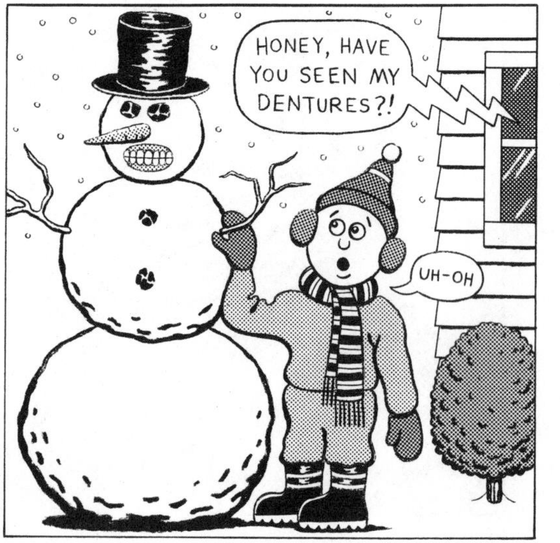
HONEY, HAVE YOU SEEN MY DENTURES?!
UH-OH

Growing Pains

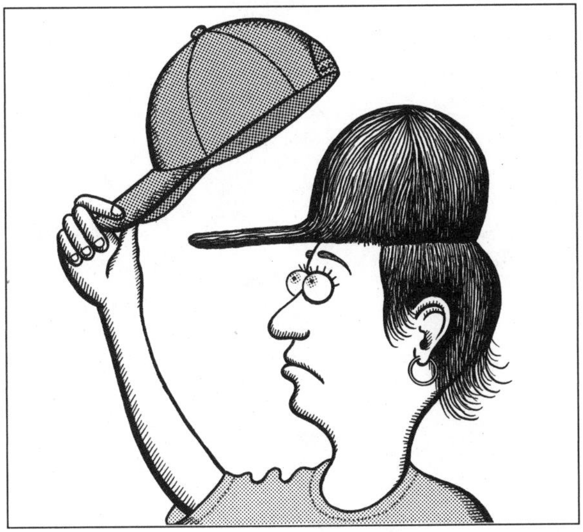

A bad case of hat hair

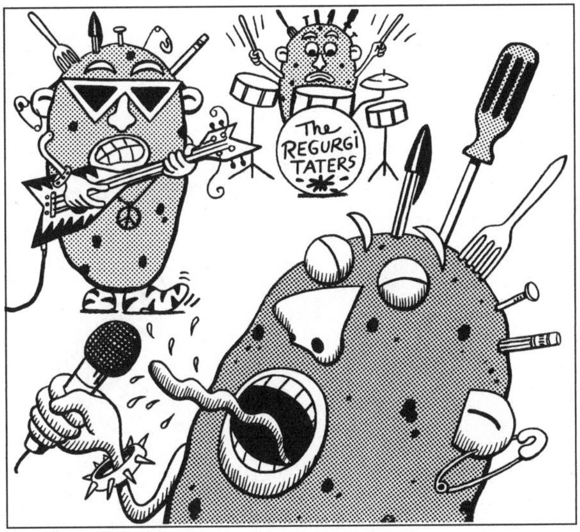
The REGURGI TATERS

The Regurgitaters. . . a punk potato band

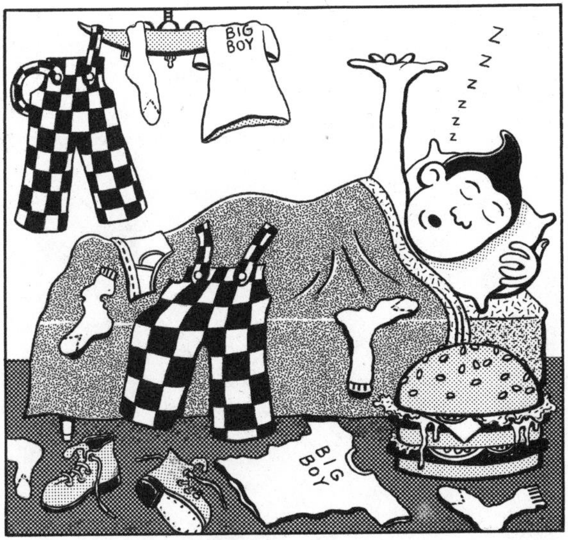
BIG BOY
Z Z Z Z Z Z Z
BIG BOY

Big Boy's room

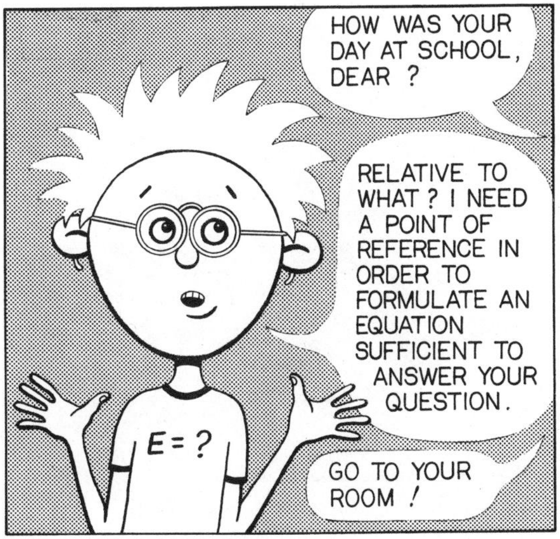
HOW WAS YOUR DAY AT SCHOOL, DEAR ?
RELATIVE TO WHAT ? I NEED A POINT OF REFERENCE IN ORDER TO FORMULATE AN EQUATION SUFFICIENT TO ANSWER YOUR QUESTION.
E = ?
GO TO YOUR ROOM !

Young Albert Einstein

Nature's Young (What We Never See)

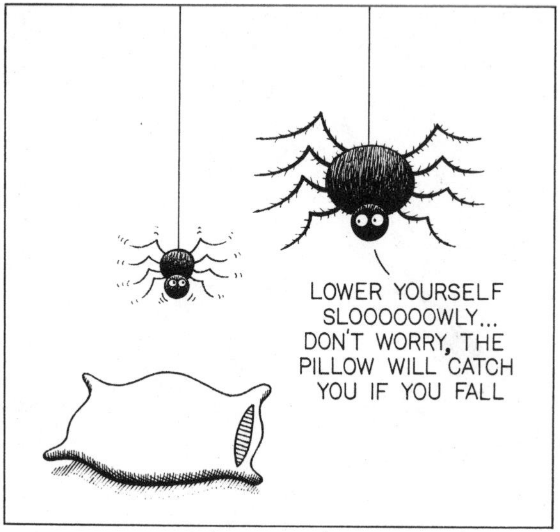
LOWER YOURSELF SLOOOOOOWLY... DON'T WORRY, THE PILLOW WILL CATCH YOU IF YOU FALL

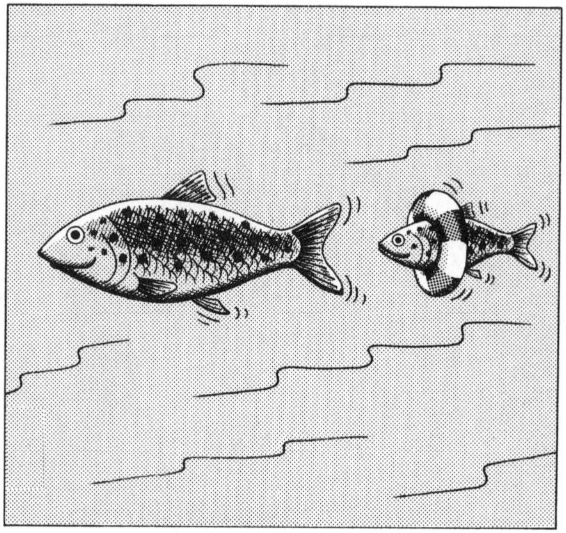

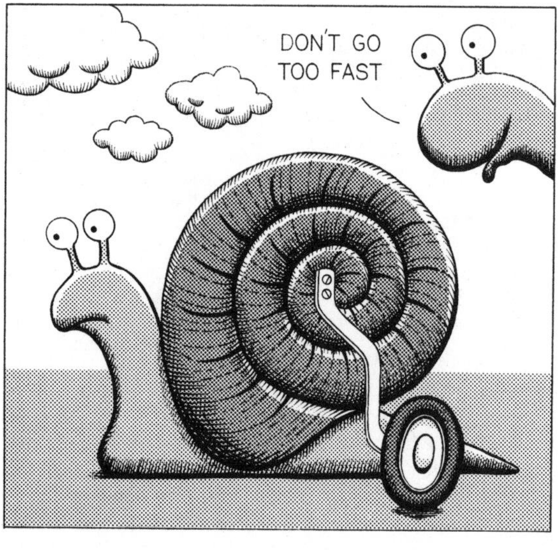
DON'T GO TOO FAST

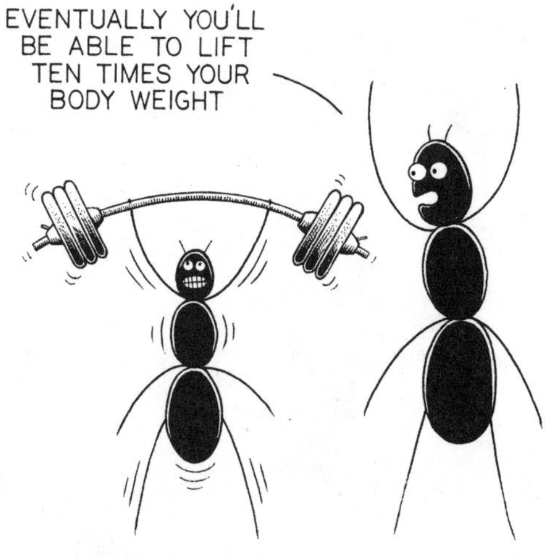
EVENTUALLY YOU'LL BE ABLE TO LIFT TEN TIMES YOUR BODY WEIGHT

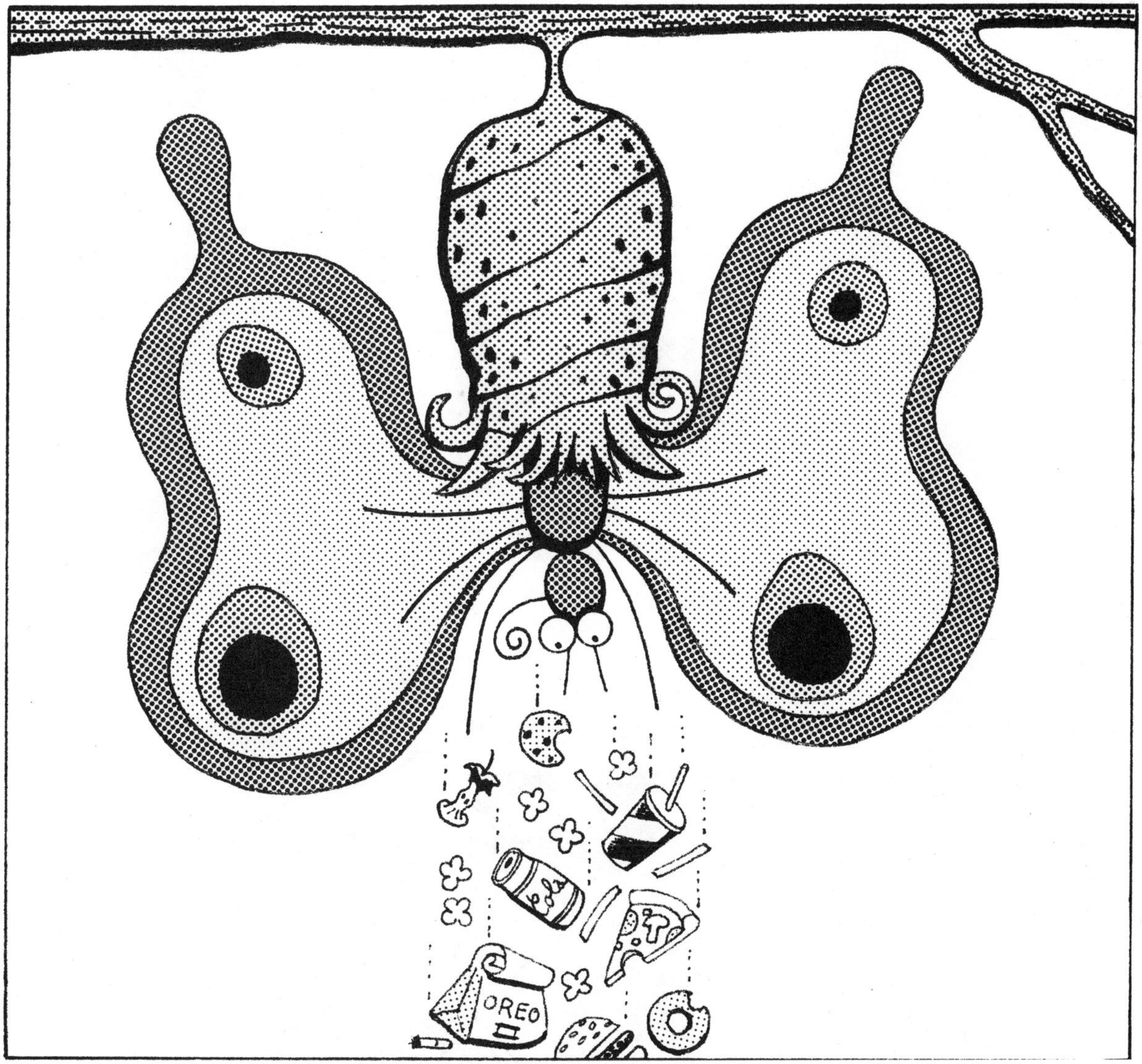
OREO

So much for the wonder of a butterfly emerging from its cocoon

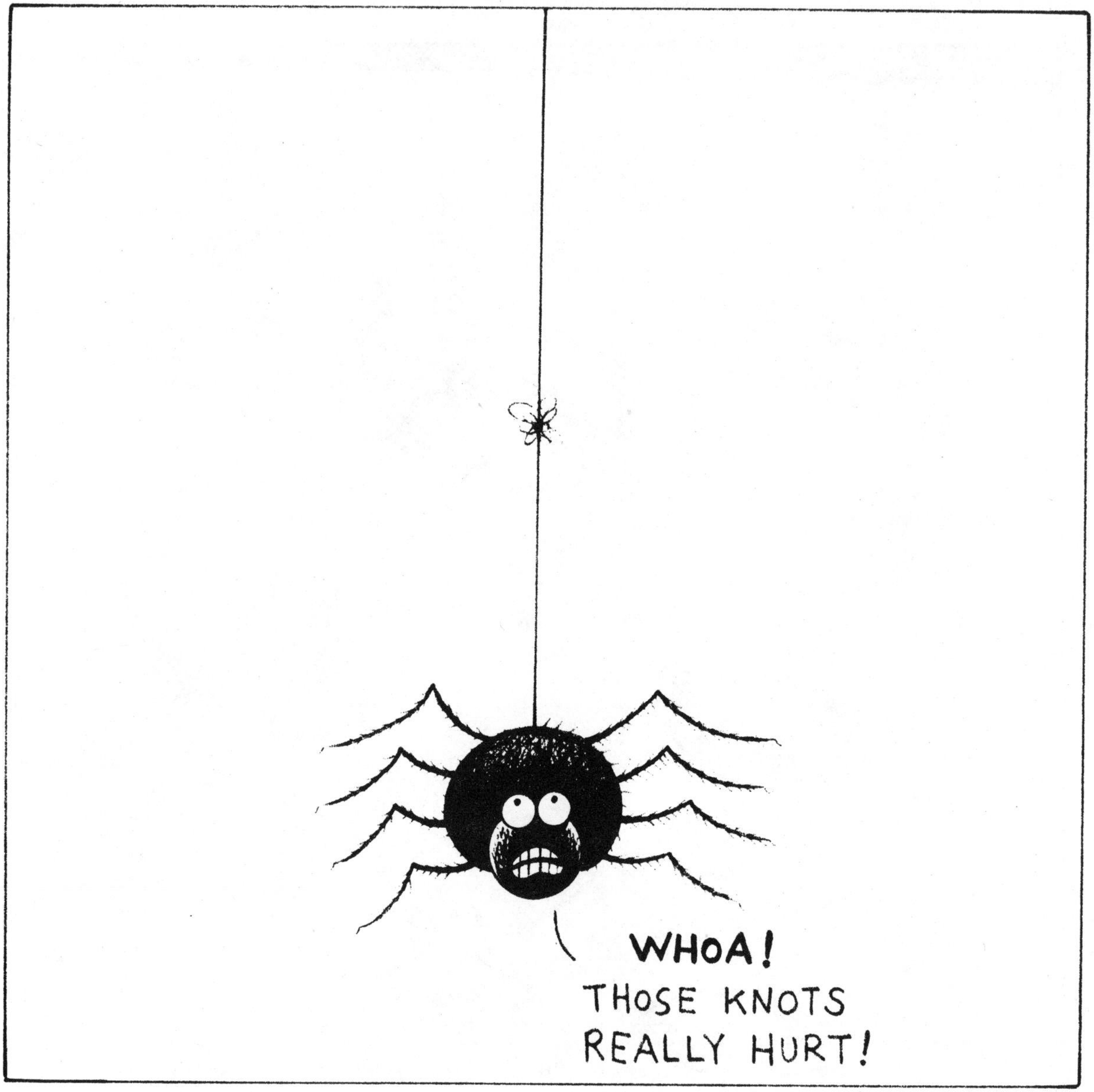
WHOA!
THOSE KNOTS
REALLY HURT!

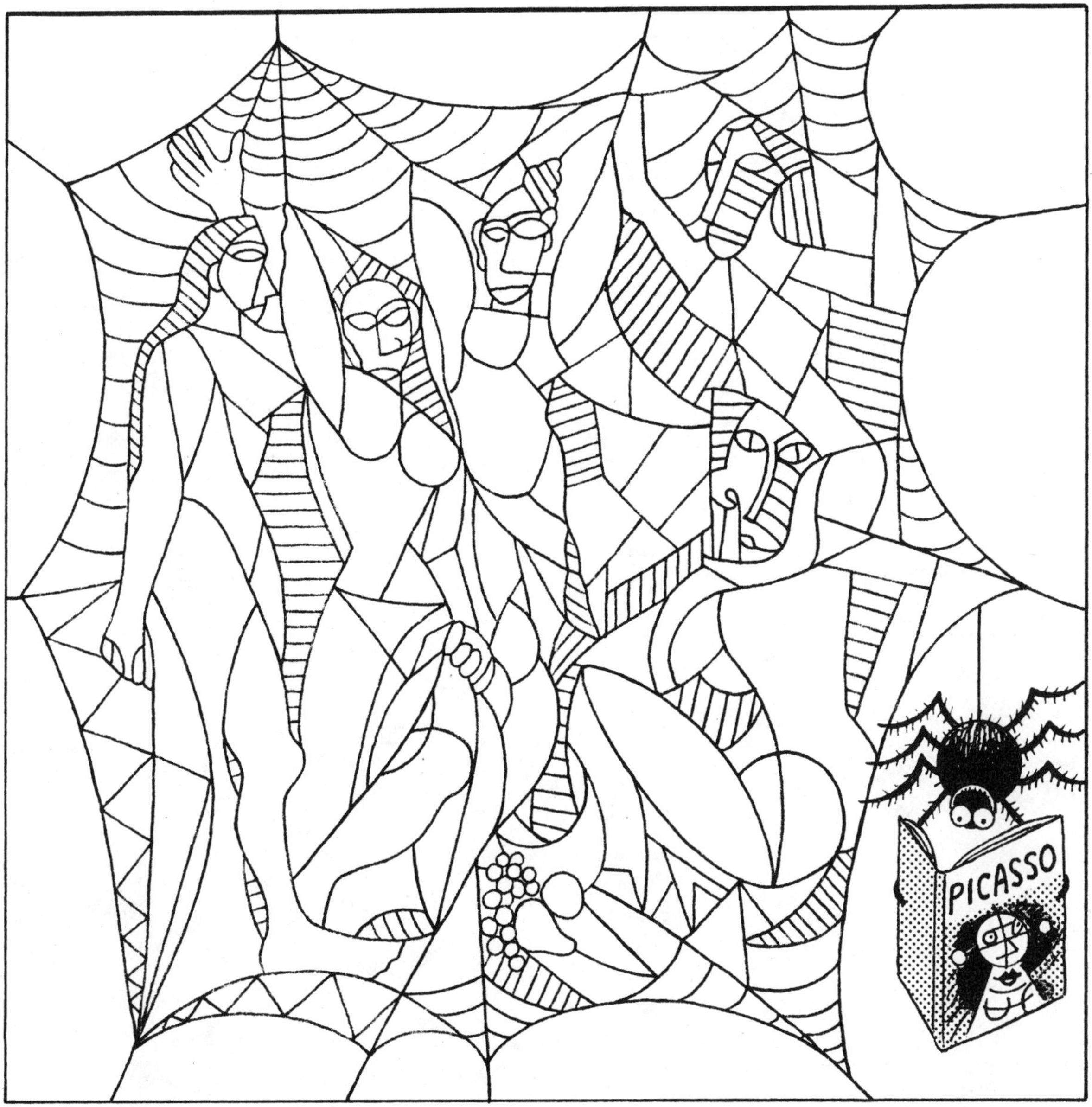
PICASSO

Dare To Be Different

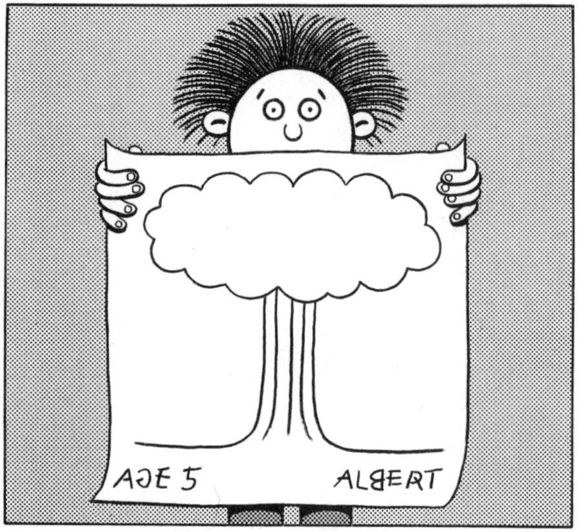
AGE 5
ALBERT

Young Albert Einstein with a drawing his teacher thought was a tree

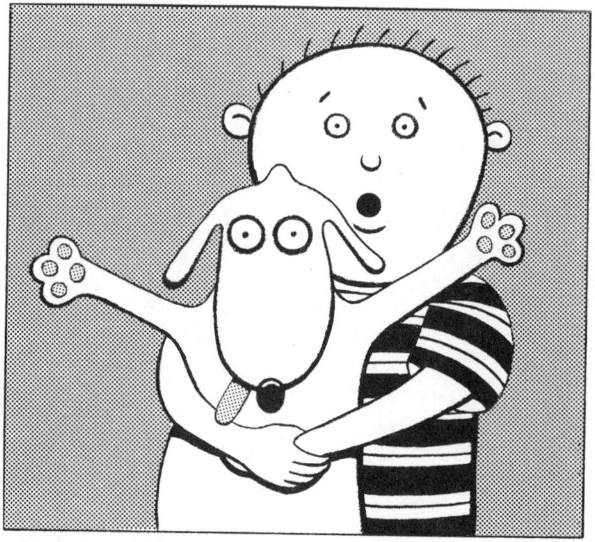

Young Heimlich tests his maneuver and gets a lap full of doggie-do

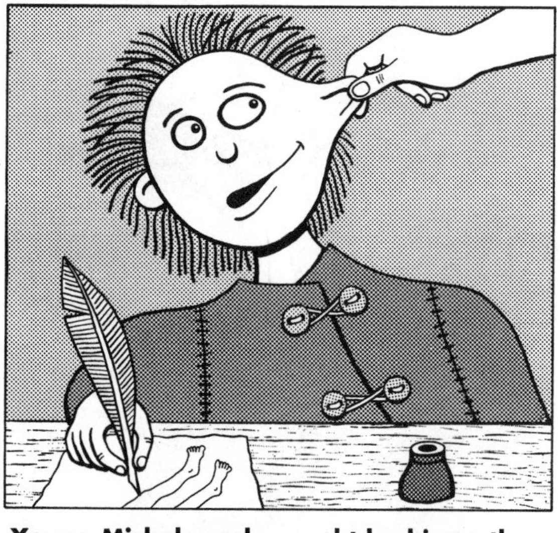

Young Michelangelo caught by his mother drawing naked people

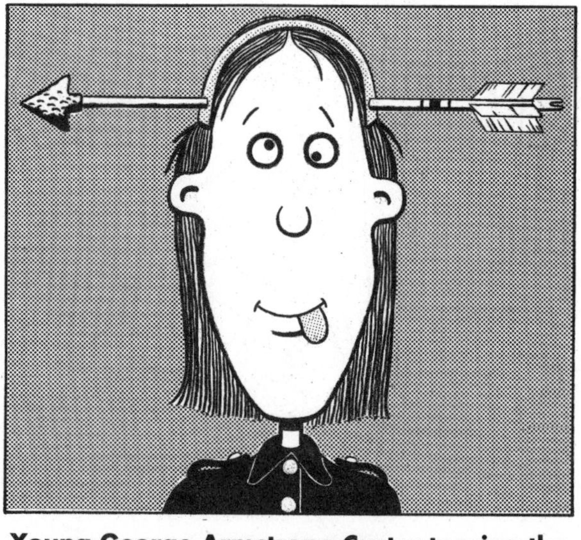

Young George Armstrong Custer teasing the girls in his class

Ancient History

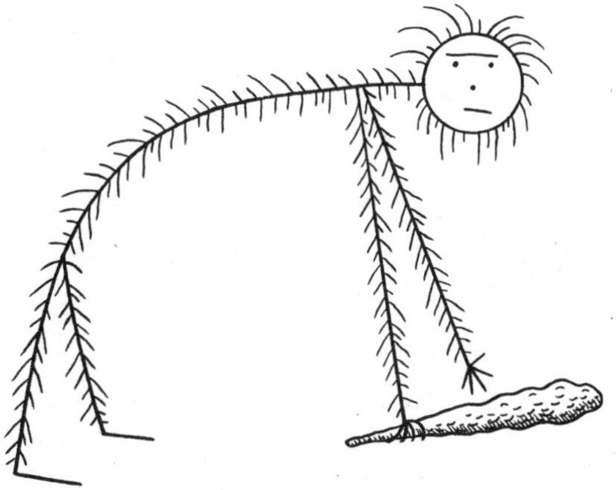

Prehistoric stick figure

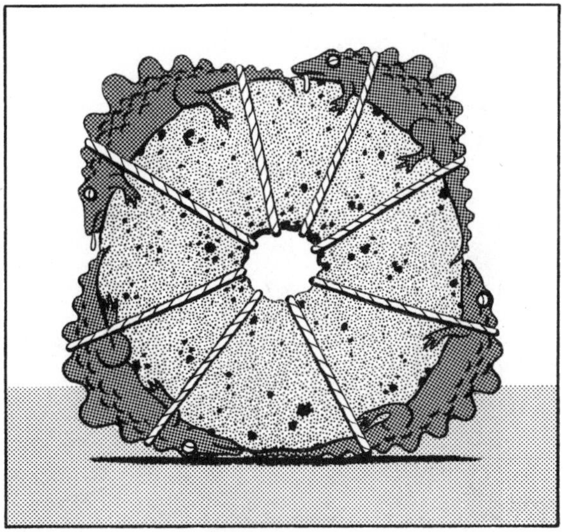

A prehistoric snow tire

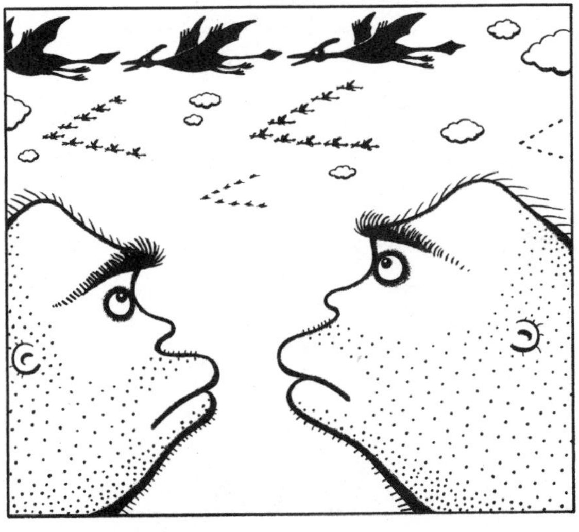

Pterodactyls flying south for the ice age

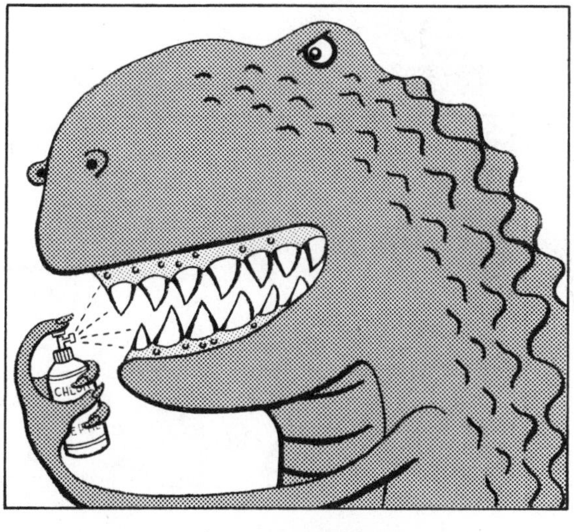

The meanest of all dinosaurs...
Cankersaurus Rex

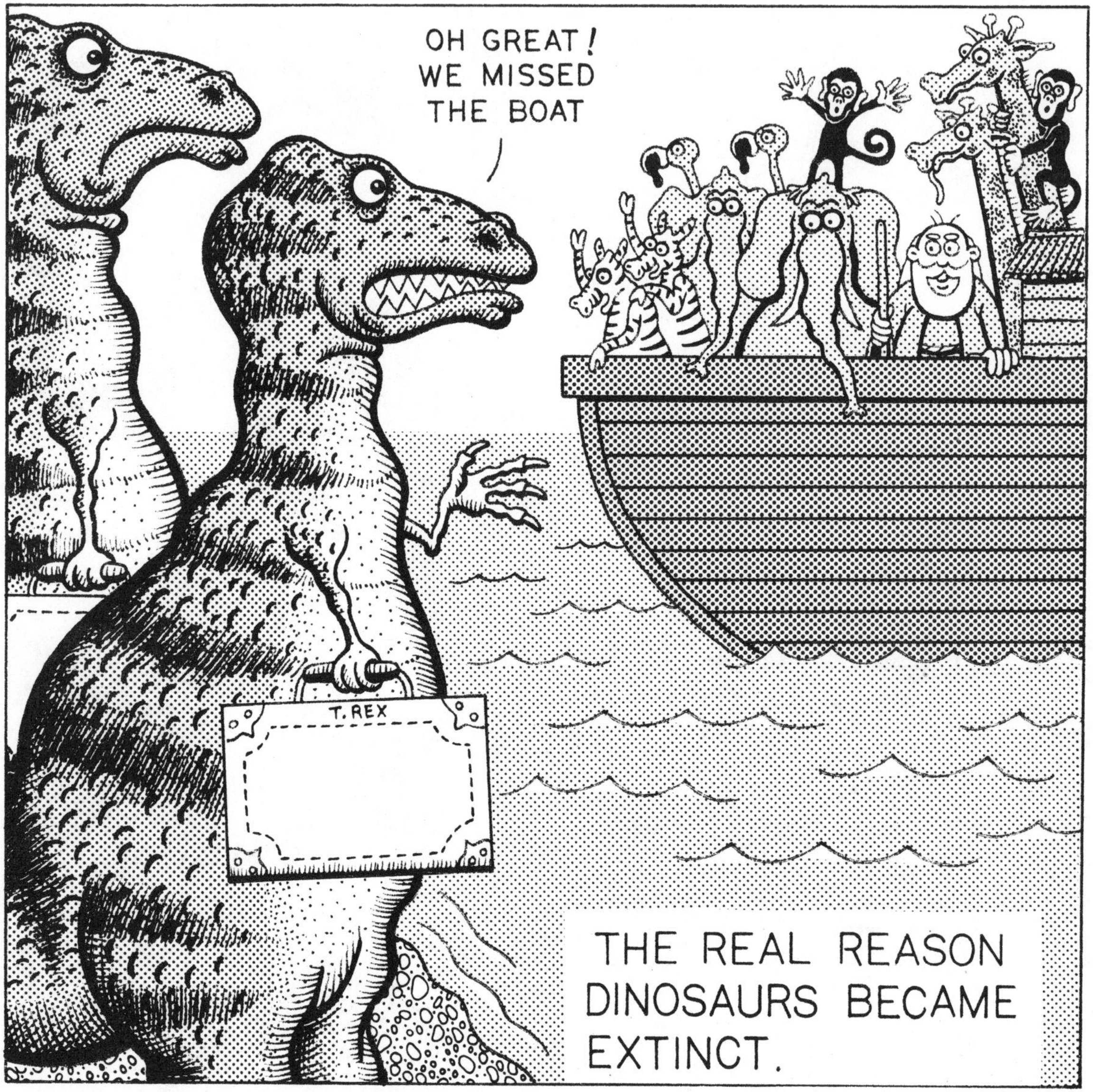
OH GREAT! WE MISSED THE BOAT
T. REX
THE REAL REASON DINOSAURS BECAME EXTINCT.

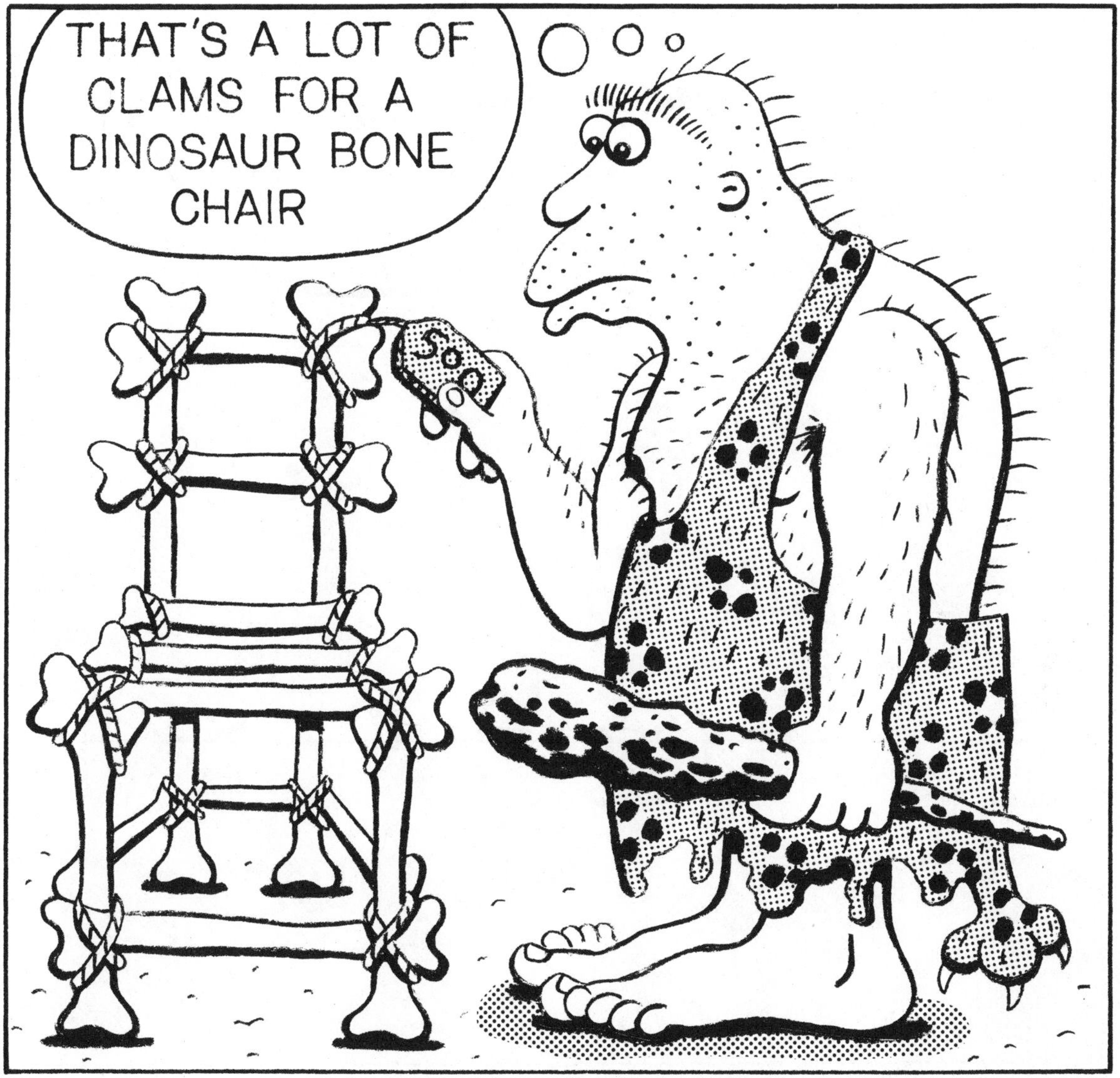
THAT'S A LOT OF CLAMS FOR A DINOSAUR BONE CHAIR
500

Did early man go antiquing?

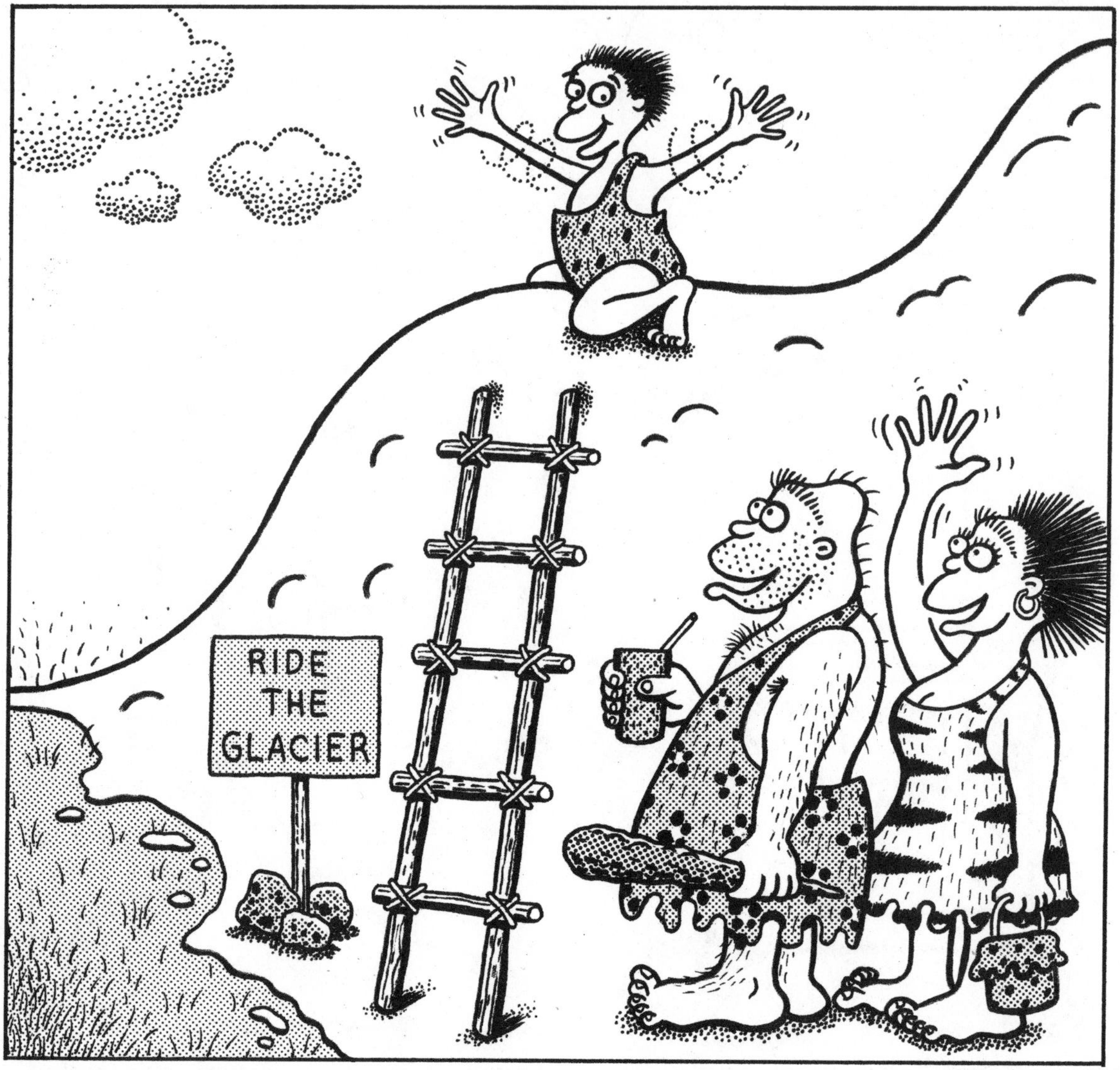
RIDE
THE
GLACIER

A prehistoric theme park

Modern History

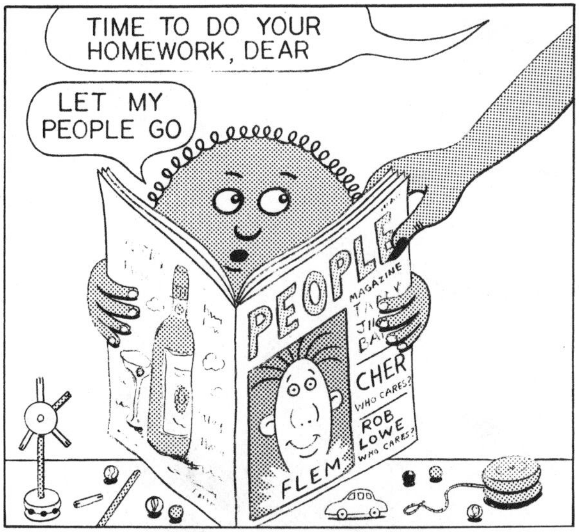
TIME TO DO YOUR HOMEWORK, DEAR
LET MY PEOPLE GO
PEOPLE
MAGAZINE
CHER
WHO CARES?
ROB LOWE
WHO CARES?
FLEM

The great, great, great, great, great, great, great, grandson of Moses

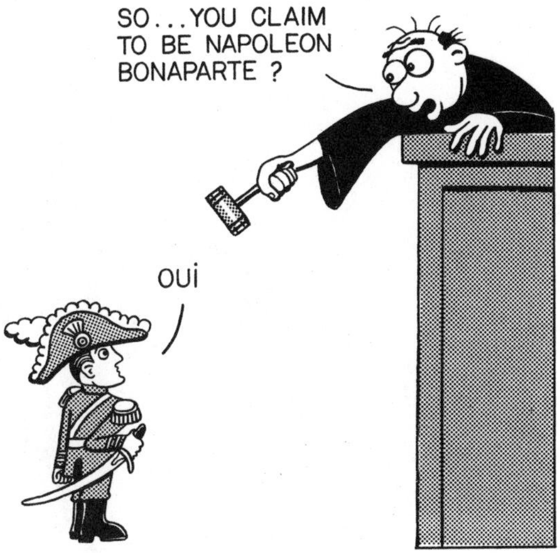
SO...YOU CLAIM TO BE NAPOLEON BONAPARTE ?
OUi

Small claims court

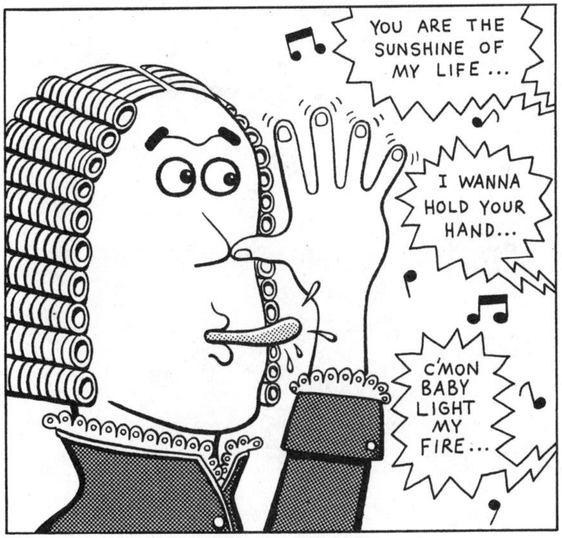
YOU ARE THE SUNSHINE OF MY LIFE...
I WANNA HOLD YOUR HAND...
C'MON BABY LIGHT MY FIRE...

Bach to the future

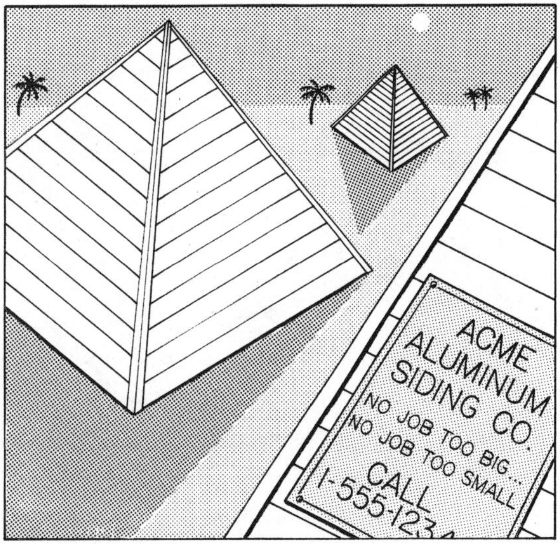
ACME ALUMINUM SIDING CO.
NO JOB TOO BIG...
NO JOB TOO SMALL
CALL

The pyramid preservation program

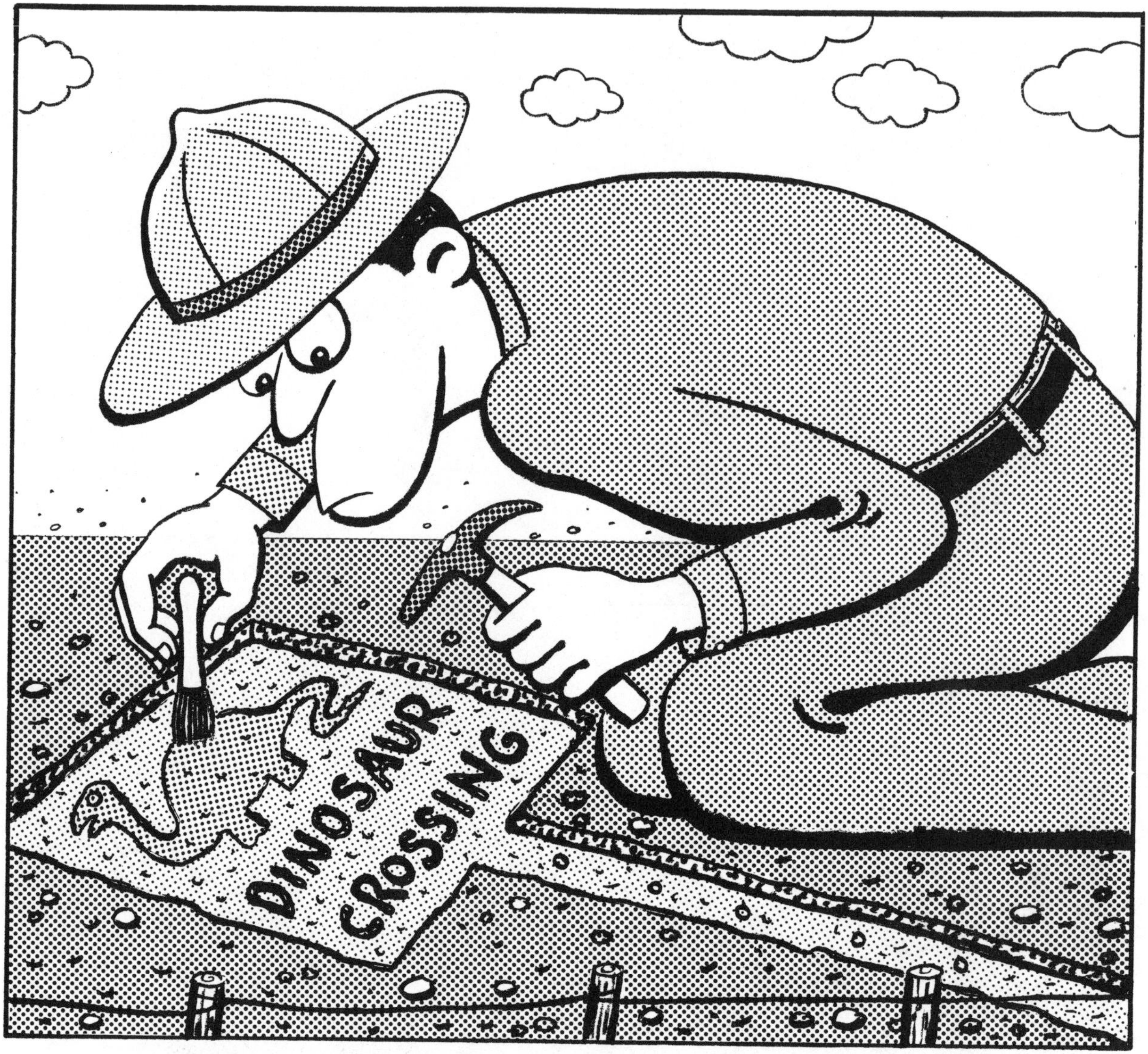
DINOSAUR
CROSSING

An archaeologist discovers an obvious sign of possible dinosaur remains

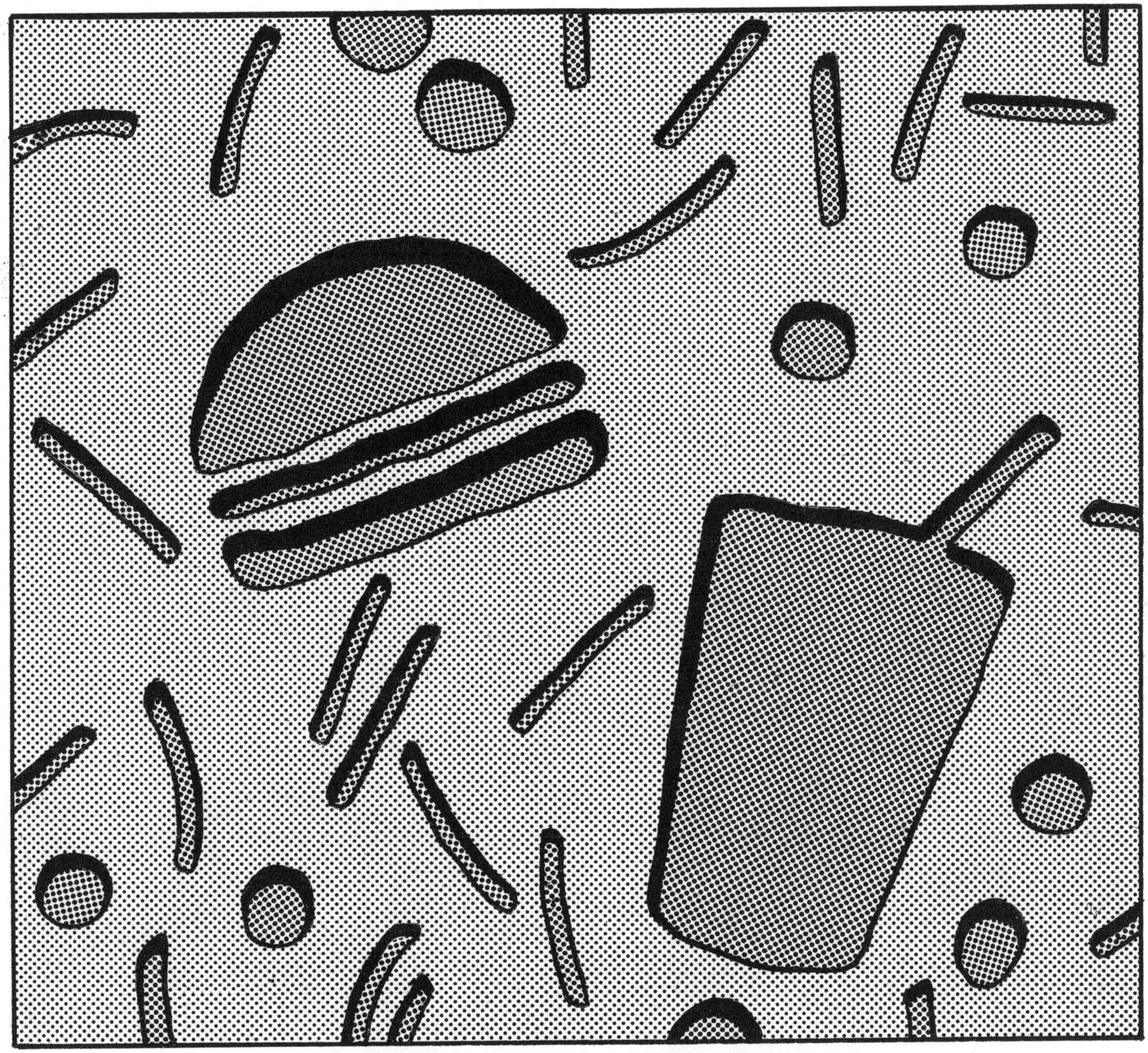

What fossils of the future will look like

Museum of Unnatural History

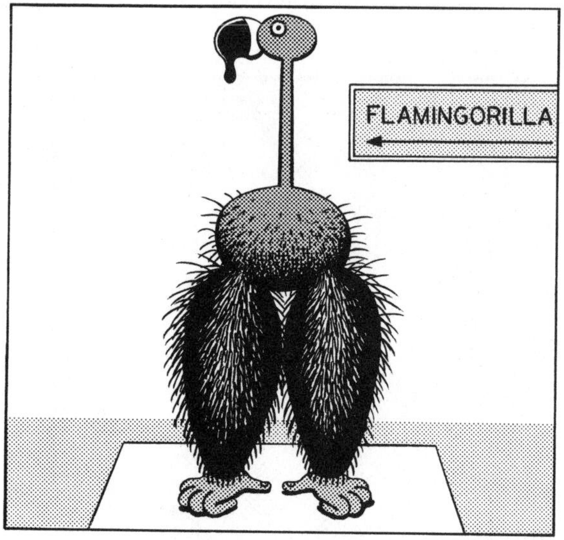
FLAMINGORILLA

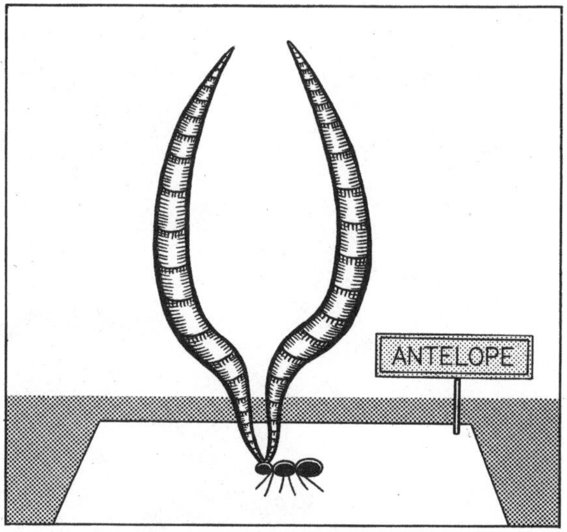
ANTELOPE

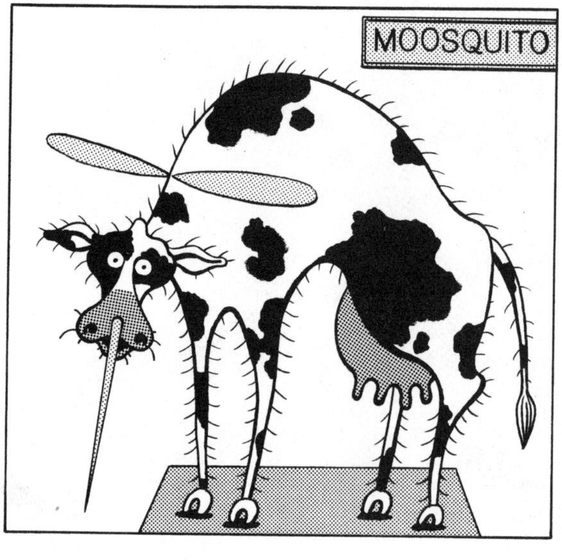
MOOSQUITO

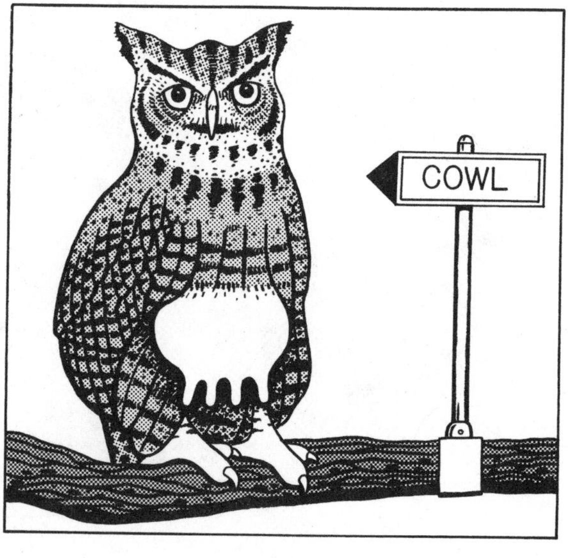
COWL

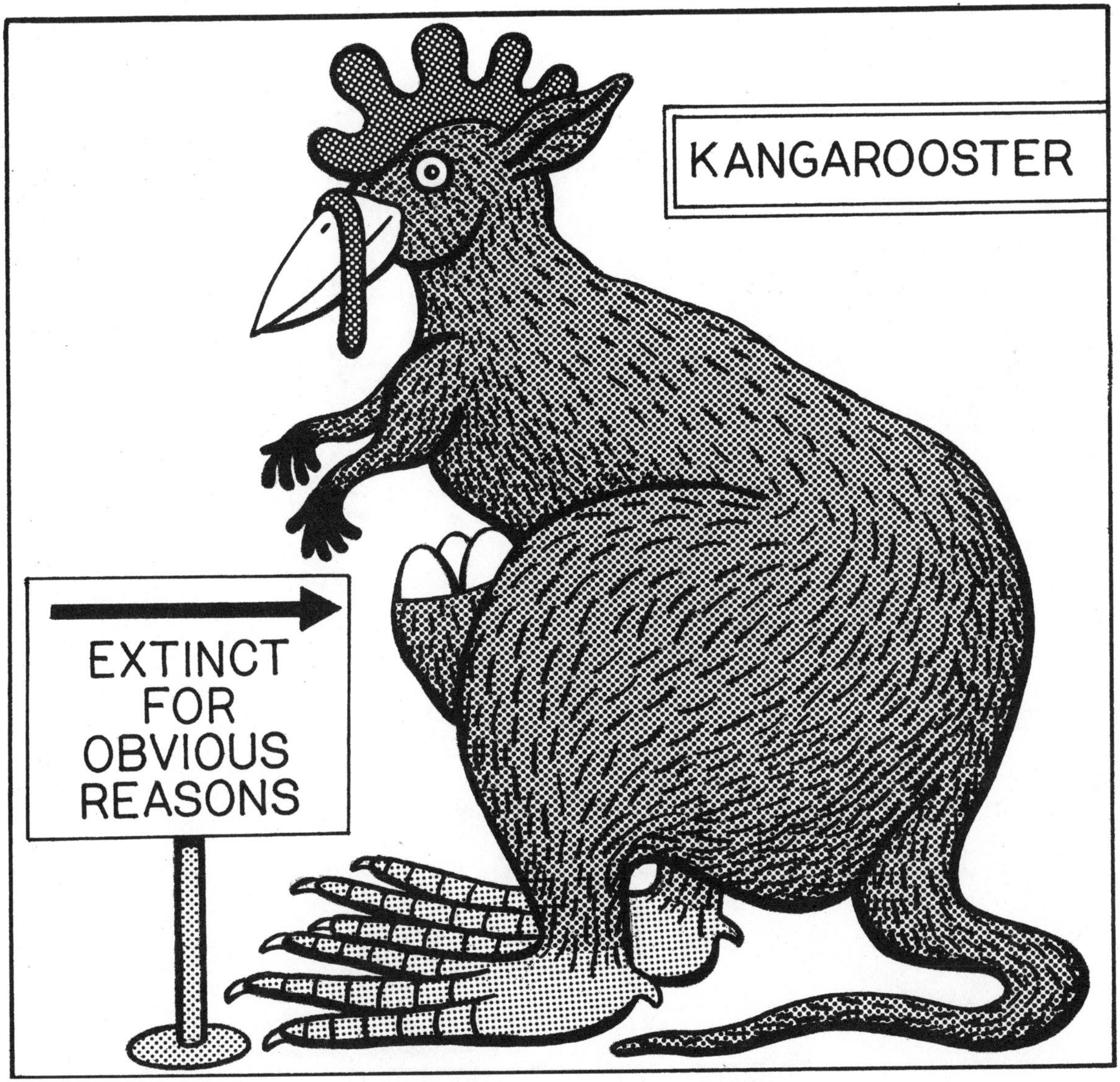
KANGAROOSTER
EXTINCT
FOR
OBVIOUS
REASONS

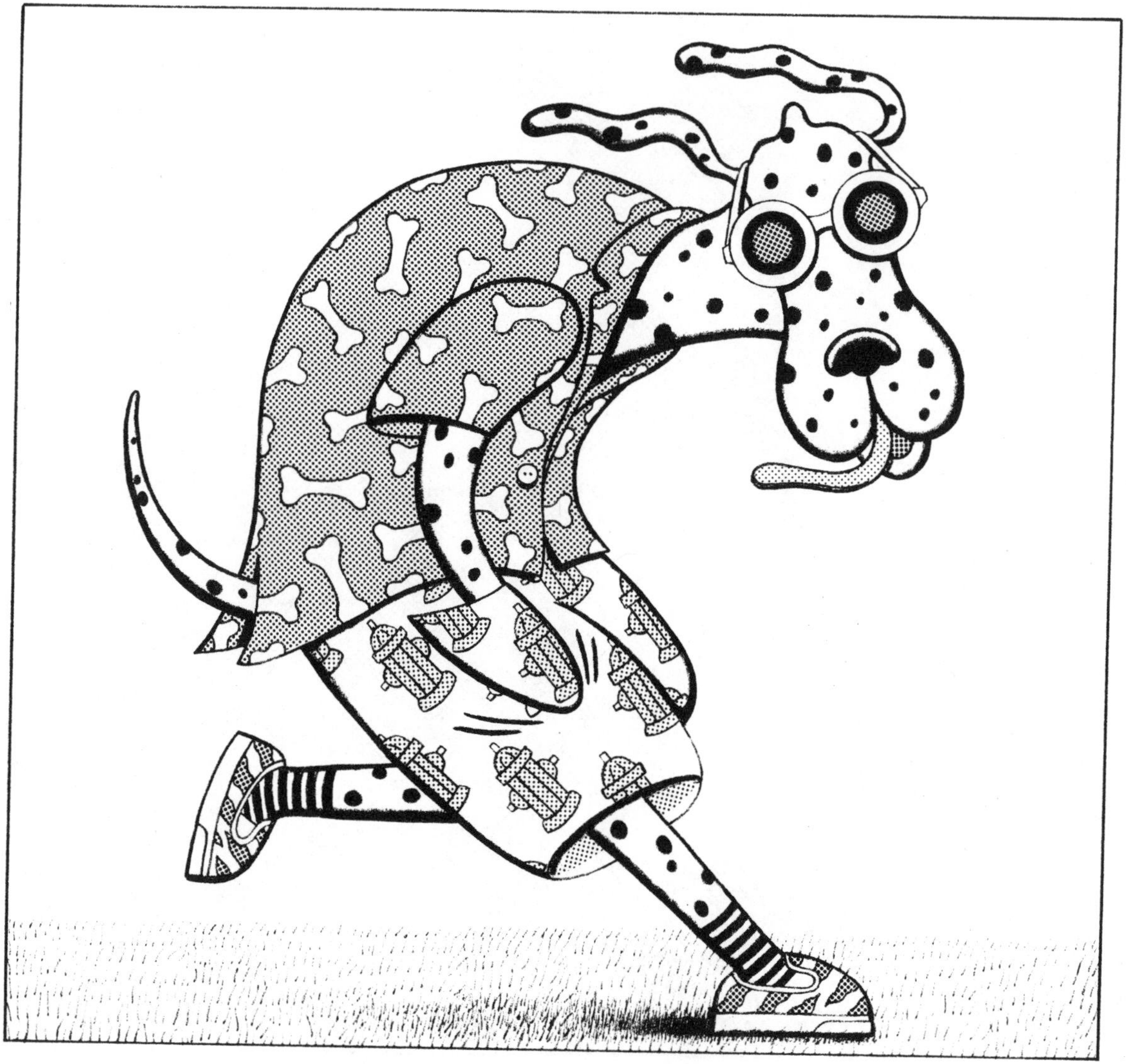

You are what you wear

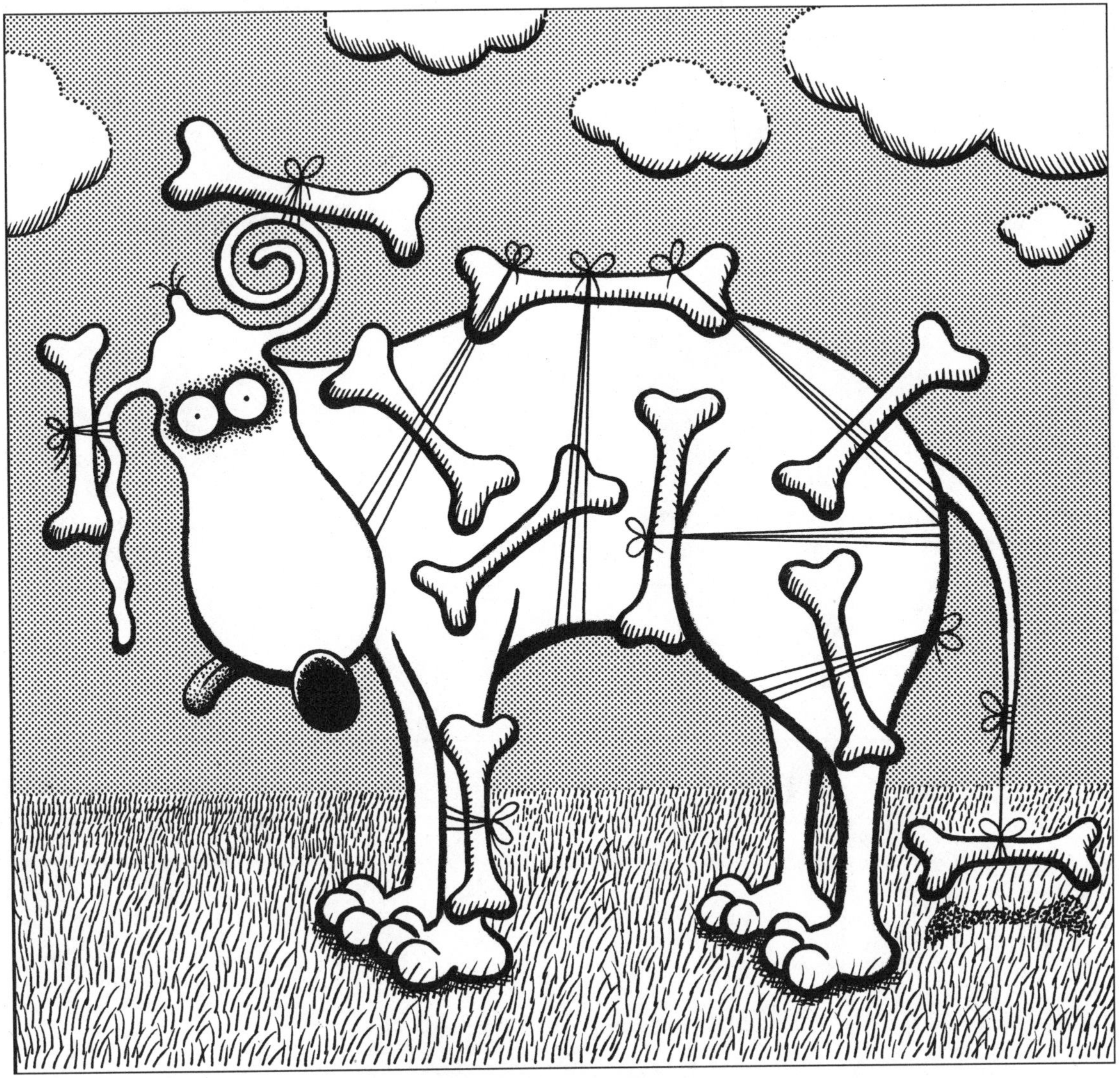

A real lonely dog

Appearances Are Everything

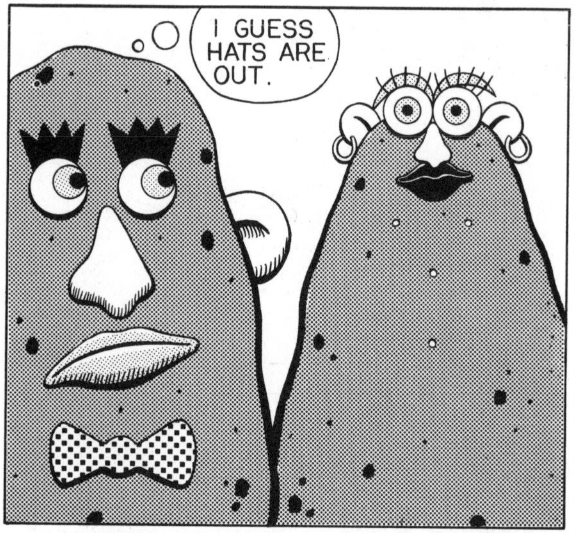
I GUESS HATS ARE OUT.

Mr. Potato Head thinks Mrs. Potato Head's new face-lift may be a little too high

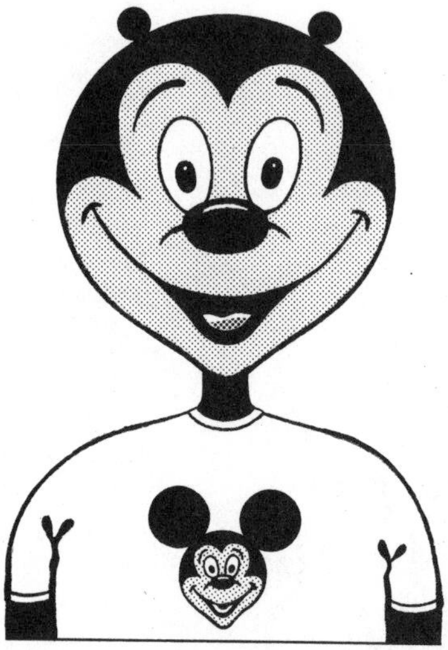

Mickey's brother, Stan, didn't have the right look for show biz

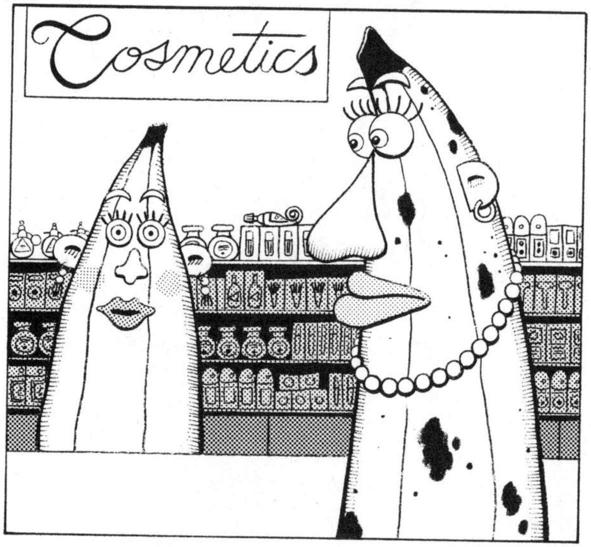
Cosmetics

Mrs. Banana looks for something to cover her brown spots

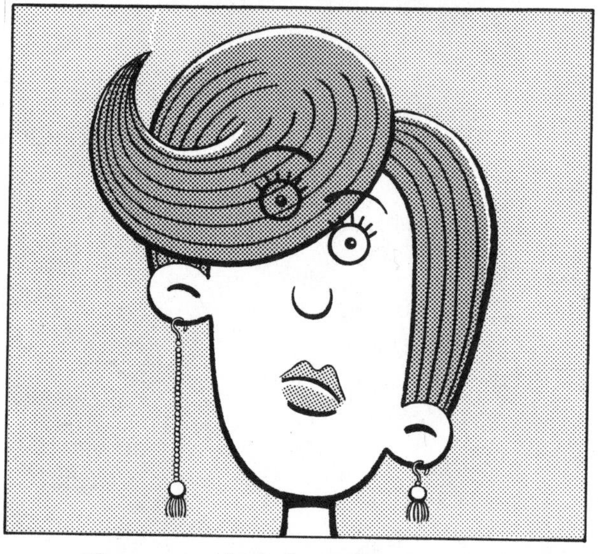

The correct hairdo and accessories can hide most flaws

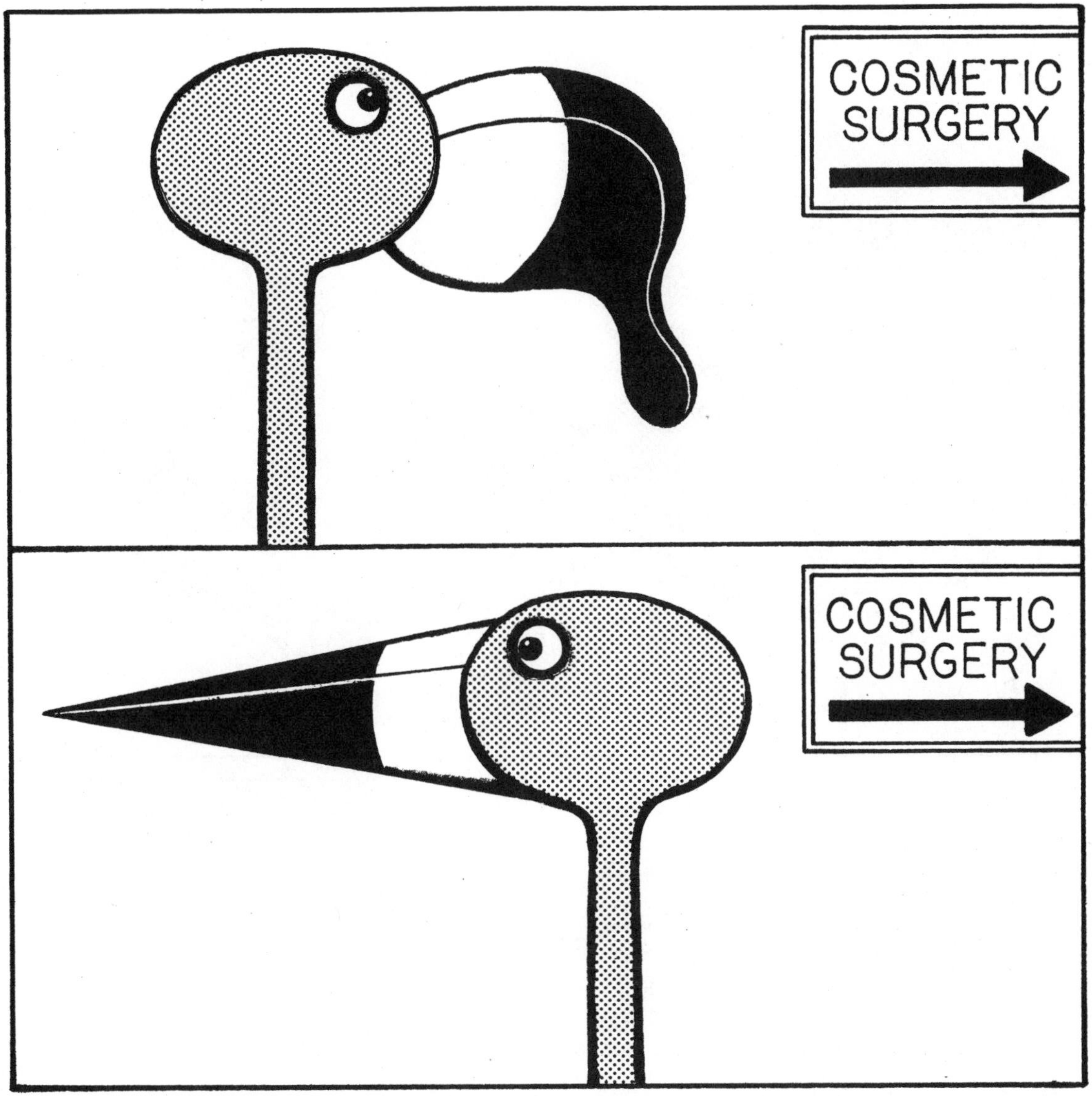
COSMETIC
SURGERY
COSMETIC
SURGERY

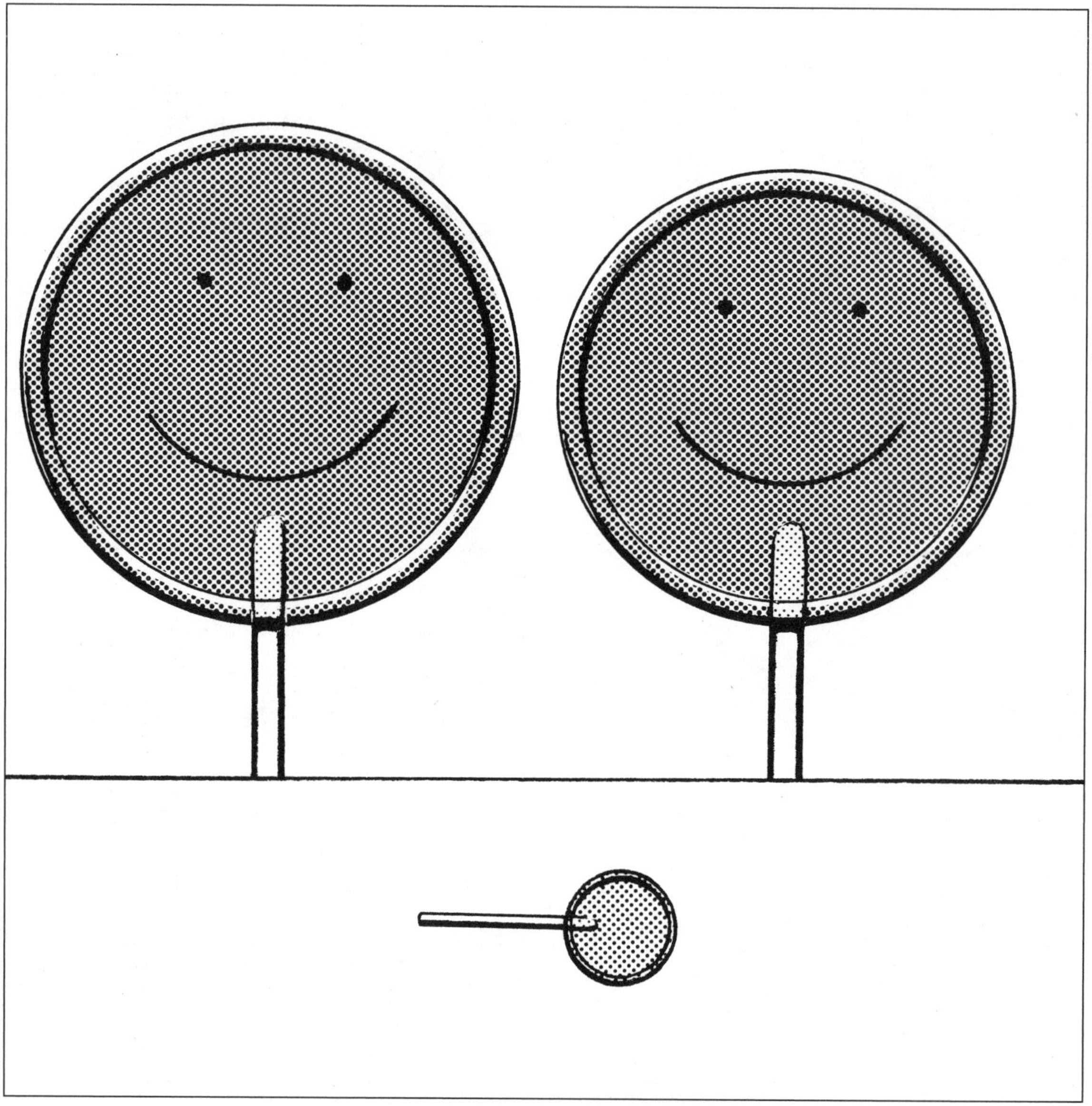

There's one born every minute

Life in the Slow Lane

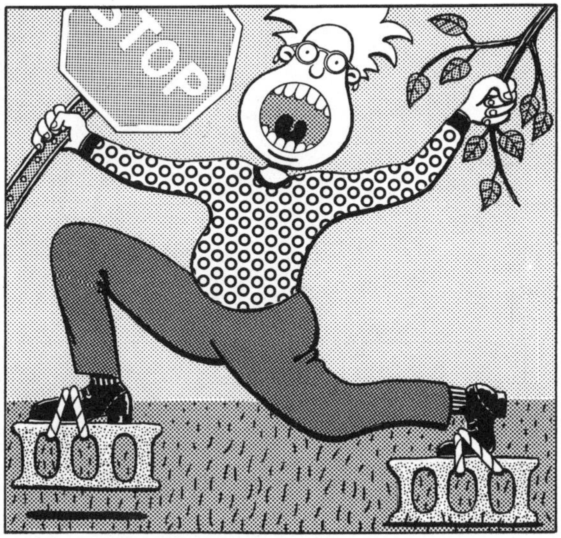
STOP

Wilbur doesn't trust gravity

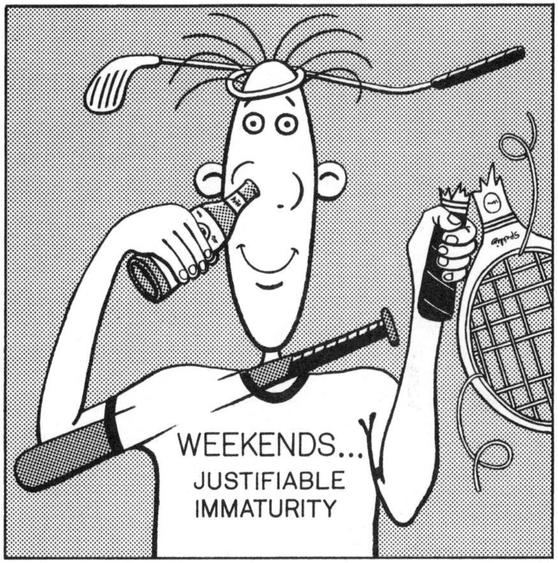
WEEKENDS...
JUSTIFIABLE
IMMATURITY

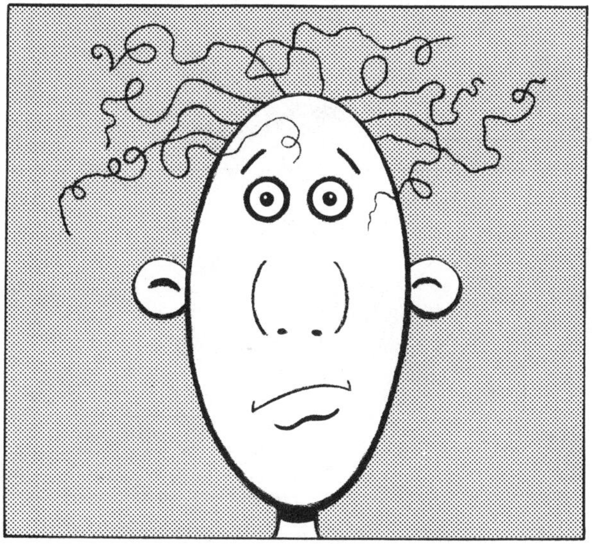

Flem hates brainstorms...they mess up his hair

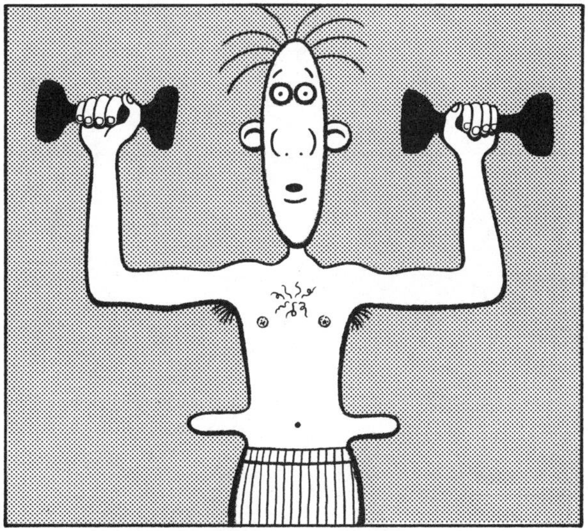

With the right exercise program, you can really develop those love handles

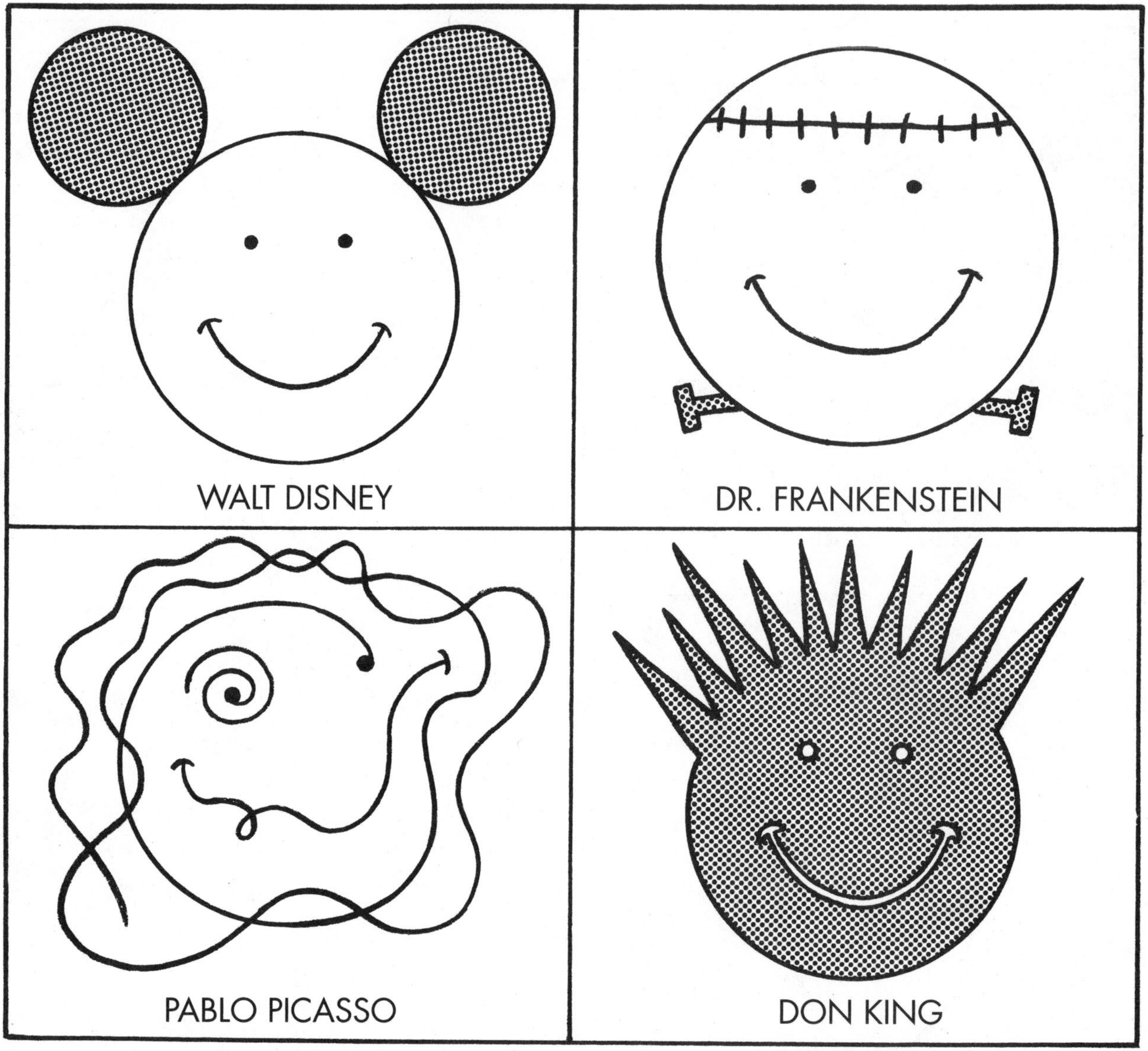
WALT DISNEY
DR. FRANKENSTEIN
PABLO PICASSO
DON KING

If other people had designed the smiley face

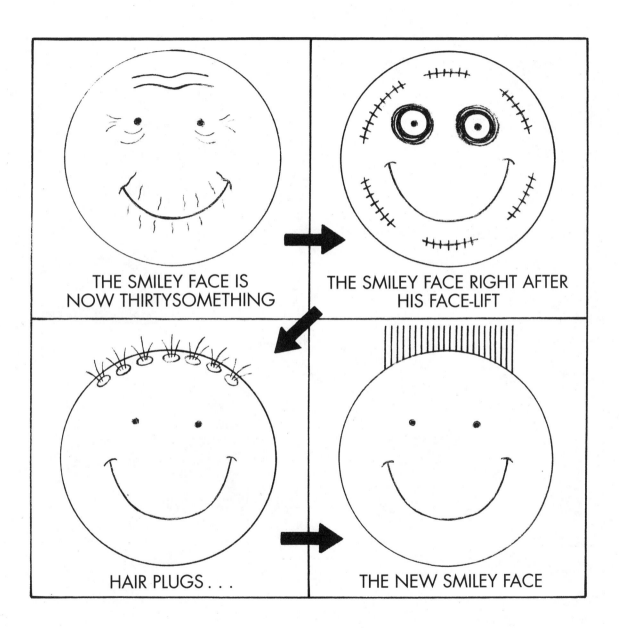

THE SMILEY FACE IS
NOW THIRTYSOMETHING

THE SMILEY FACE RIGHT AFTER
HIS FACE-LIFT

HAIR PLUGS . . .

THE NEW SMILEY FACE

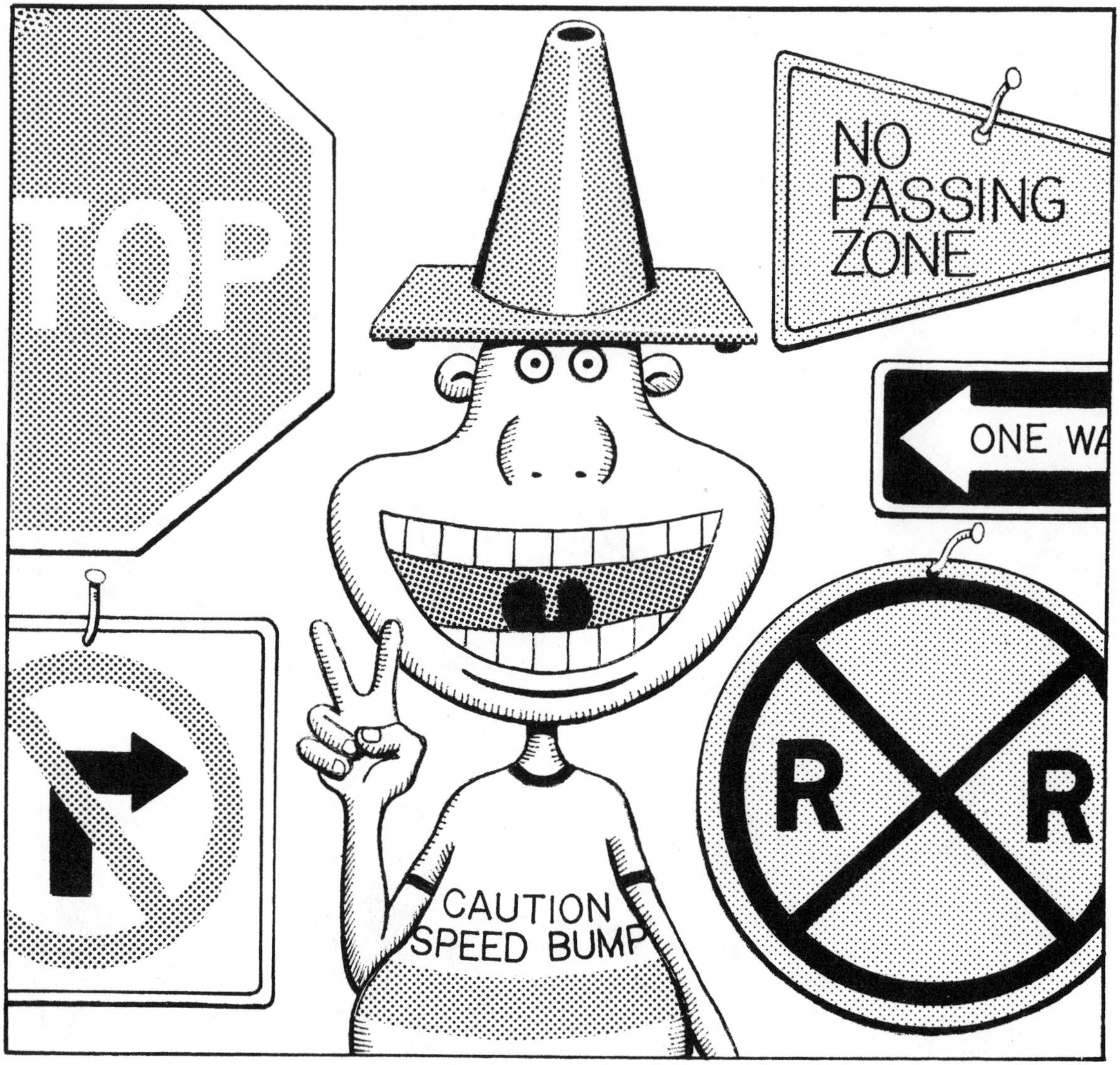
TOP
NO PASSING ZONE
ONE WA
R
R
CAUTION SPEED BUMP

A roads scholar

Time Out

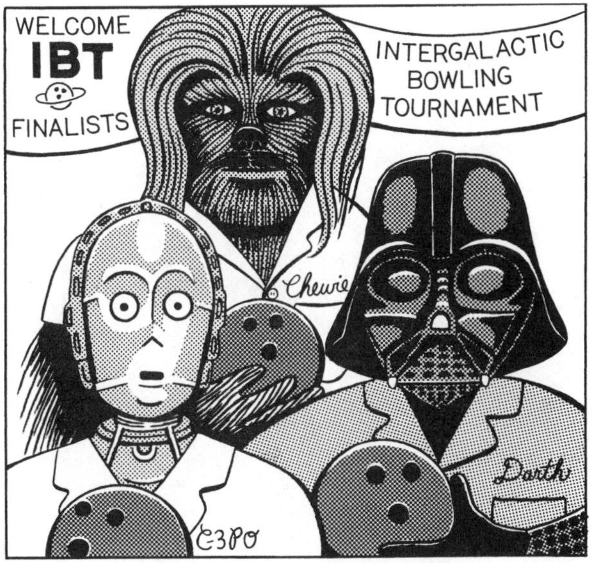
WELCOME
IBT
FINALISTS
INTERGALACTIC
BOWLING
TOURNAMENT
Chewie
Darth
C3PO

The empire strikes back

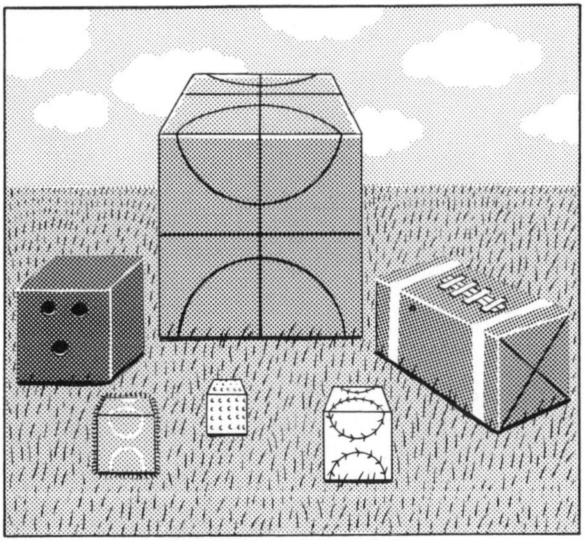

Sports equipment before round was discovered

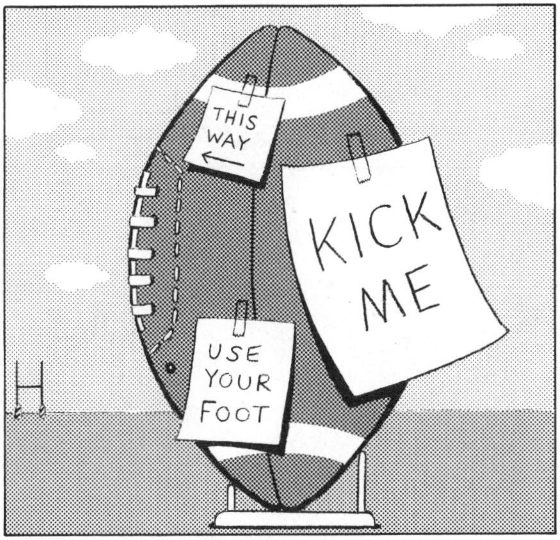
THIS WAY
KICK ME
USE YOUR FOOT

The first day of football practice

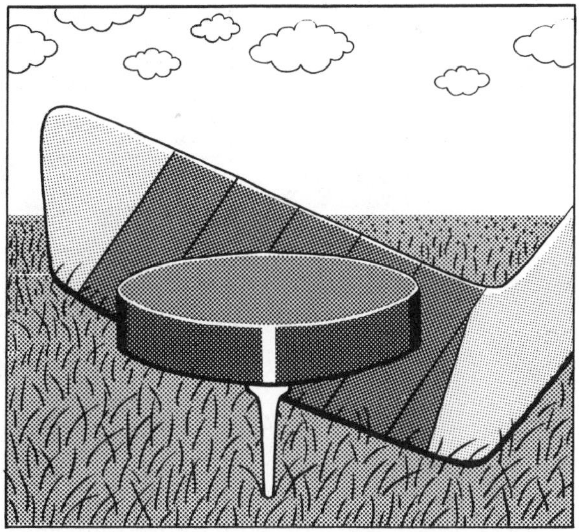

If golf had been invented by Canadians

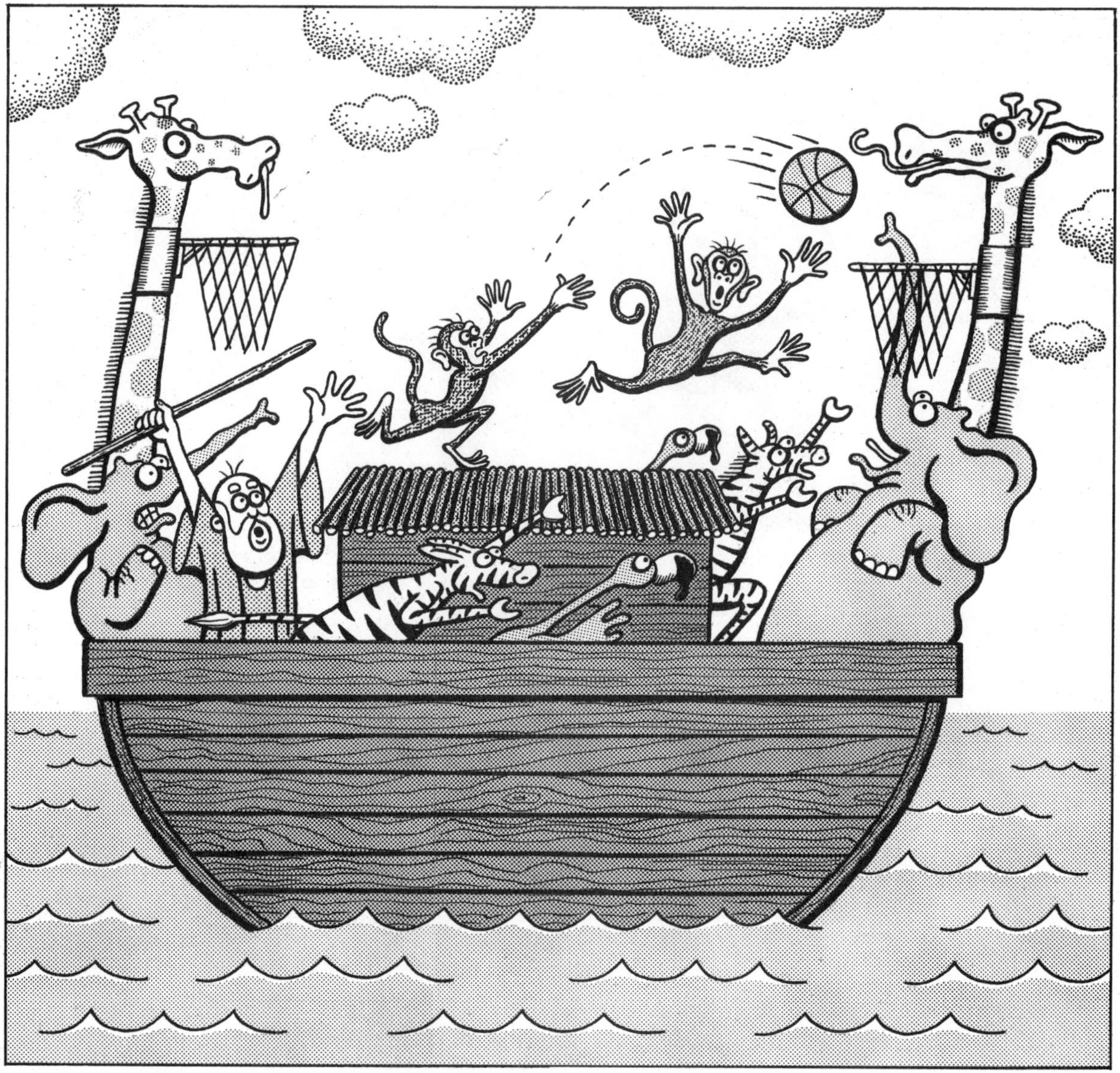

If Noah had been into sports

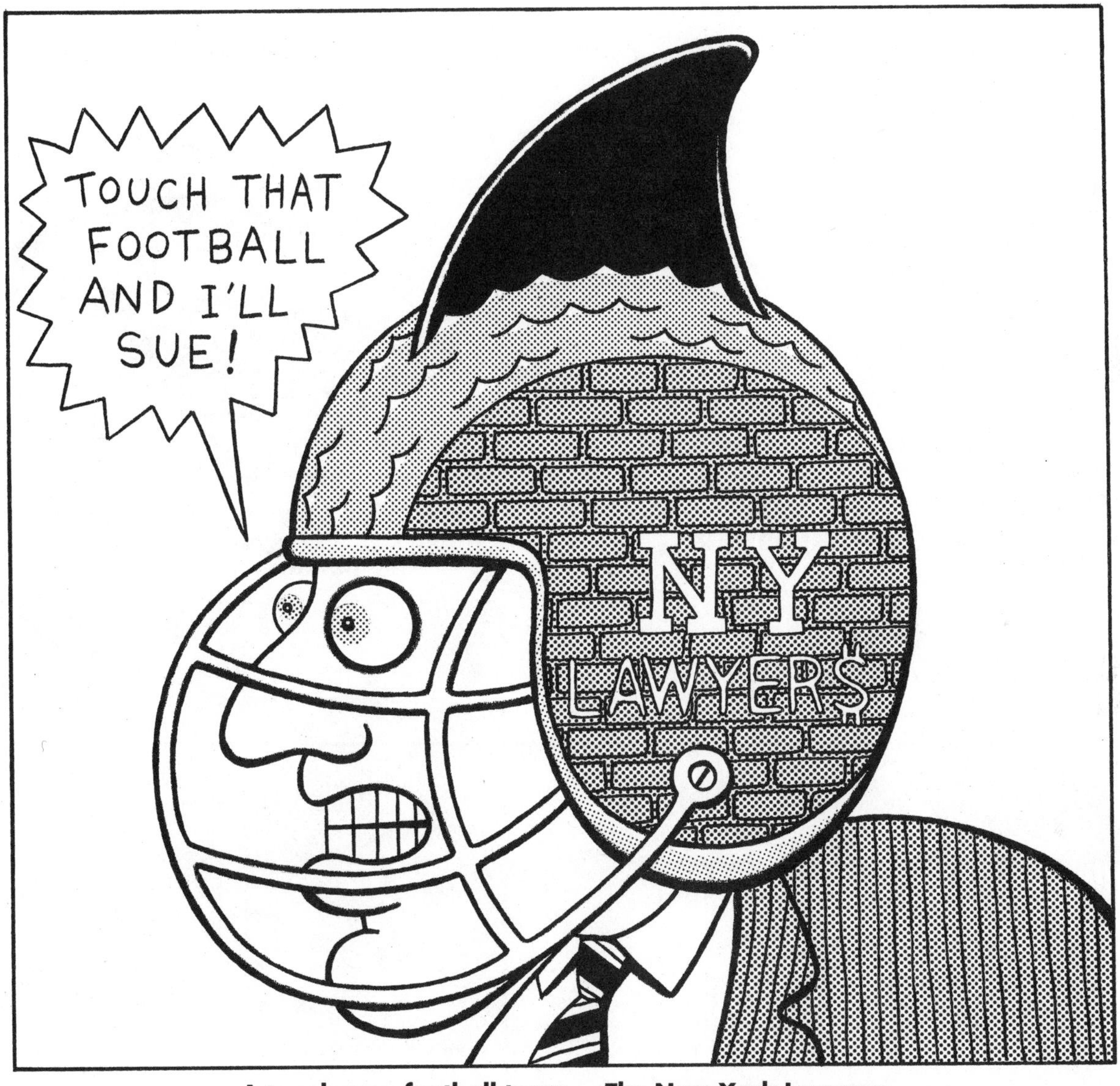
TOUCH THAT FOOTBALL AND I'LL SUE!
NY
LAWYER$

A tough new football team. . .The New York Lawyers

Patent Pending

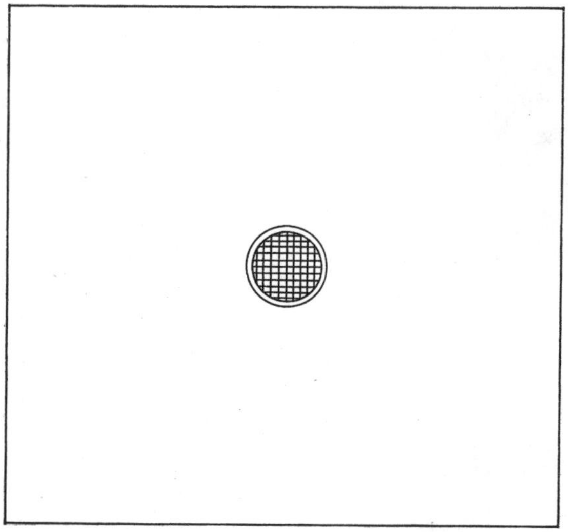

Belly button lint screen

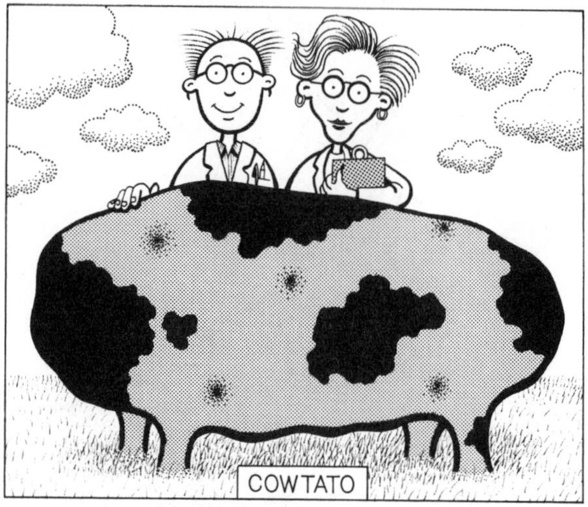
COWTATO

Scientists have successfully crossed a potato with a cow. Now you can have your meat and potatoes at the same time

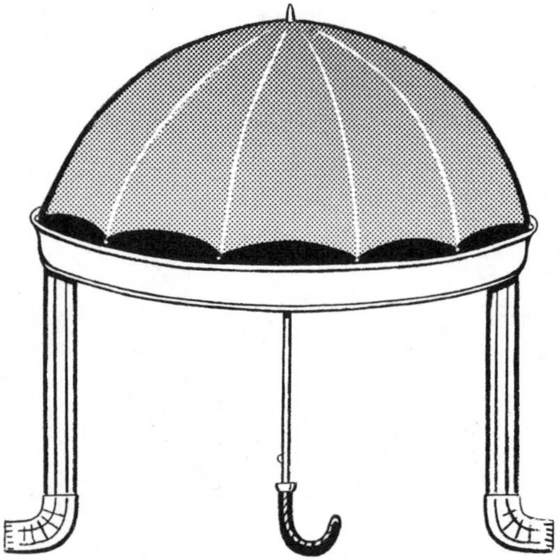

Improved umbrella with gutter and downspouts

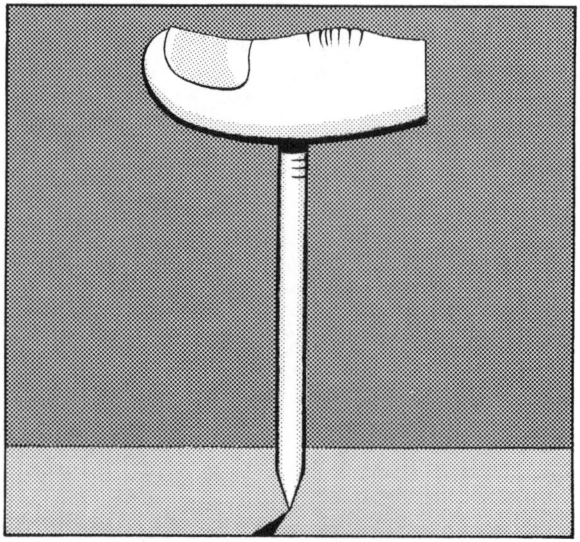

The newly designed, never-miss nail

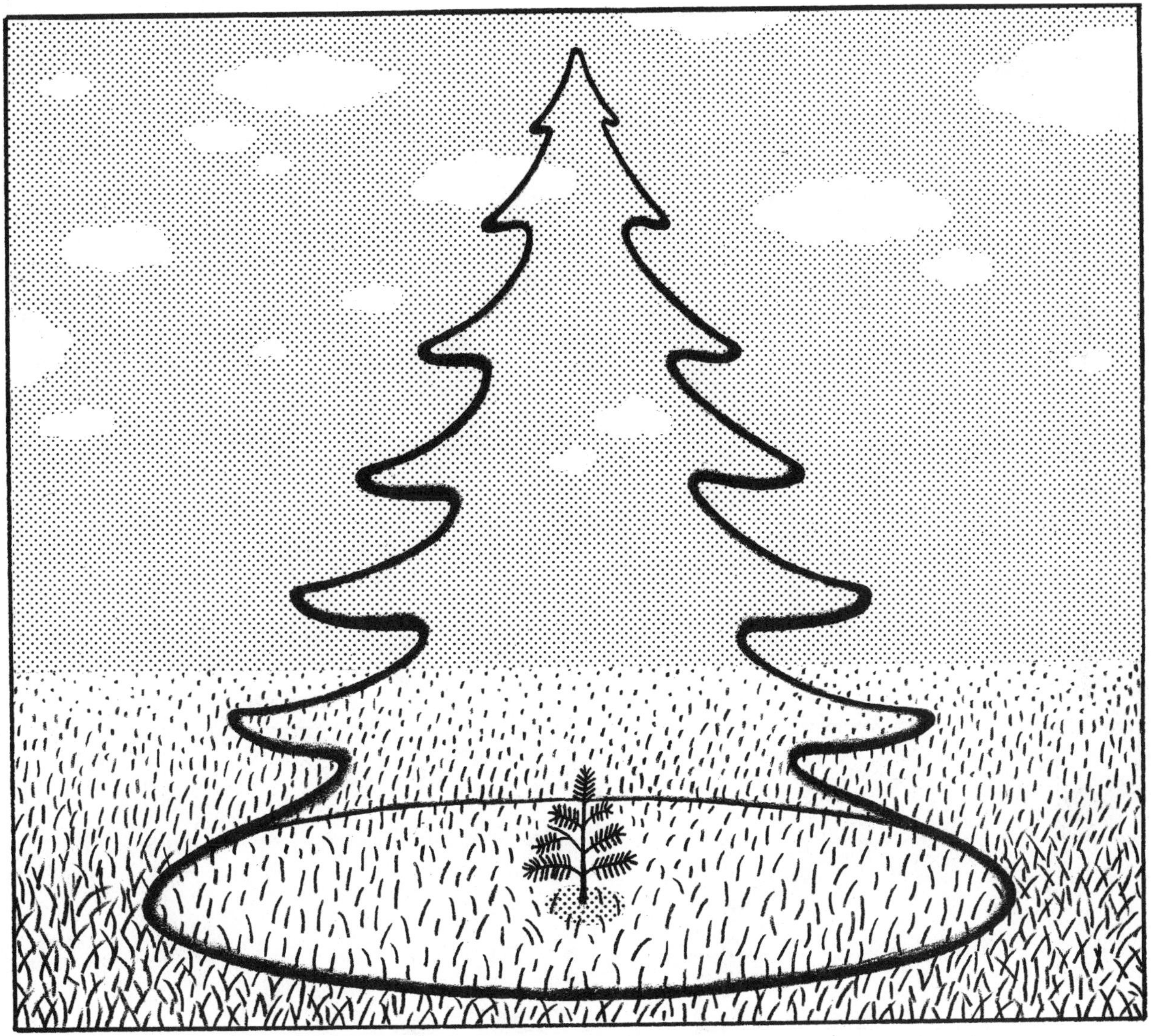

A clear mold for growing perfect Christmas trees

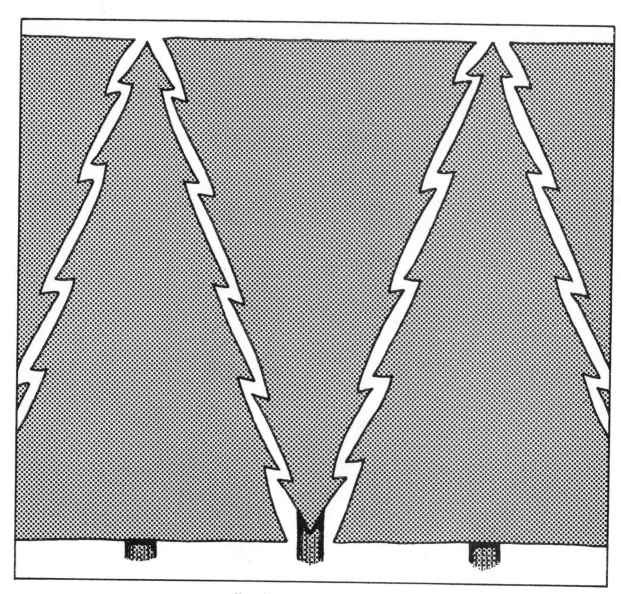

A really efficient Christmas tree farm

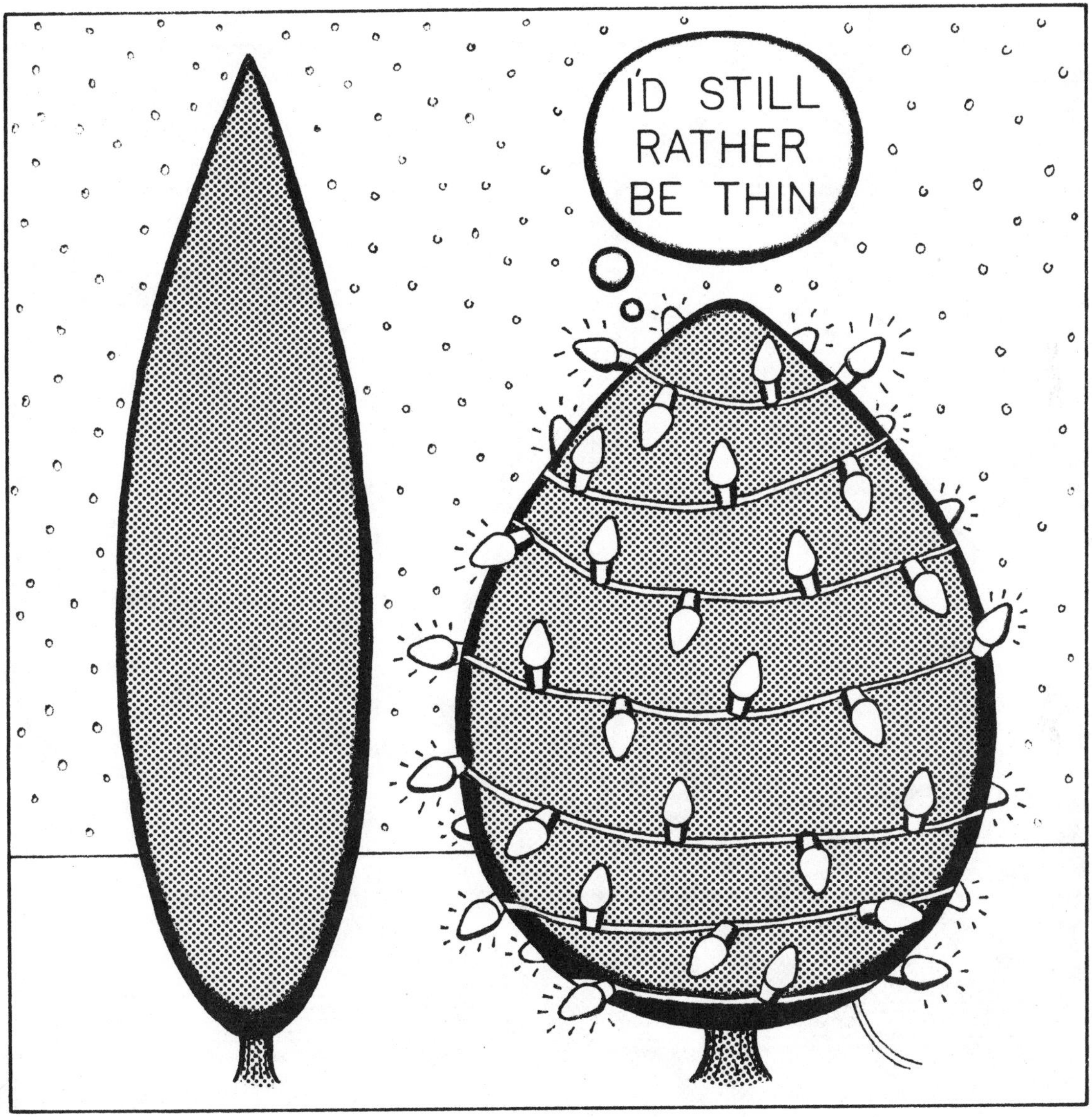
I'D STILL RATHER BE THIN

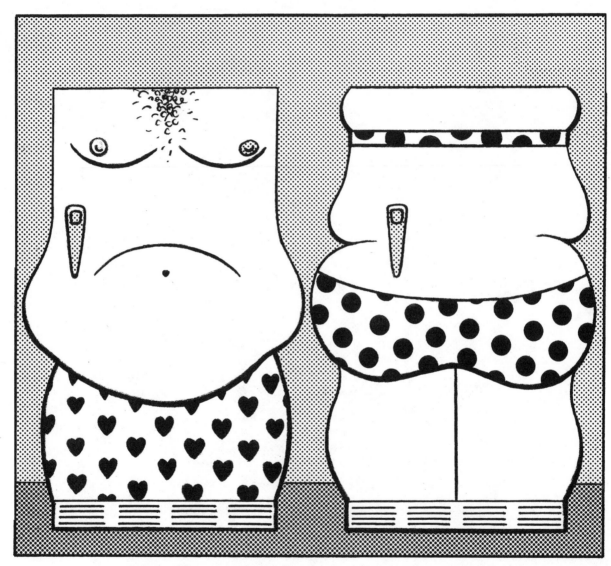

New refrigerator doors designed to discourage overeating

Losing It

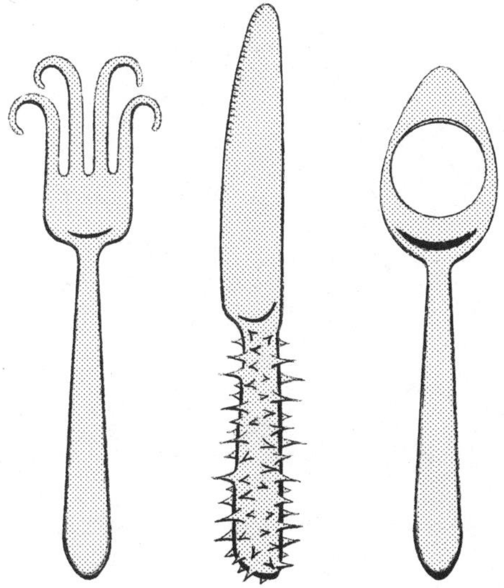

Silverware for dieting

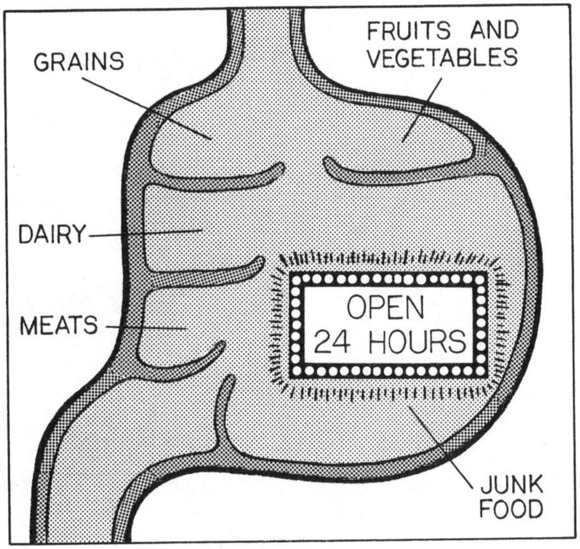
GRAINS
FRUITS AND VEGETABLES
DAIRY
MEATS
OPEN 24 HOURS
JUNK FOOD

Inside the stomach

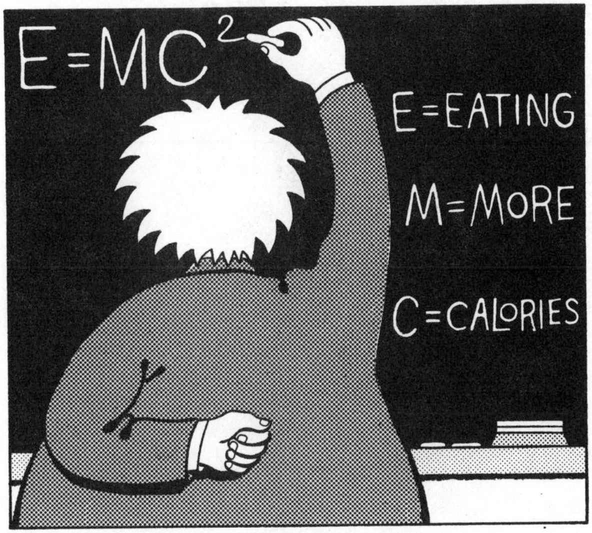
E=MC²
E=EATING
M=MORE
C=CALORIES

Einstein finally figures out why he's been gaining weight

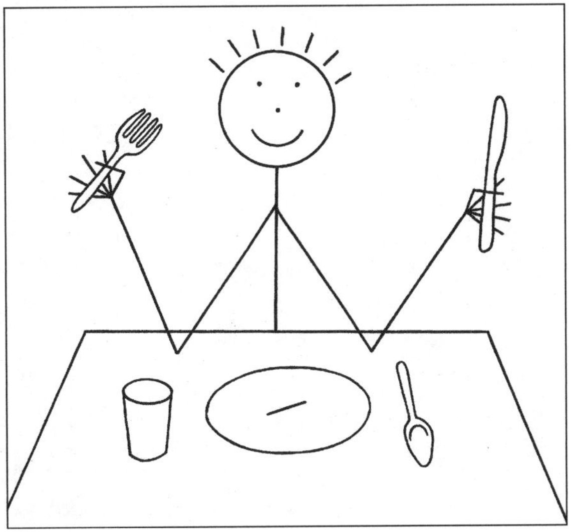

Lean cuisine

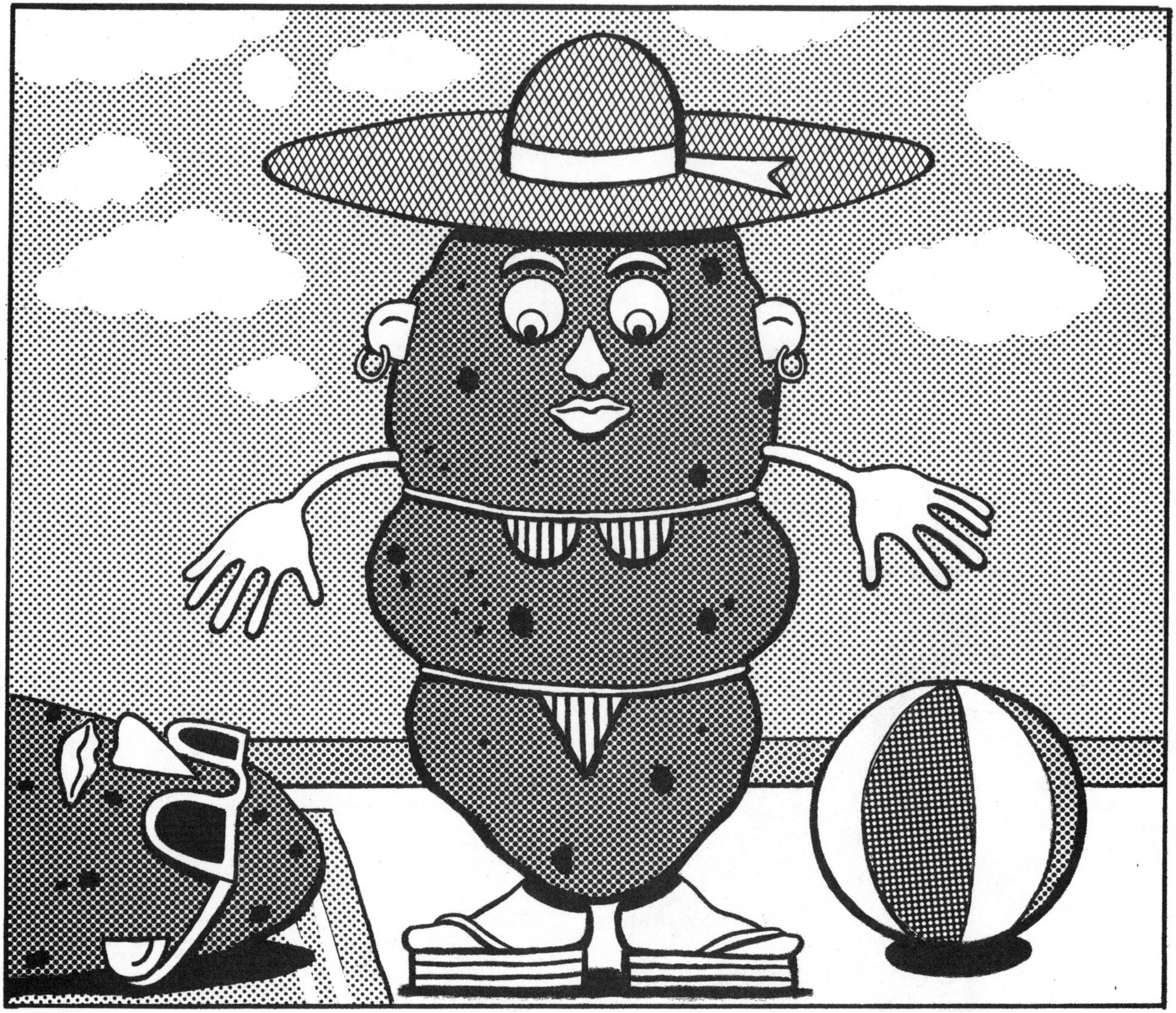

Mrs. Potato Head discovers that you can't put 10 lbs. of potatoes in a 5 lb. sack

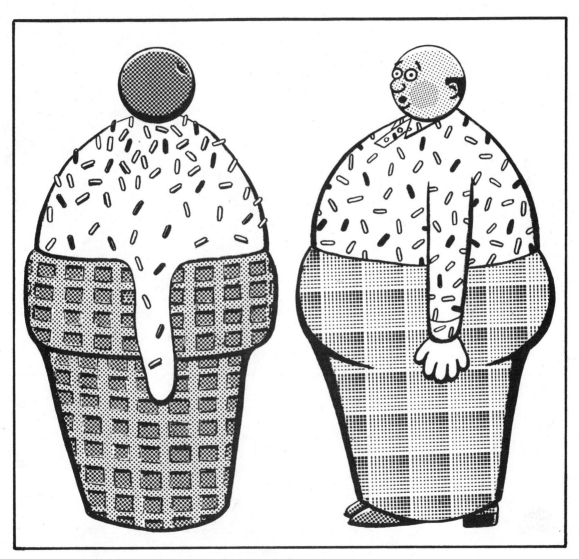

You are what you eat

Faceless Food

I THINK...
THEREFORE
I YAM

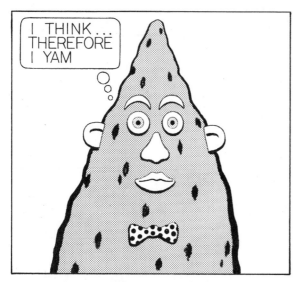

Transcendental vegetation

NEW
LIFESAVERS
NATURAL FLAVORS:
100%
LIMA BEANS, ASPARAGUS
SQUASH AND BROCCOLI
VEGGIE
JUICERS

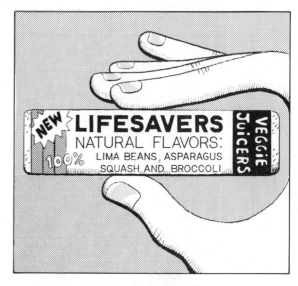

Lifesavers' only flop

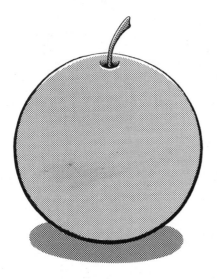

A pear holding its breath

OLIVE
TOMATO
CABBAGE
PEPPER
STUFFED
PEPPERS
OUR
SPECIALTY
Les Pulp
TAXIDERMY

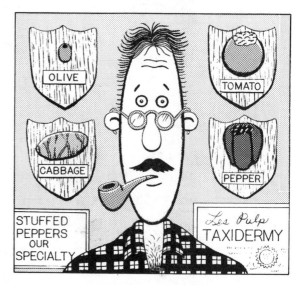

Vegetarian taxidermist

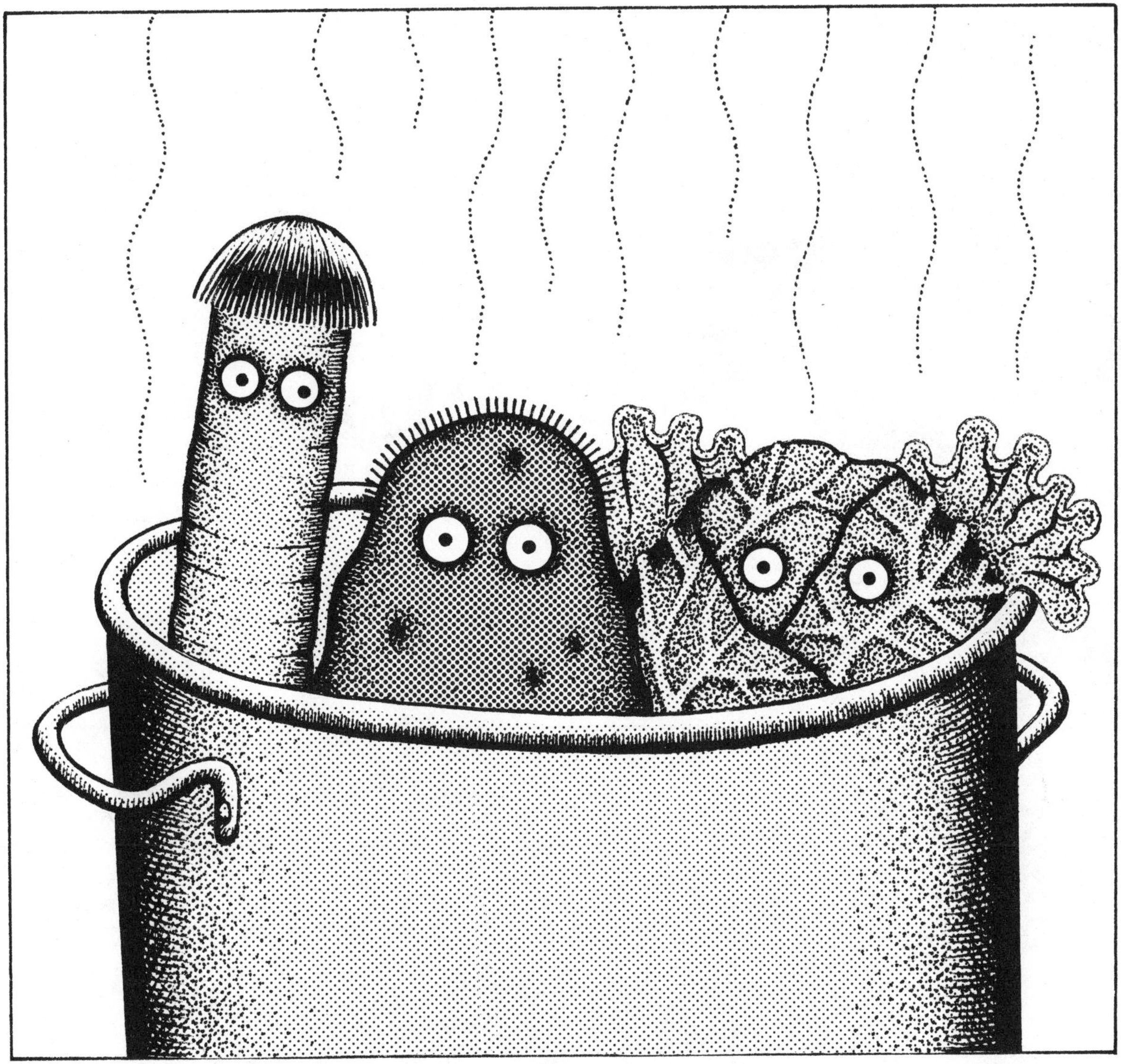

The three stewges

Second Helping

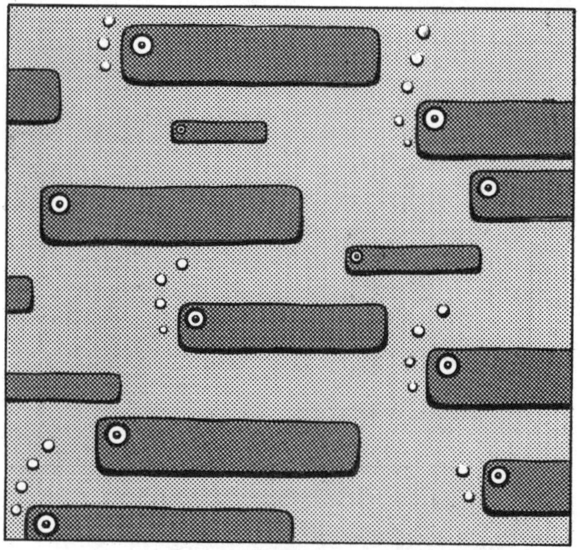

A school of fish sticks

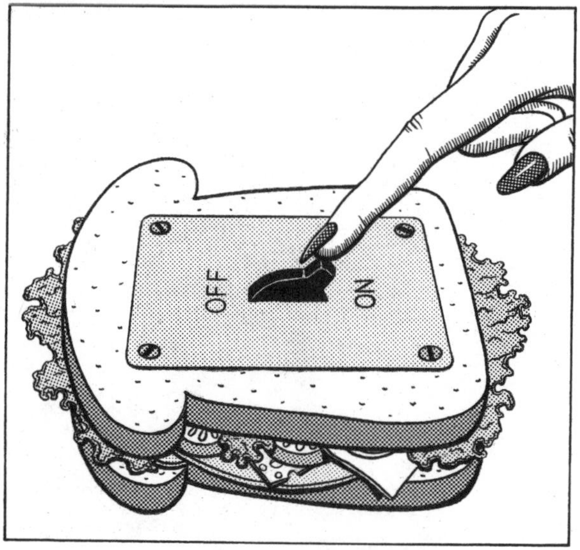
OFF
ON

Starting lunch

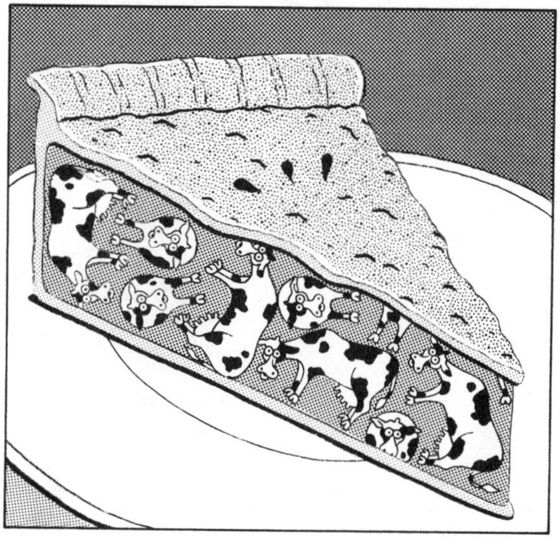

Cow pie

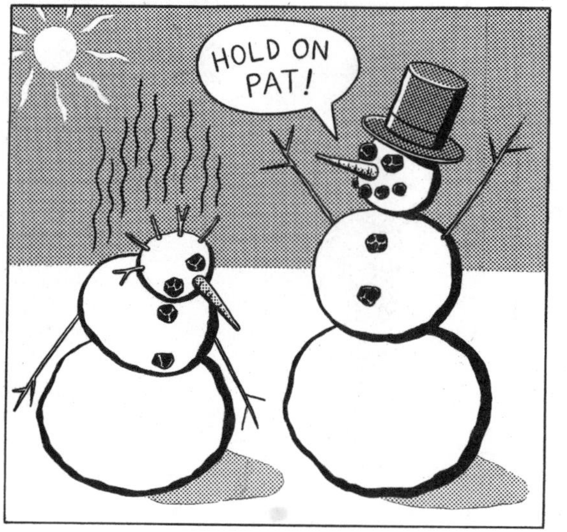
HOLD ON PAT!

Patty melt

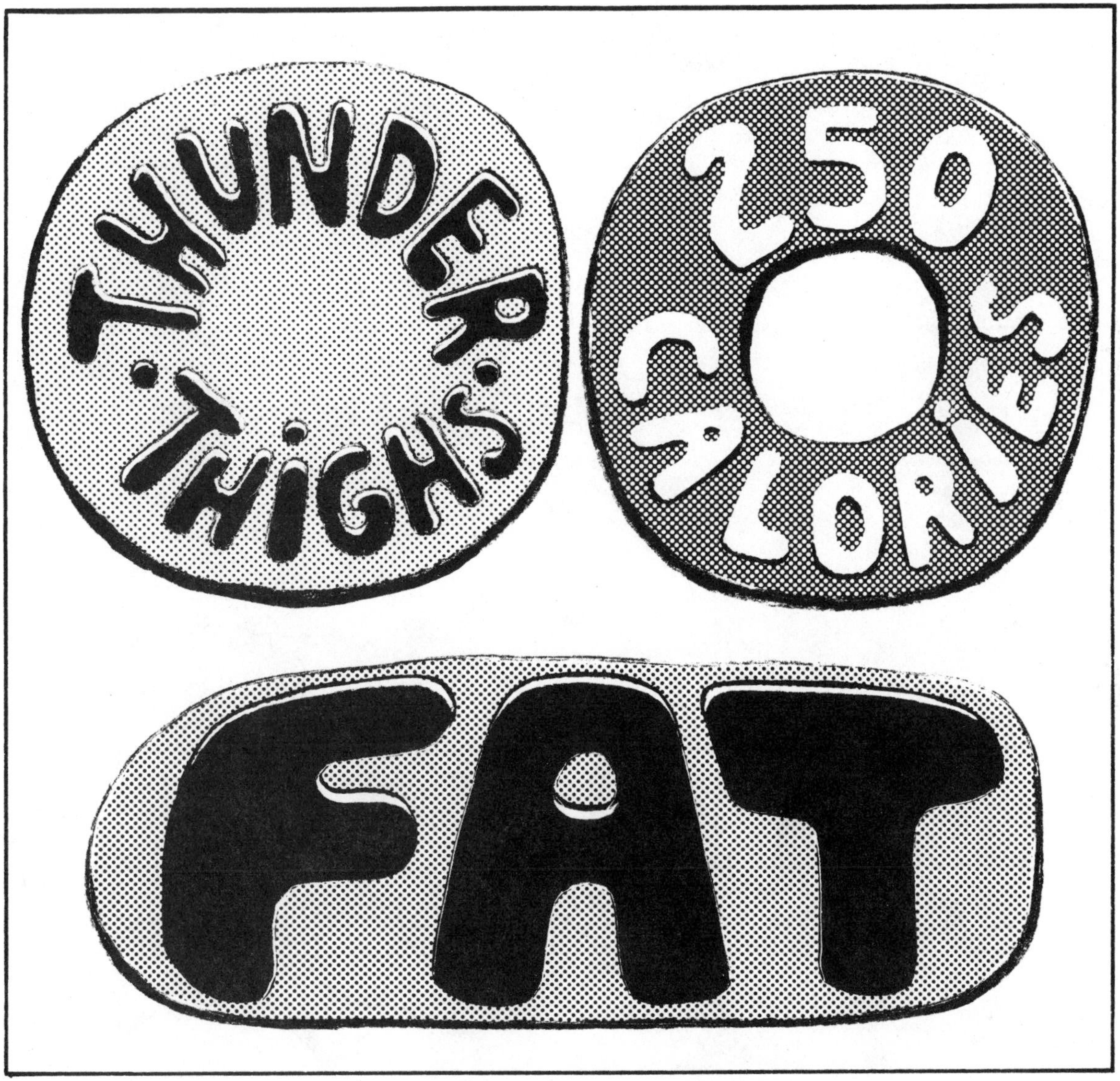
THUNDER THIGHS
250 CALORIES
FAT

Donuts should come with warning labels

Lawyers riding to work

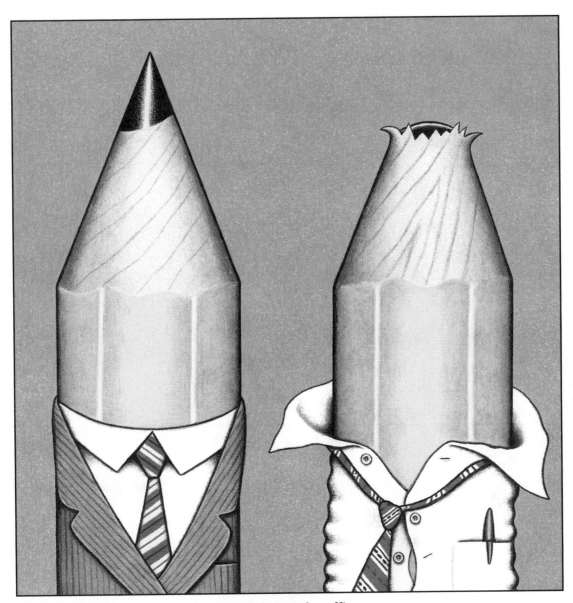

Hard day at the office

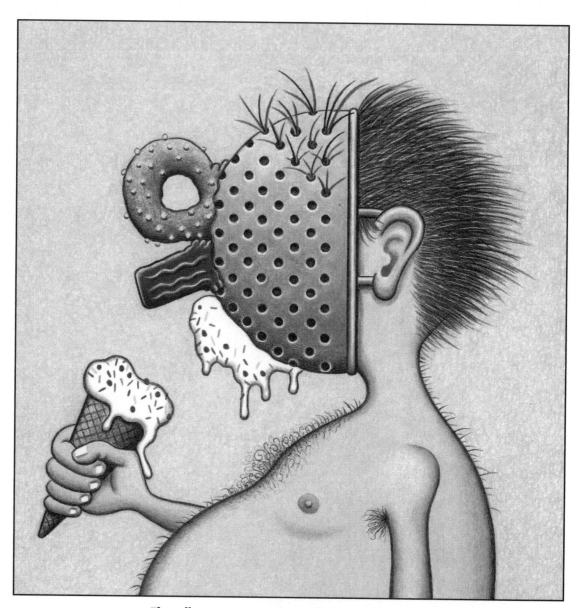

The all-you-can-eat-through-a-colander diet

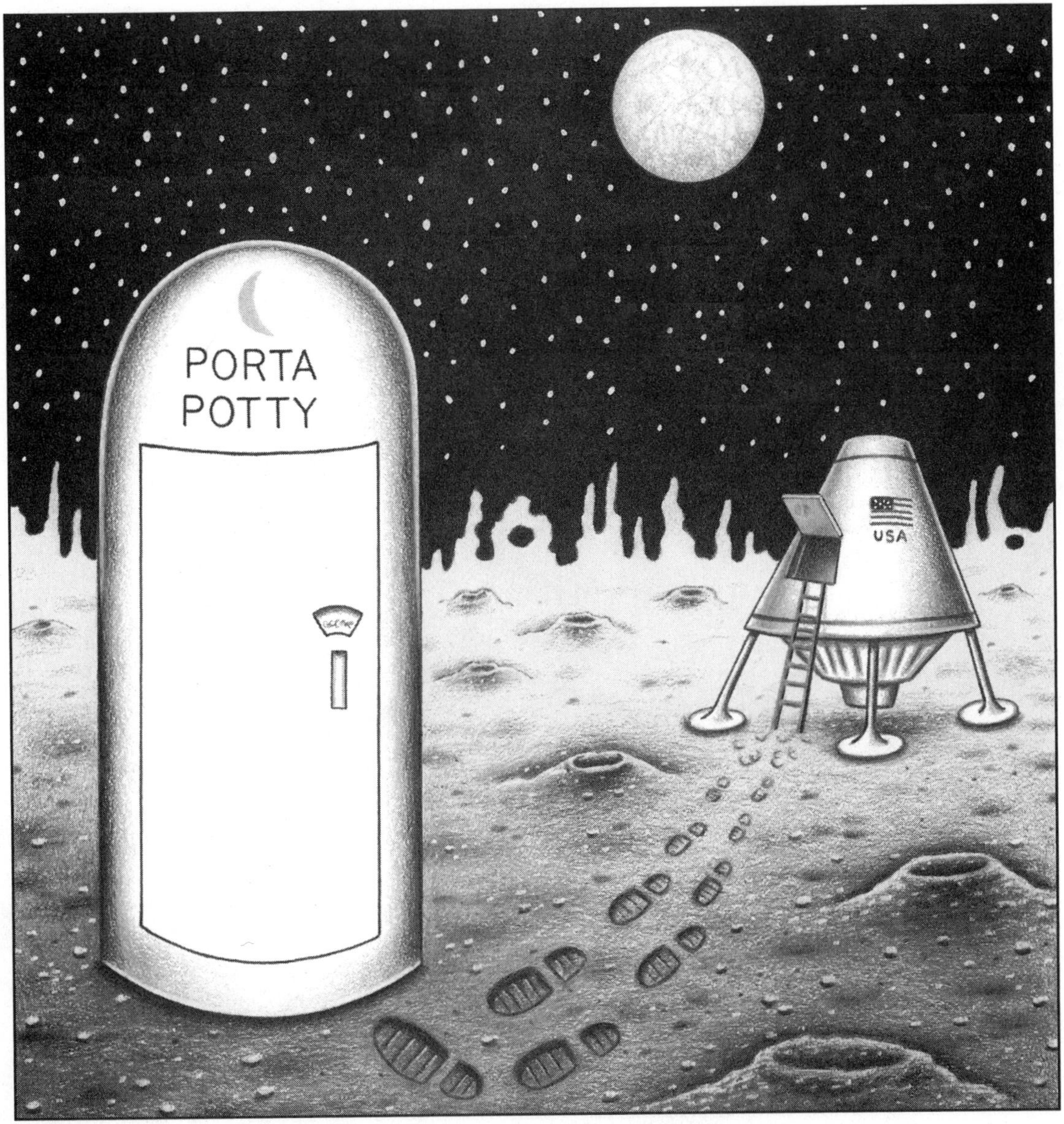
PORTA
POTTY
USA

To boldly go where no man has gone before

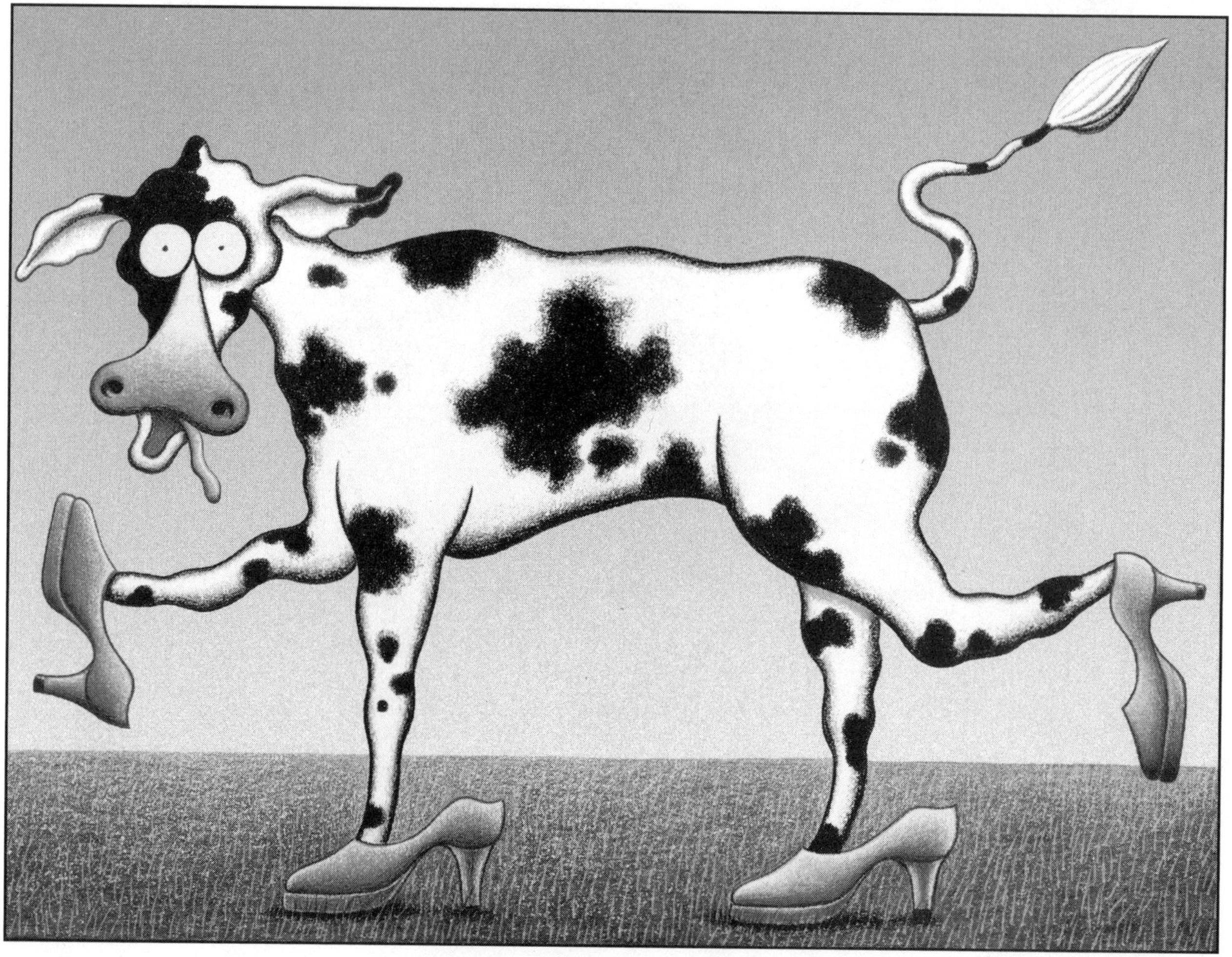

High heels make your calves look sexy

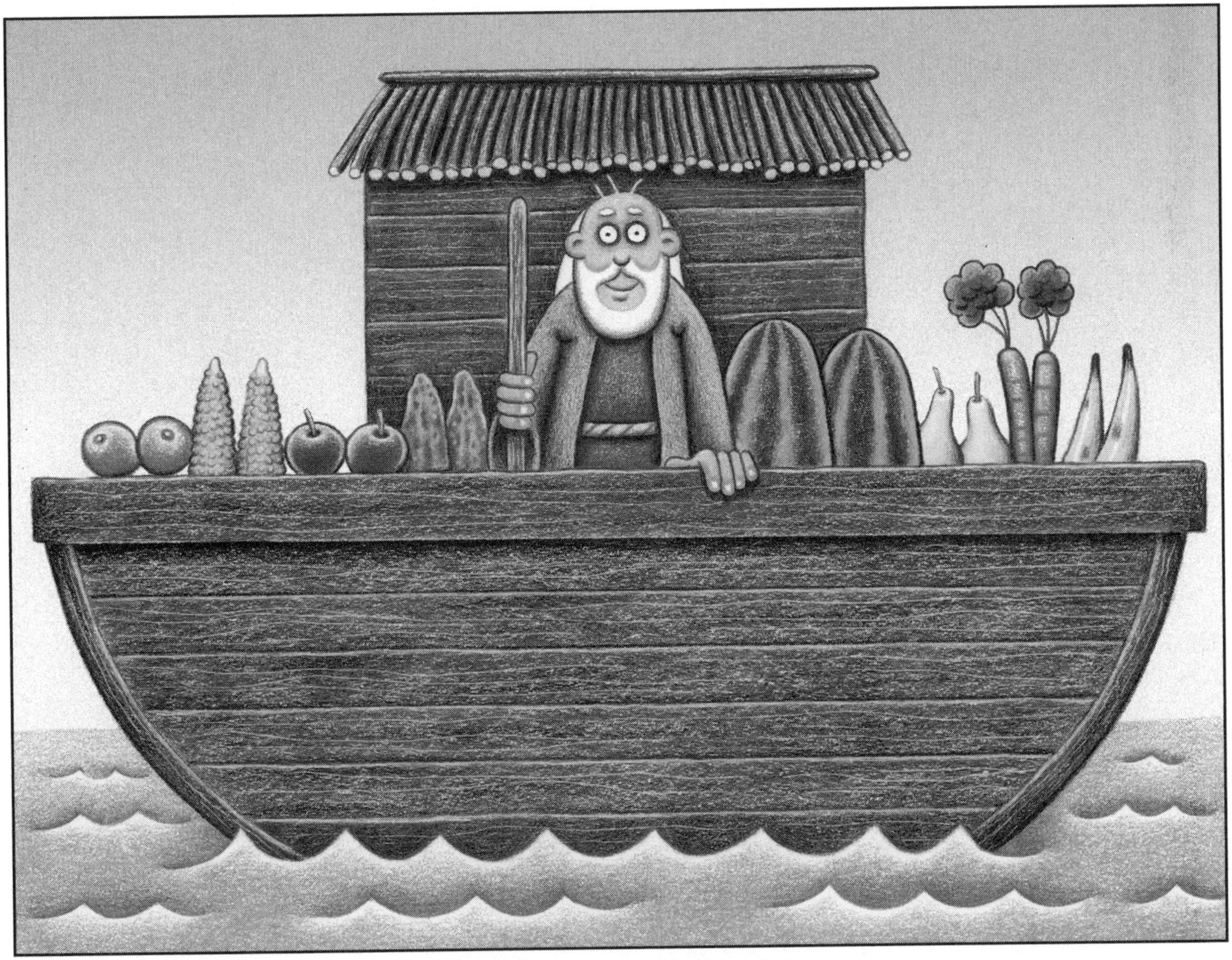

If Noah had been a vegetarian

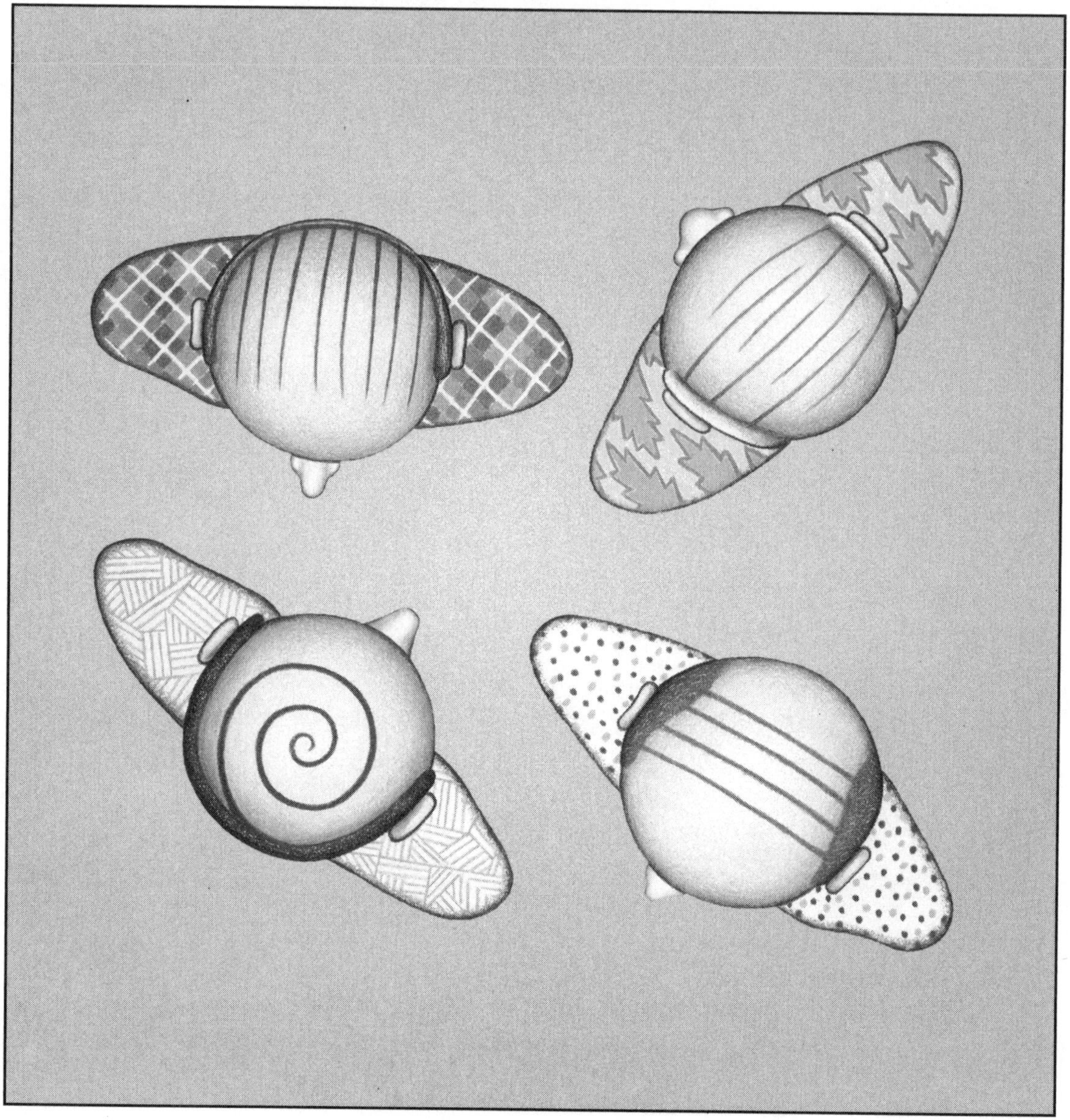

Aerial view of bald men cover-up techniques

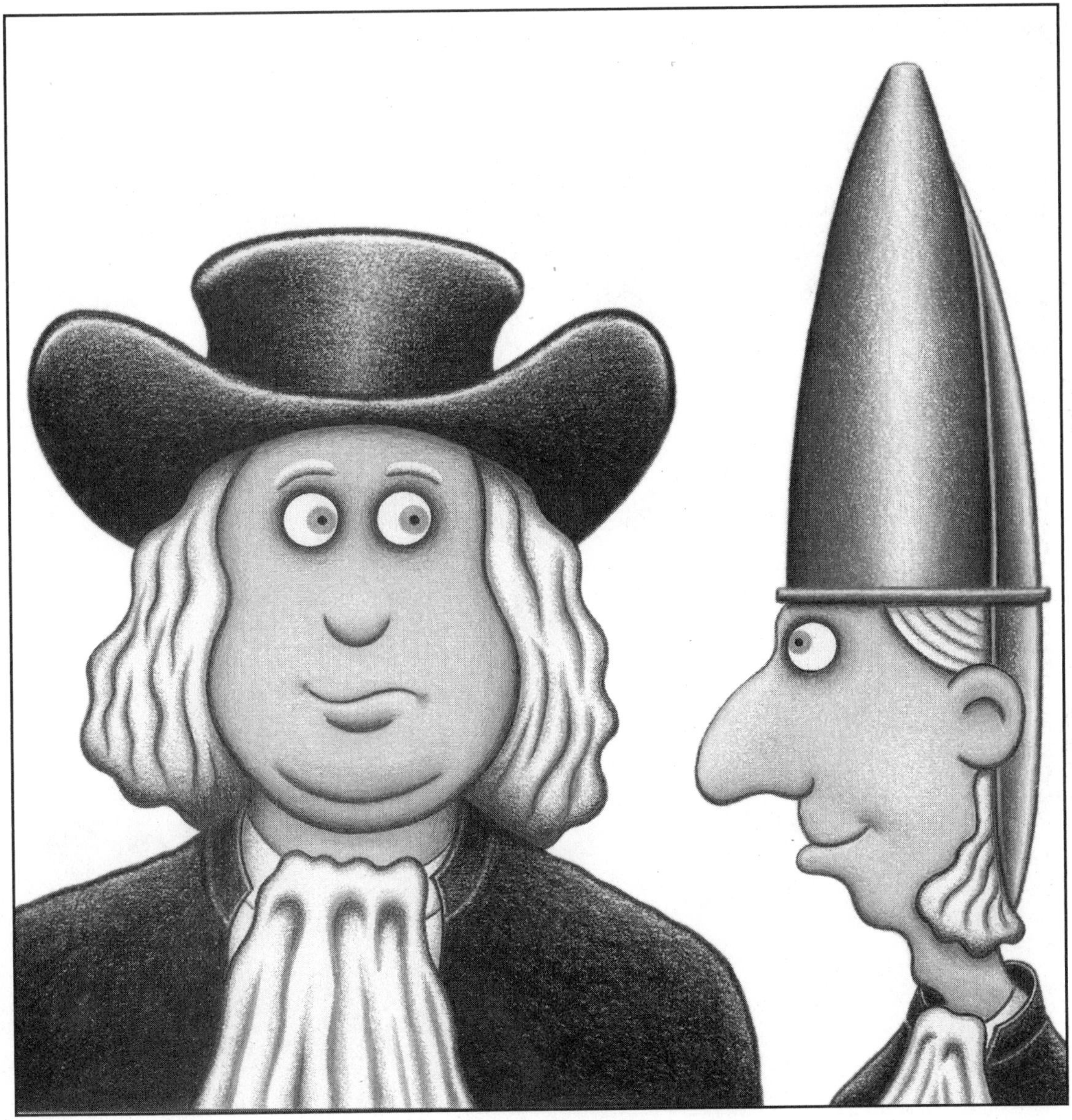

William Penn and his brother Bic

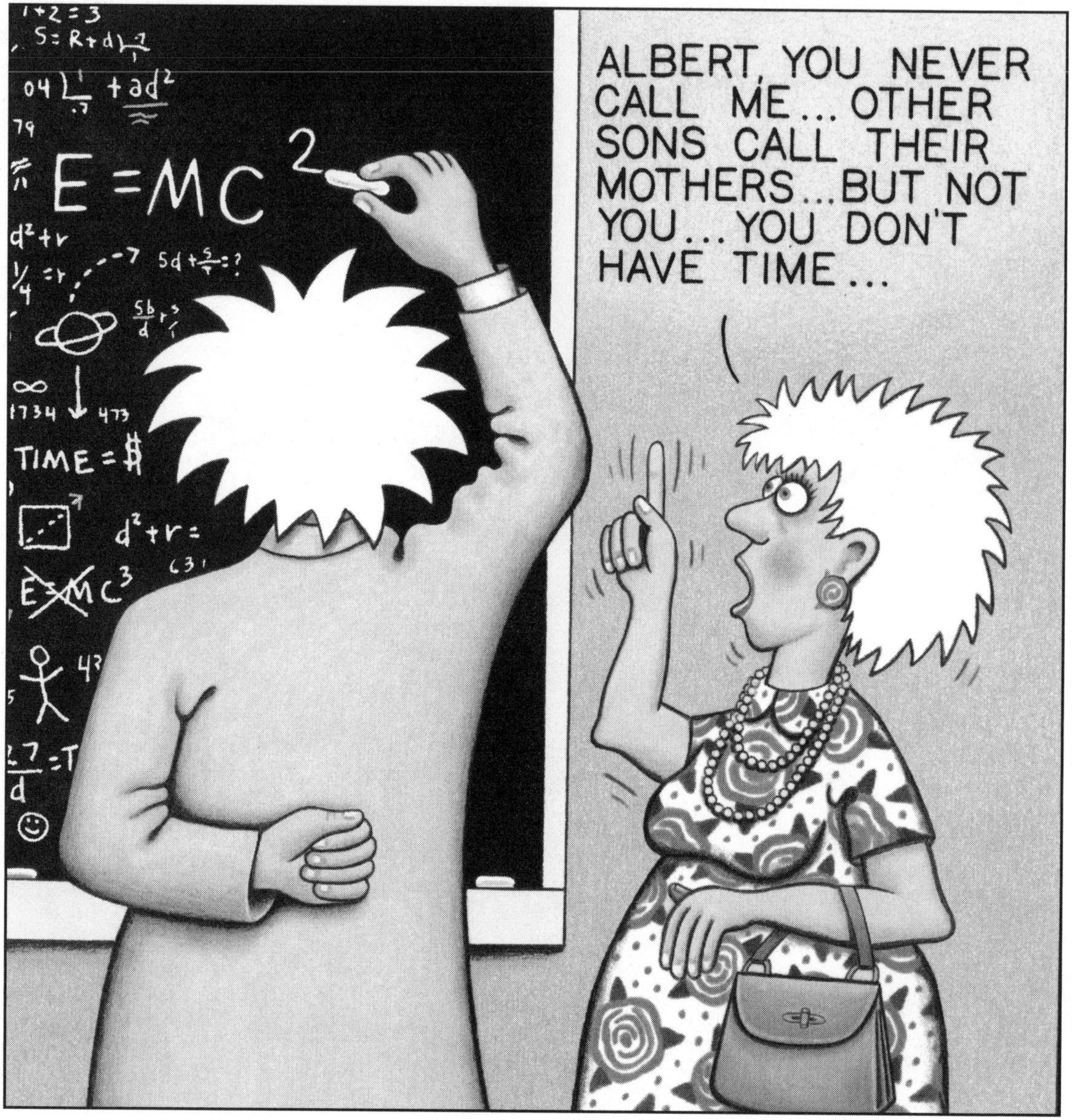
ALBERT, YOU NEVER CALL ME... OTHER SONS CALL THEIR MOTHERS...BUT NOT YOU... YOU DON'T HAVE TIME...
E = MC²
TIME = $

Einstein discovers that sound and guilt travel at the same speed

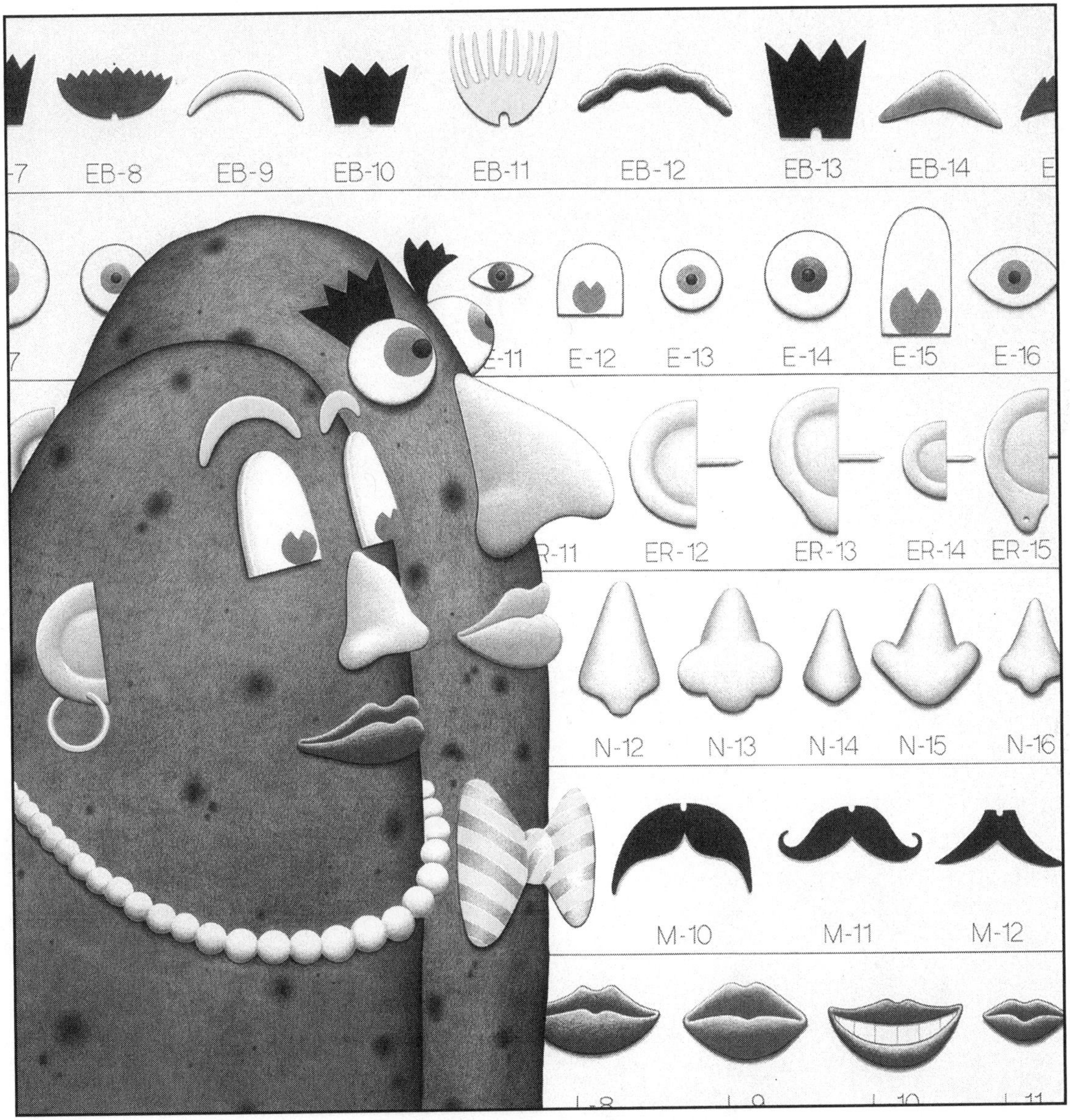
EB-8
EB-9
EB-10
EB-11
EB-12
EB-13
EB-14
E-12
E-13
E-14
E-15
E-16
ER-12
ER-13
ER-14
ER-15
N-12
N-13
N-14
N-15
N-16
M-10
M-11
M-12

Mr. & Mrs. Potato Head consider plastic surgery

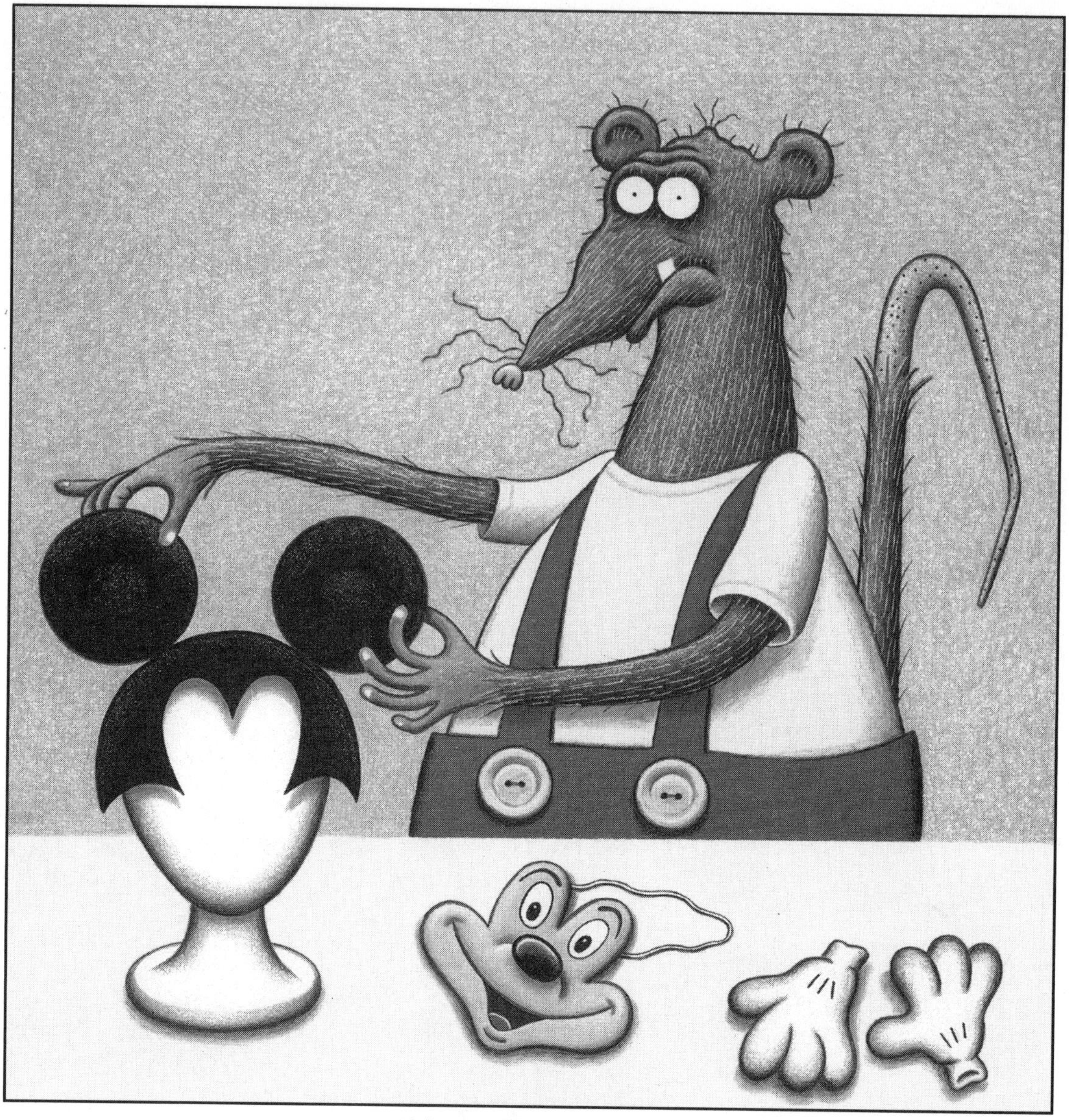

Mickey without make-up

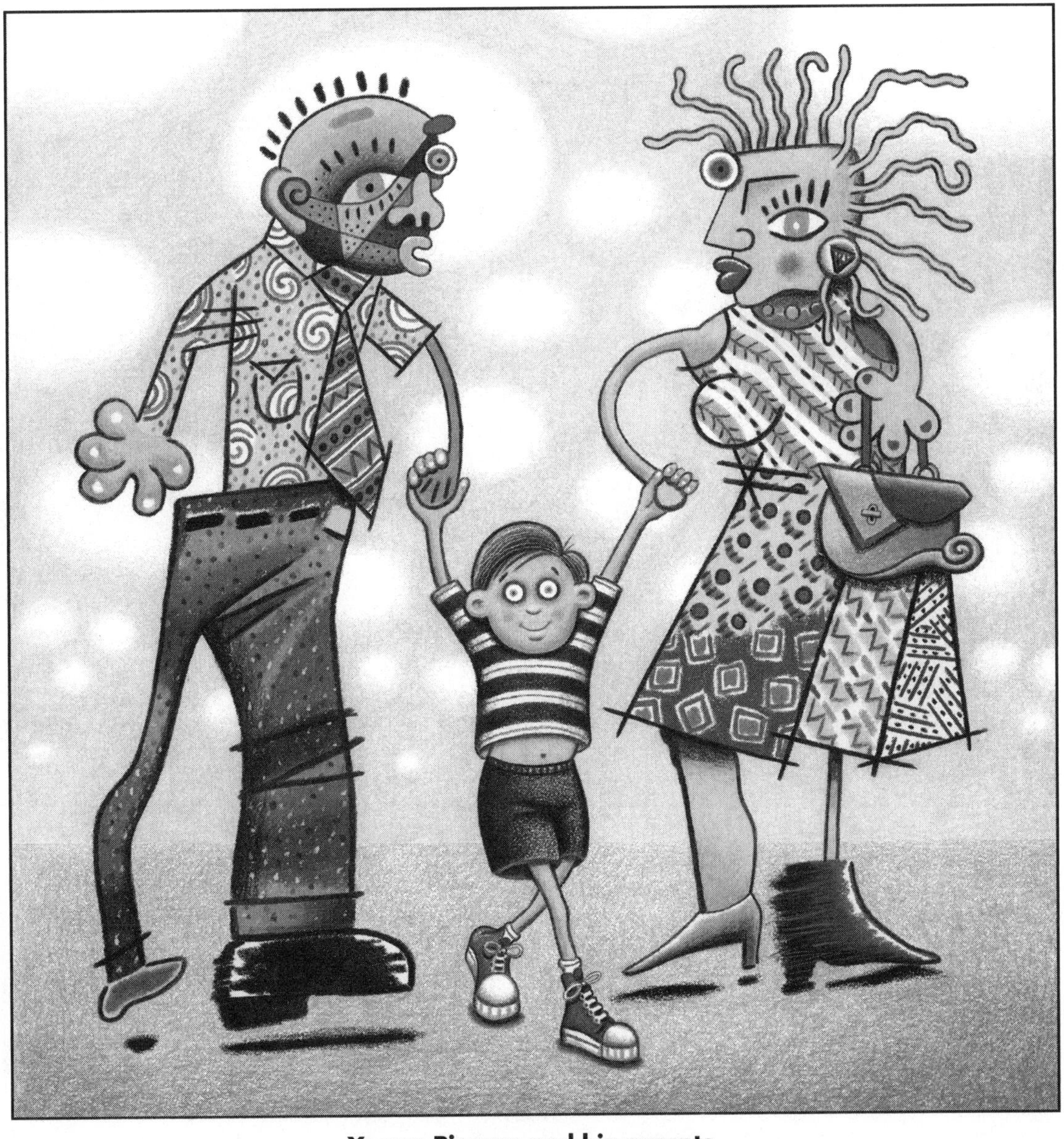
Young Picasso and his parents

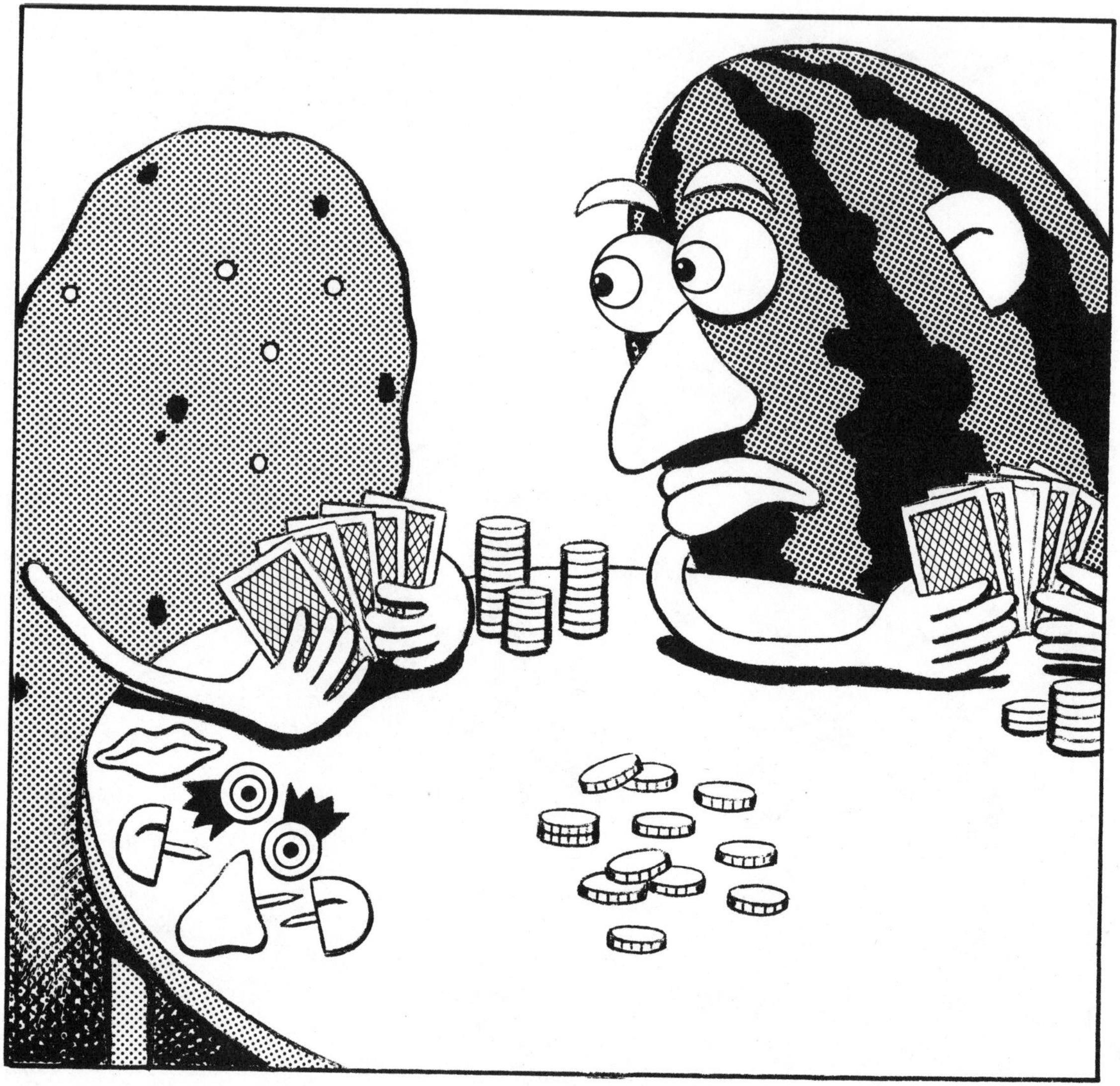

Mr. Potato Head has an excellent poker face

American Icons

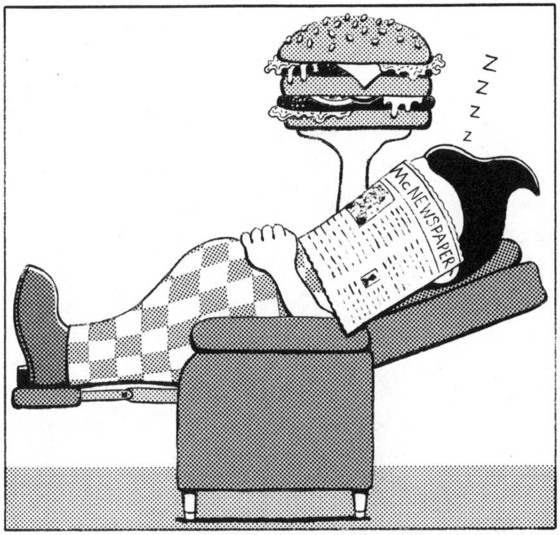
Z
Z
Z
Z
Z
McNEWSPAPER

Lazy Boy

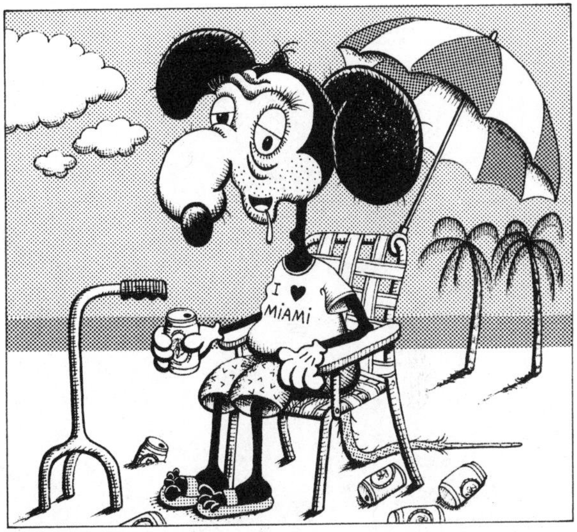
I ♥
MIAMI

The real Mickey is retired and living in Miami

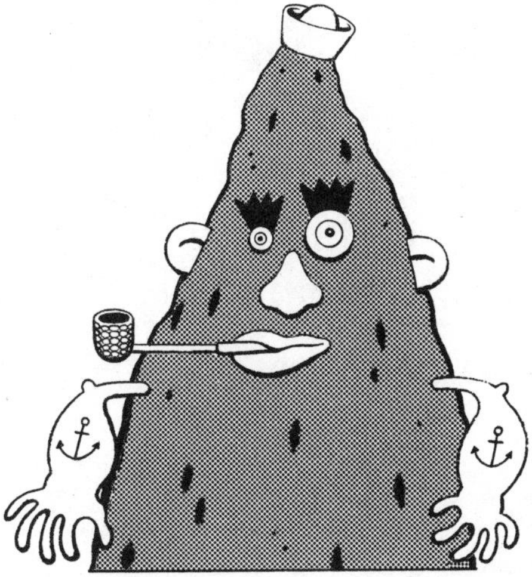

I yam what I yam and that's all that I yam

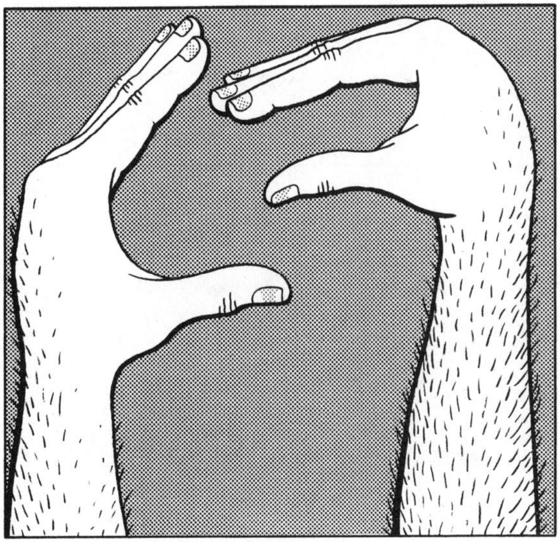

Kermit and Miss Piggy nude

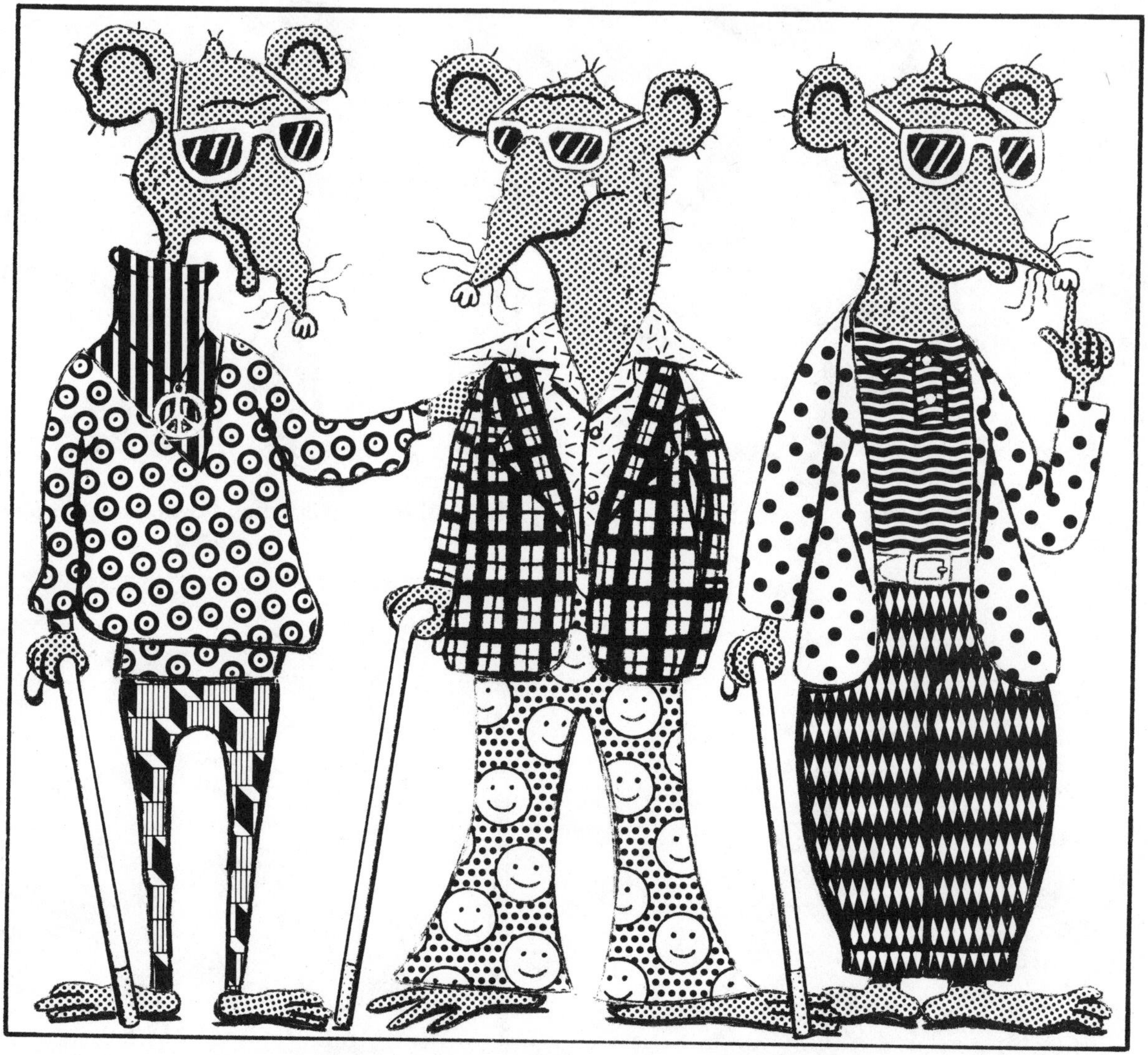

The Three Blind Mice dressed accordingly

Thin is in . . .

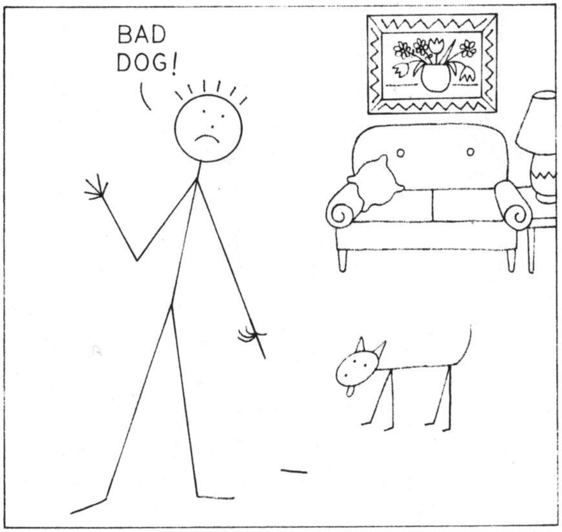
BAD
DOG!

Mr. Stickfigure's dog has an accident

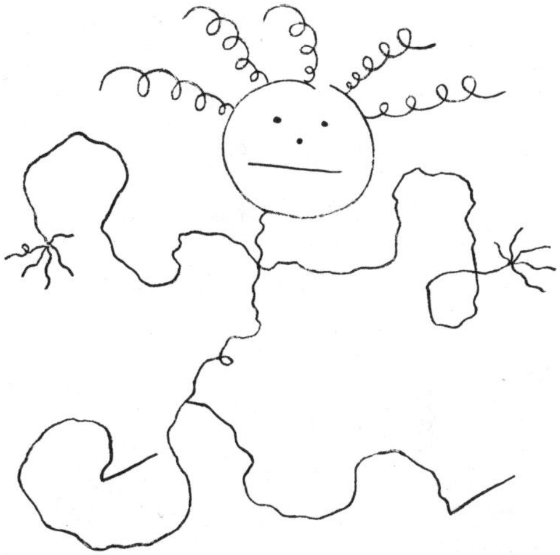

When the humidity goes up . . . Mrs. Stickfigure gets frizzy

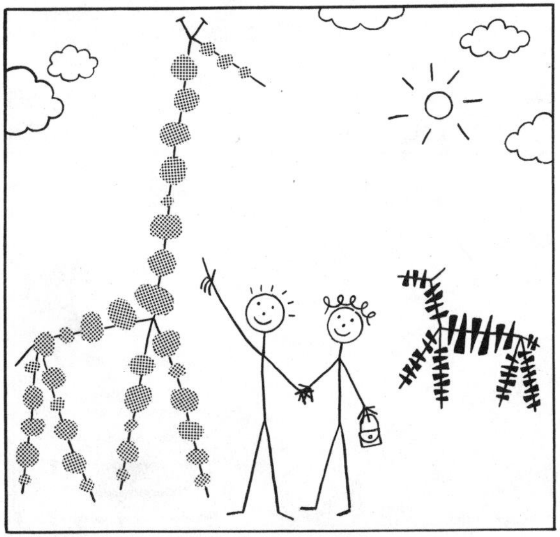

Mr. and Mrs. Stickfigure go to the zoo

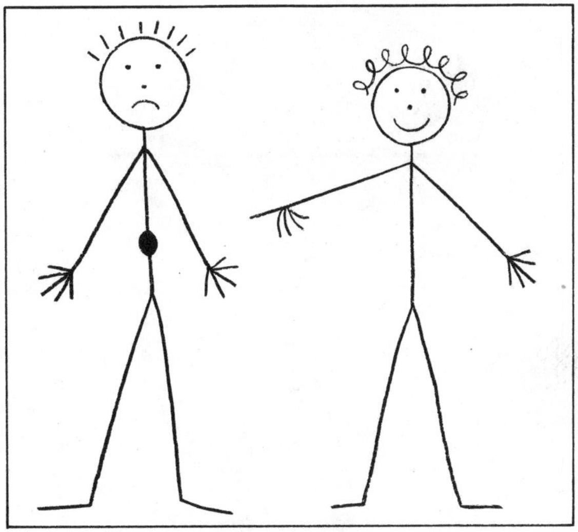

Mrs. Stickfigure making fun of Mr. Stickfigure's love handles

The Write Stuff

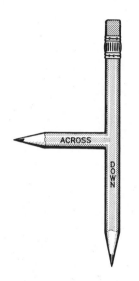

A crossword puzzle pencil

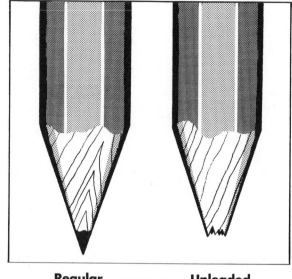

Regular ———— Unleaded

TRANSYLVANIA

PENCILVANIA

Early signs of lead poisoning

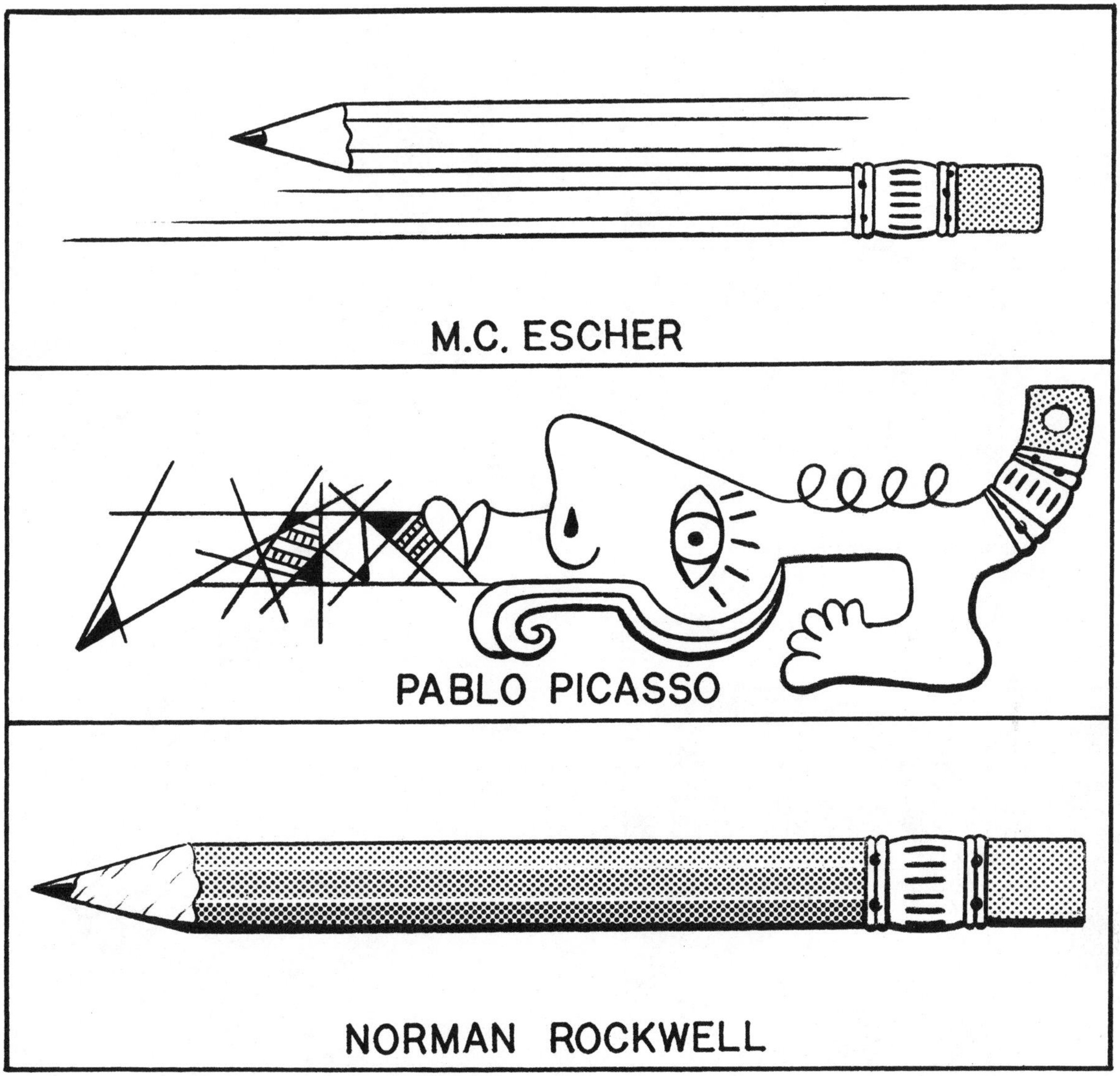

M.C. ESCHER
PABLO PICASSO
NORMAN ROCKWELL

Pencils of famous artists

Imagine That

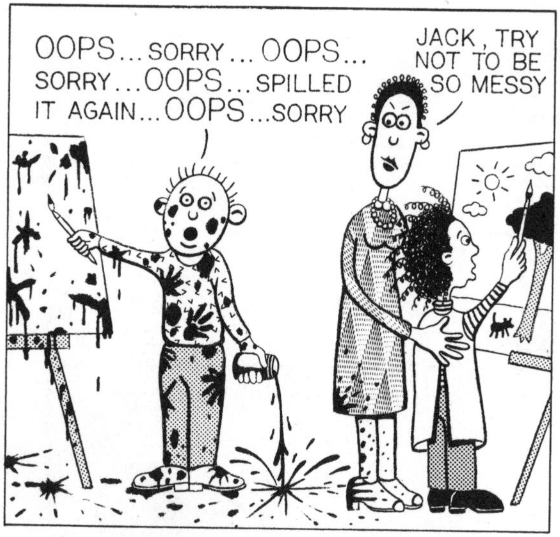
OOPS... SORRY... OOPS... SORRY... OOPS... SPILLED IT AGAIN... OOPS... SORRY
JACK, TRY NOT TO BE SO MESSY

Young Jackson Pollock

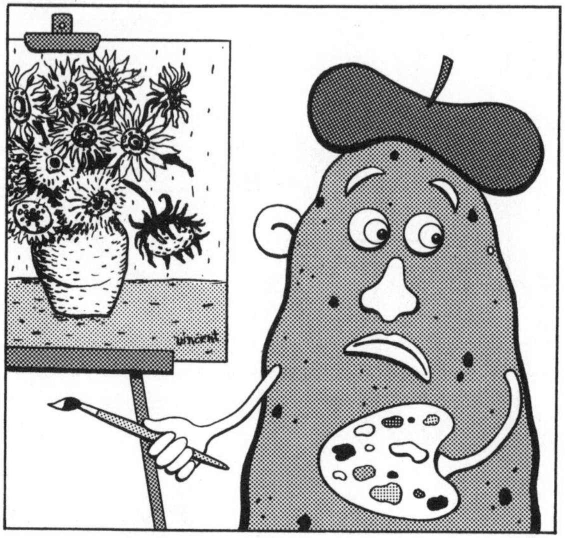
VINCENT

Vincent van Potatogh

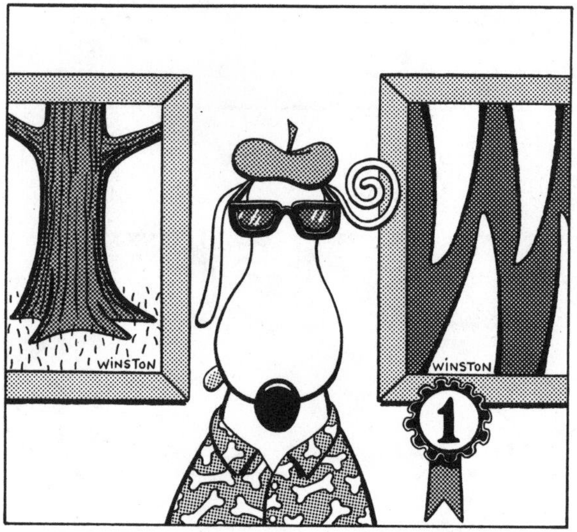
WINSTON
WINSTON
1

Winston's bark is worse than his bite

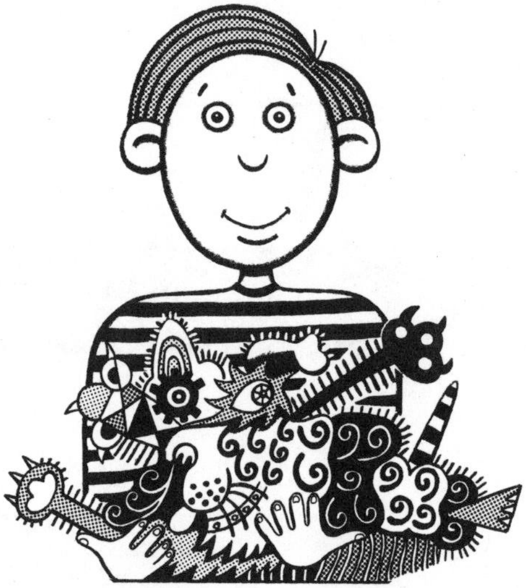

Young Picasso with his dog...or cat...or...

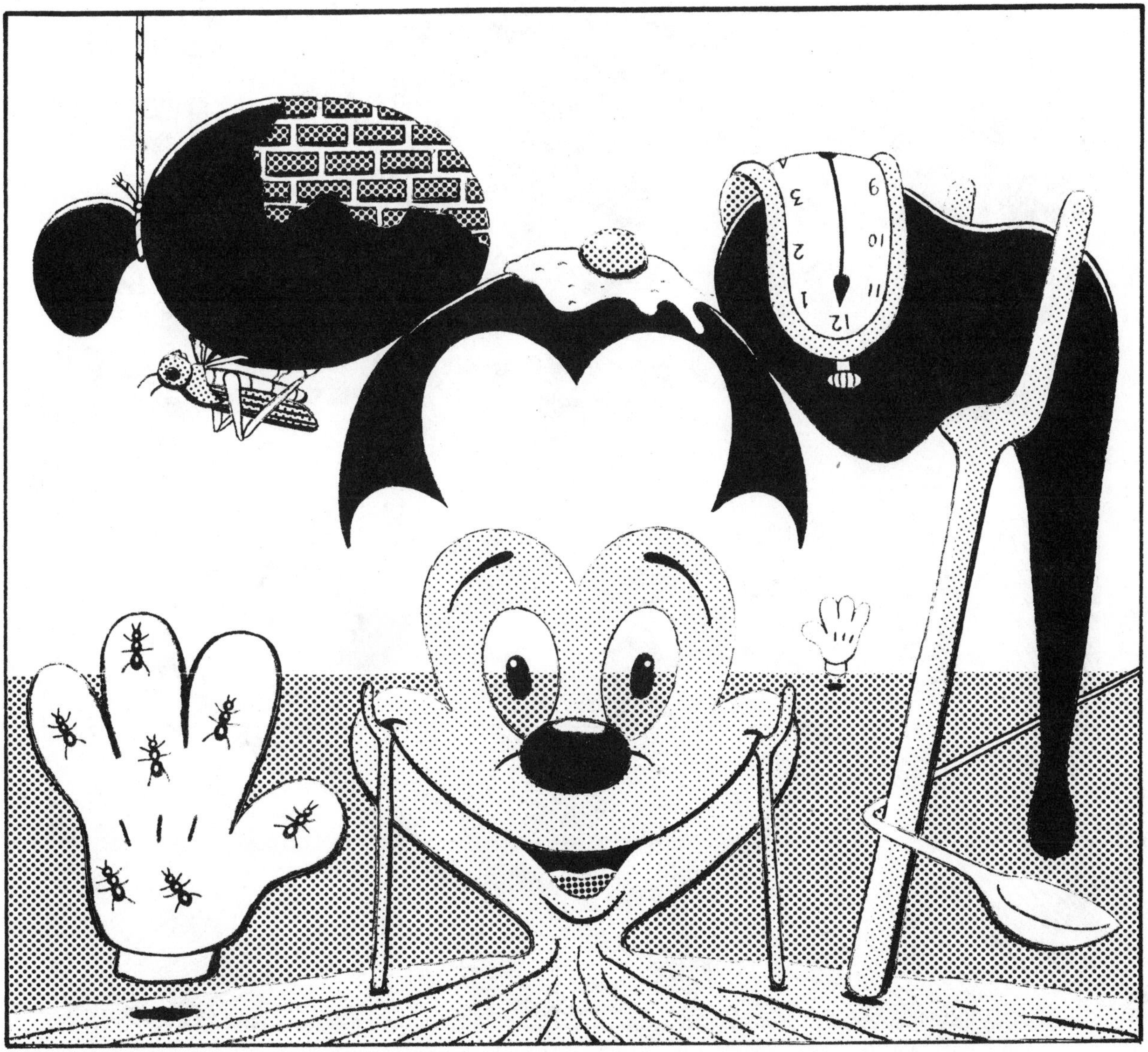

3
9
2
10
1
11
12

If Mickey had been created by Salvador Dali

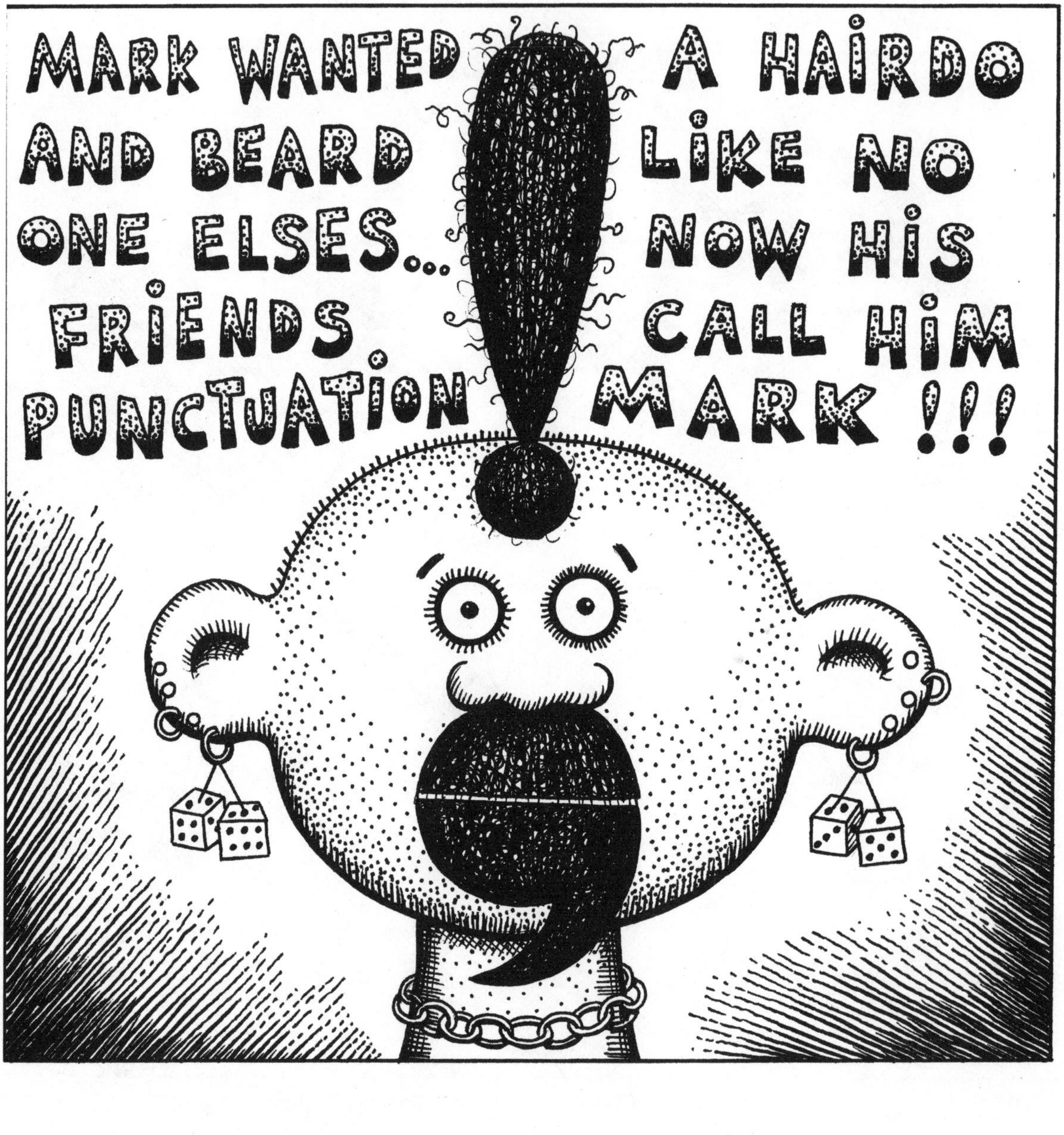
MARK WANTED A HAIRDO AND BEARD LIKE NO ONE ELSES... NOW HIS FRIENDS CALL HIM PUNCTUATION MARK!!!

Creature Comforts

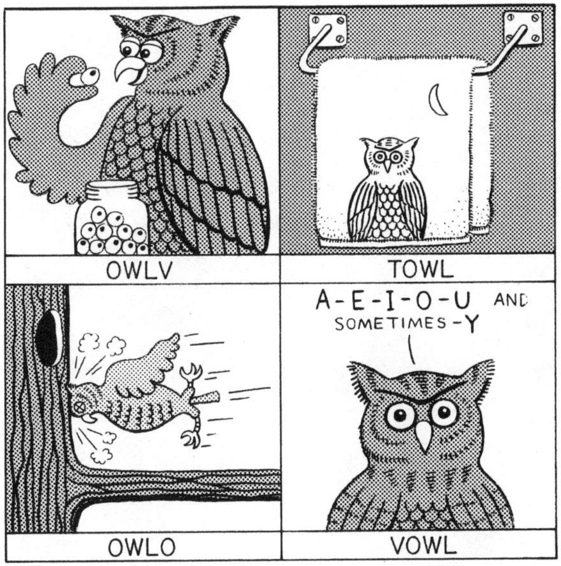
OWLV
TOWL
OWLO
A-E-I-O-U AND
SOMETIMES-Y
VOWL

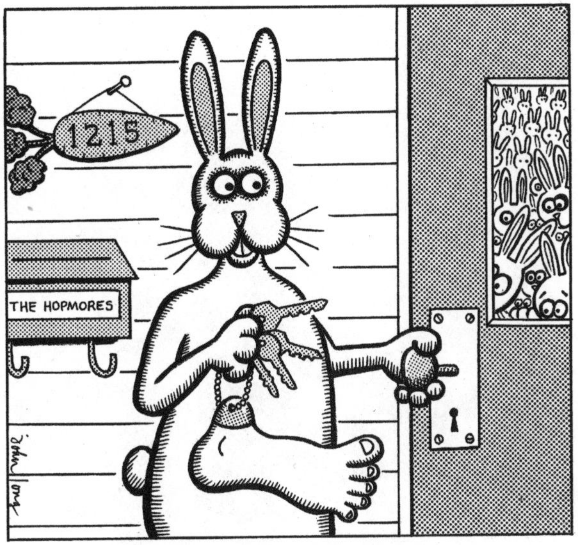
1215
THE HOPMORES

Rabbit with a lucky people's foot

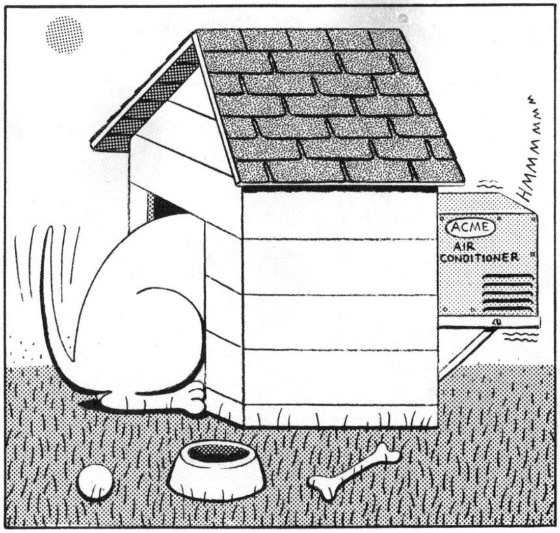
HMMMMMMMM
ACME
AIR
CONDITIONER

Home improvement

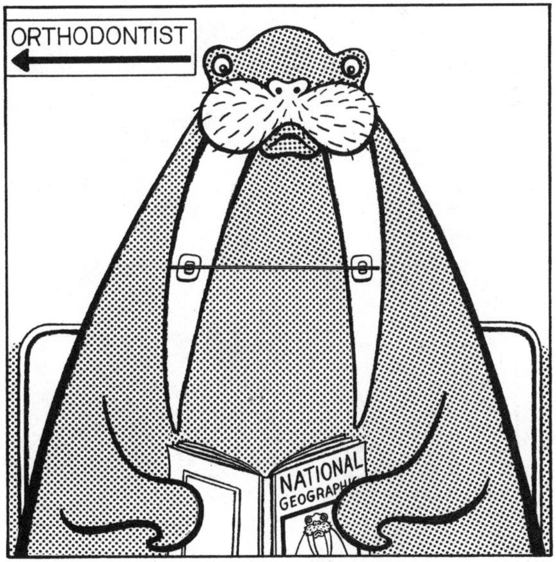
ORTHODONTIST
NATIONAL
GEOGRAPH

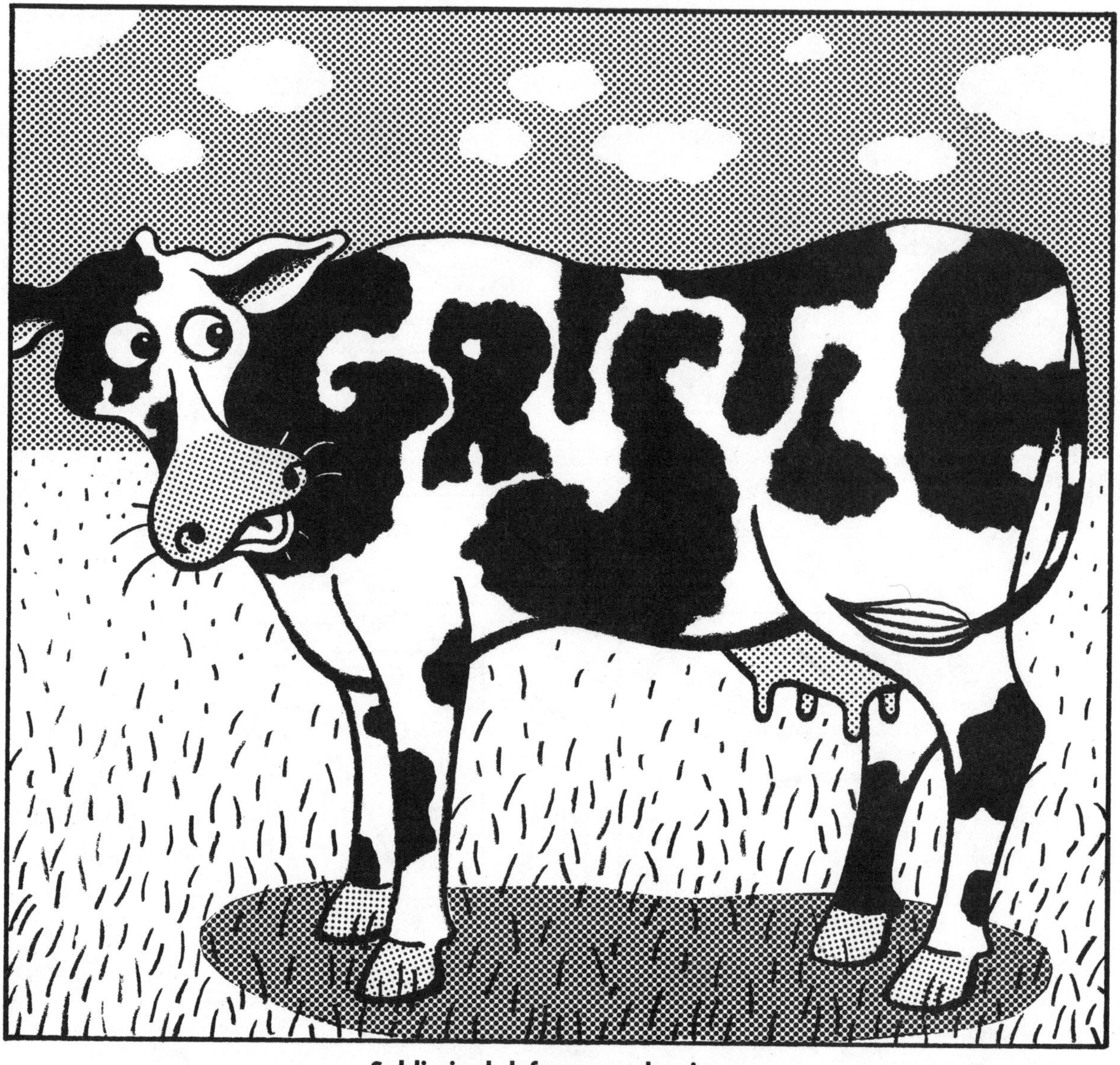

Subliminal defense mechanism

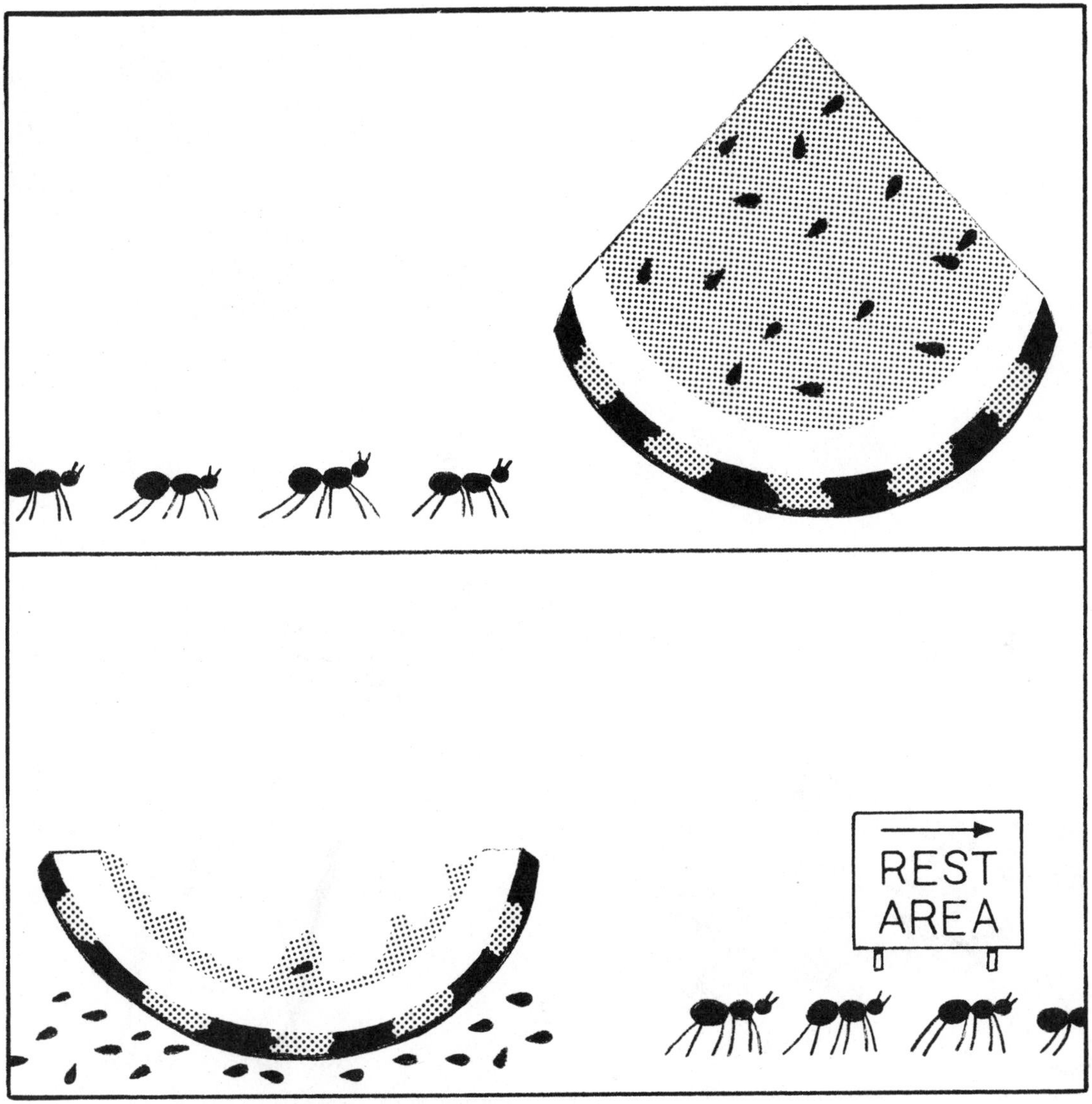
REST
AREA

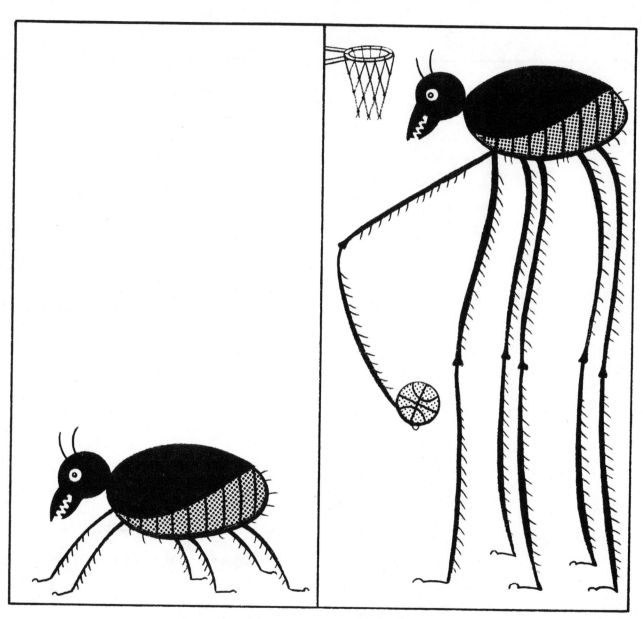

A regular tick ——————— A celtic

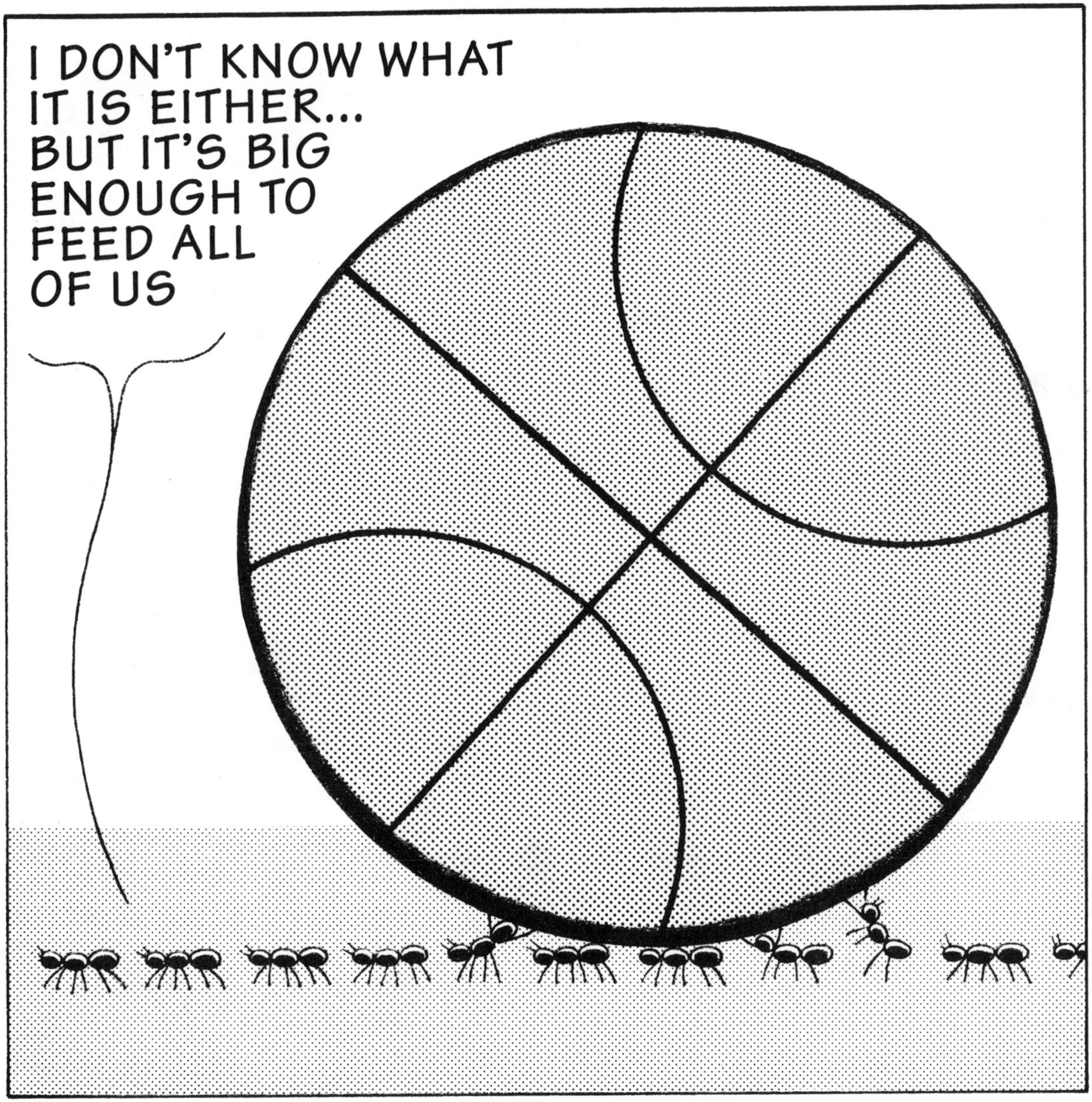
I DON'T KNOW WHAT IT IS EITHER... BUT IT'S BIG ENOUGH TO FEED ALL OF US

Little Buggers

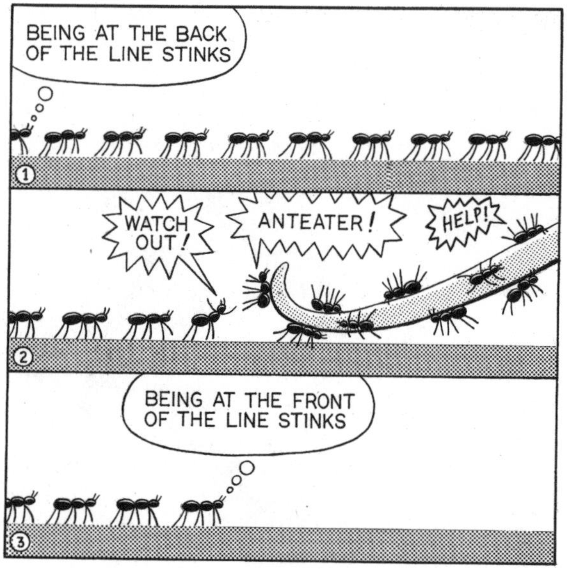

BEING AT THE BACK OF THE LINE STINKS
1
WATCH OUT!
ANTEATER!
HELP!
2
BEING AT THE FRONT OF THE LINE STINKS
3

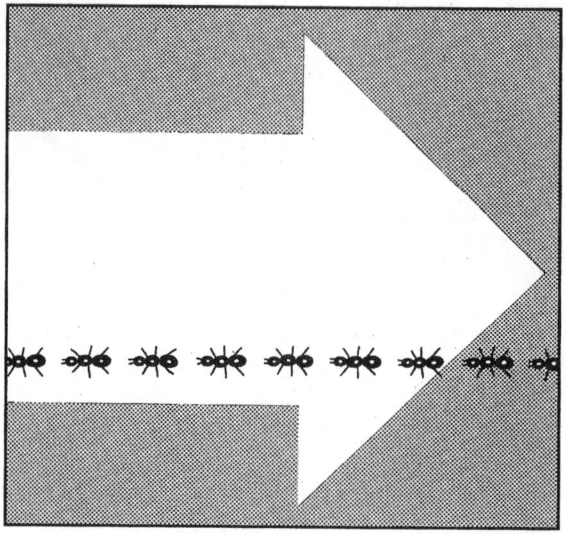

Anti-establishment

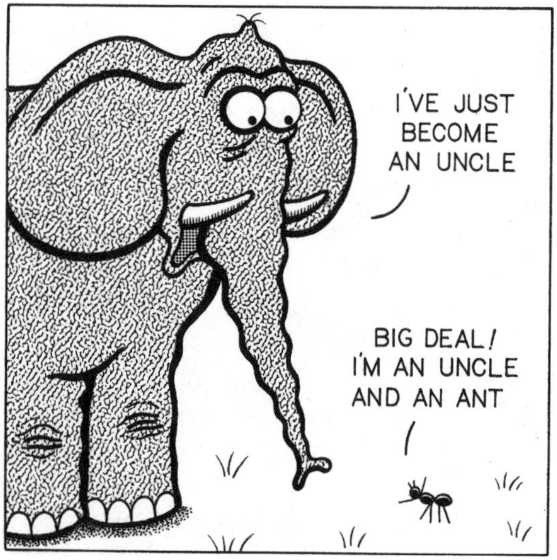

I'VE JUST BECOME AN UNCLE
BIG DEAL! I'M AN UNCLE AND AN ANT

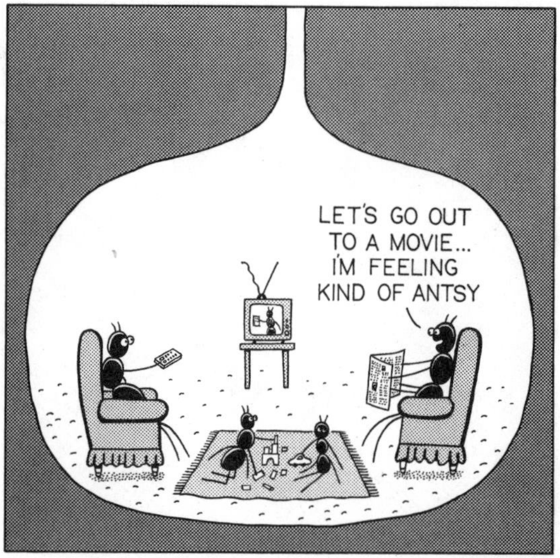

LET'S GO OUT TO A MOVIE... I'M FEELING KIND OF ANTSY

Grass Stains

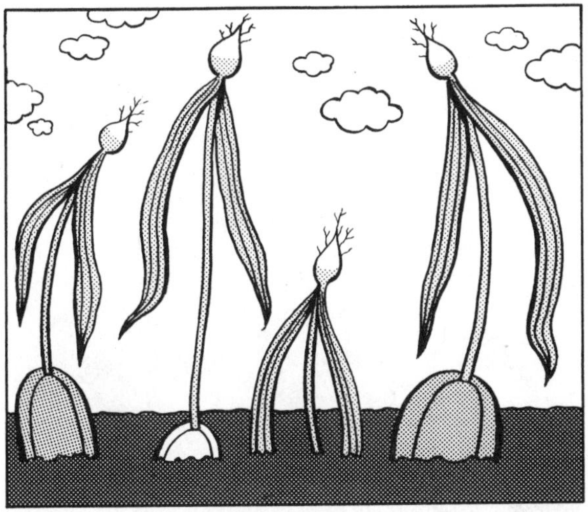

You really feel stupid when you realize that you've planted your tulip bulbs upside down

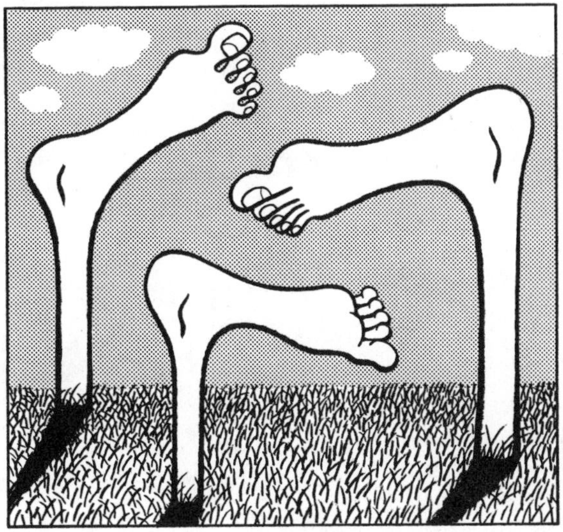

There are three feet in a yard

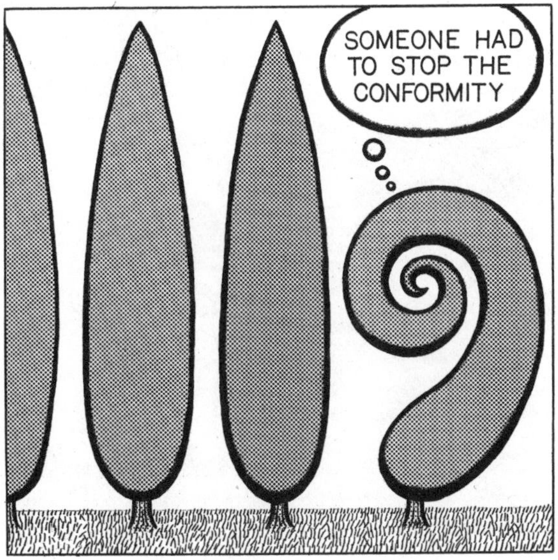
SOMEONE HAD TO STOP THE CONFORMITY

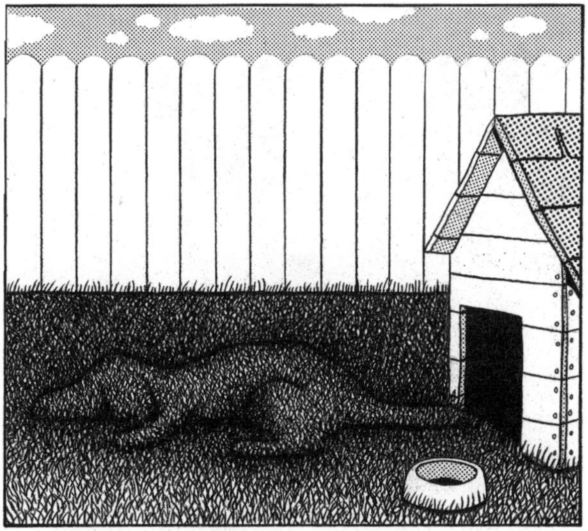

The dog disappeared right after the new sod was laid

The Hunt

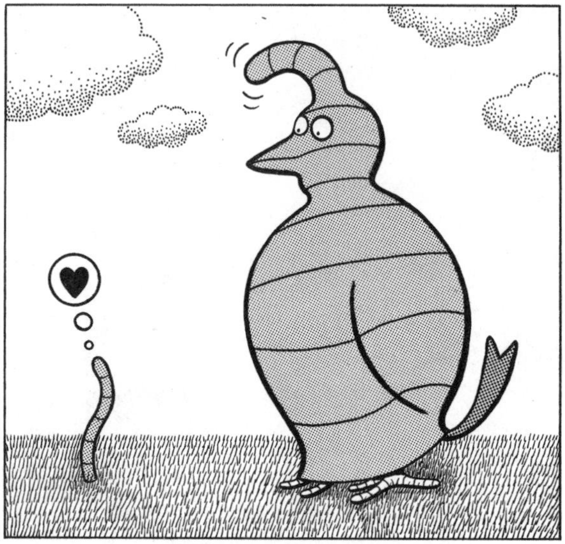

Robin using the fake-worm attack maneuver

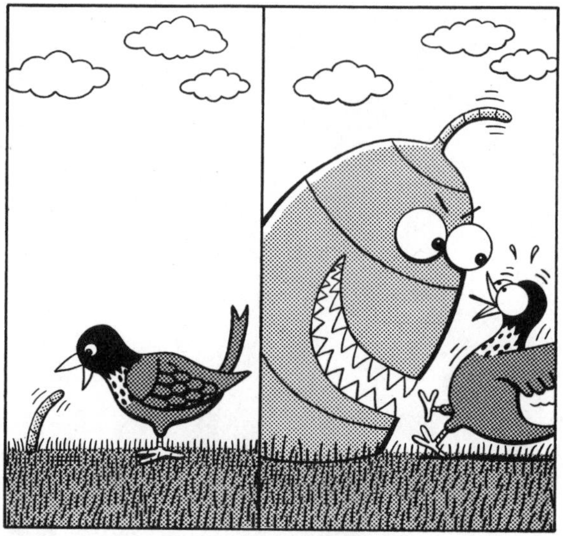

The worm turns

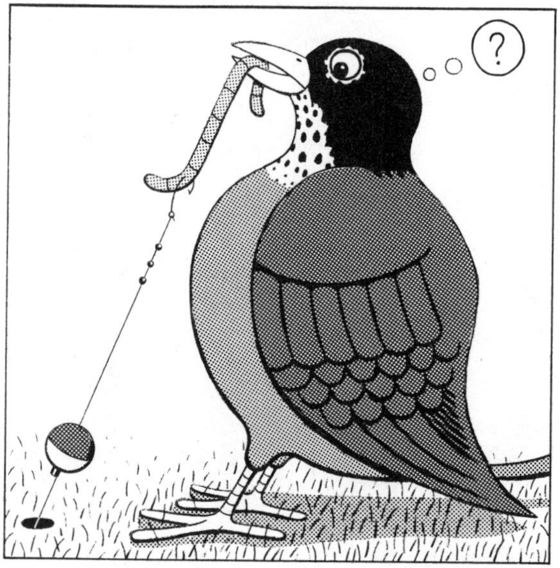

?

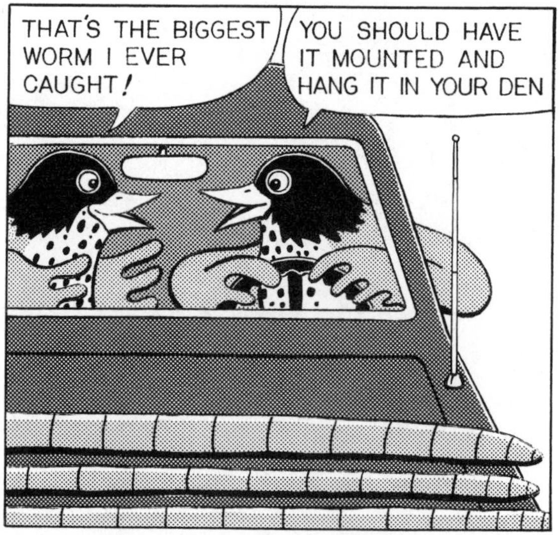

THAT'S THE BIGGEST WORM I EVER CAUGHT!
YOU SHOULD HAVE IT MOUNTED AND HANG IT IN YOUR DEN

Robins returning from the hunt

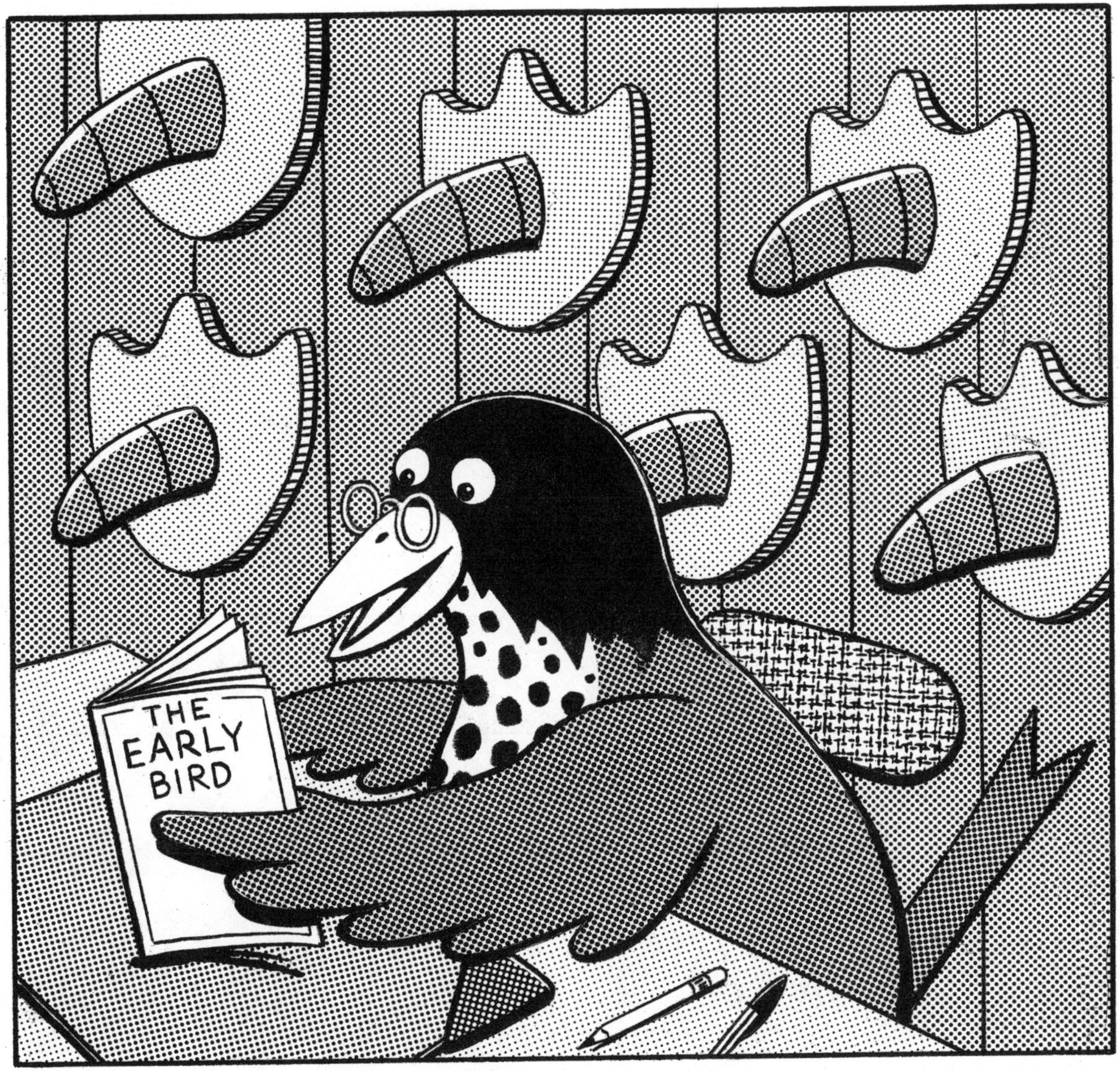
THE
EARLY
BIRD

Mr. Robin's den

Weather You Like It or Not

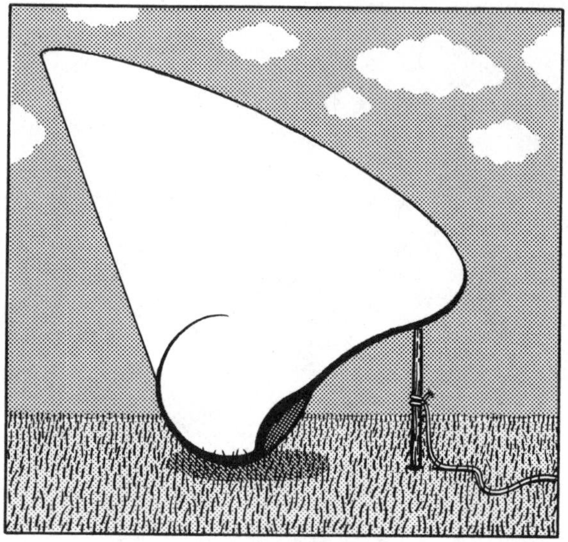

Catching a cold

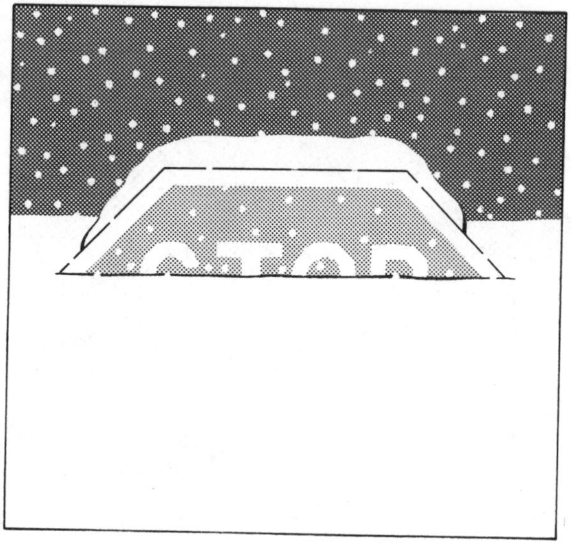

No sign of stopping

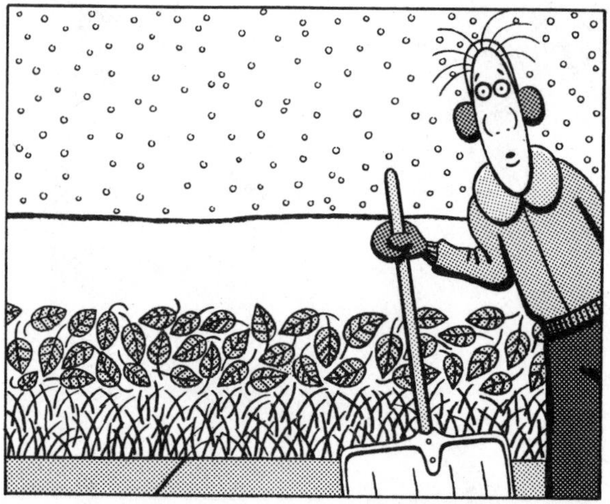

Flem's a little behind...while shoveling the snow, he discovers that he hasn't even cut the grass or raked the leaves yet

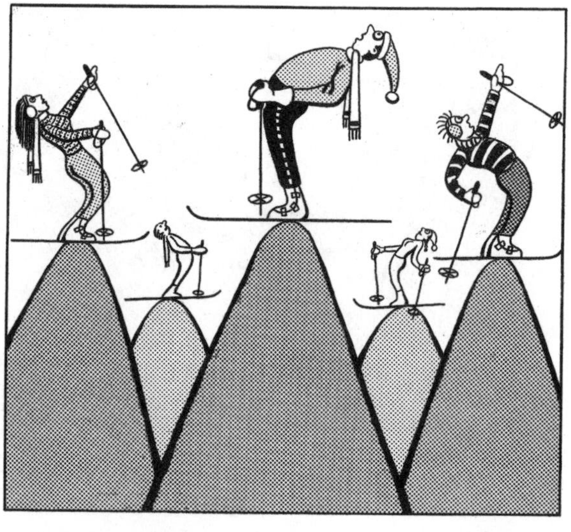

Skiers watching for the first sign of snow

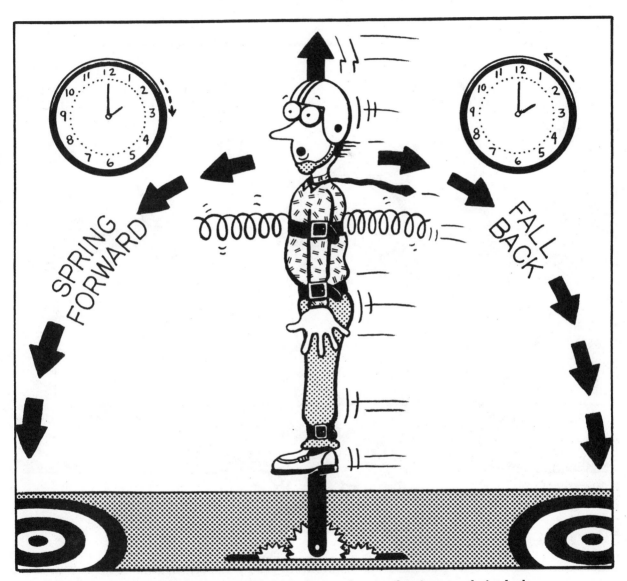

SPRING FORWARD

FALL BACK

Some people need a subtle reminder to change the time on their clocks

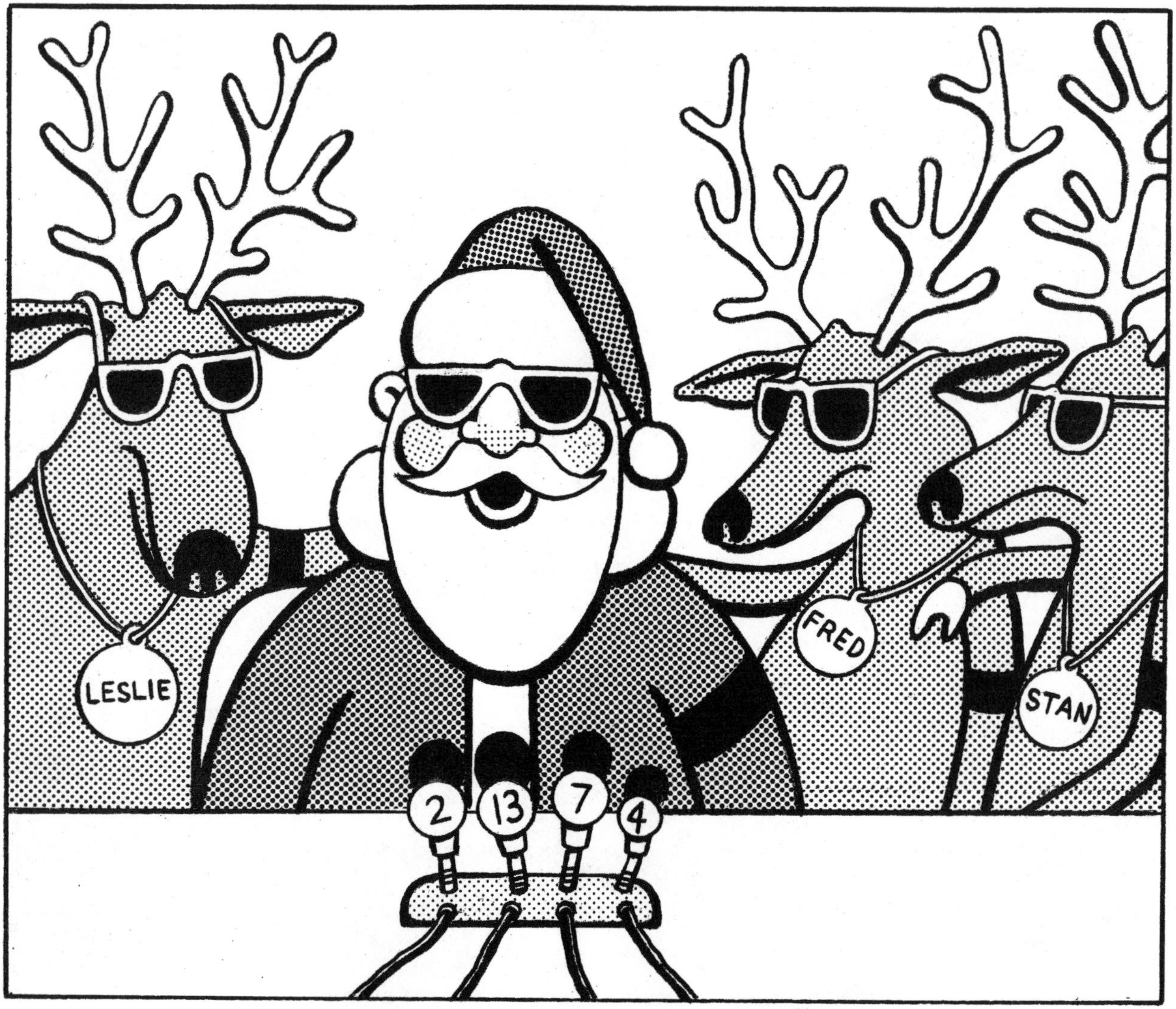
LESLIE
FRED
STAN
2
13
7
4

"Due to deer hunting season, Blitzen, Comet and Prancer will be replaced by Leslie, Fred and Stan."

Out of the Ordinary

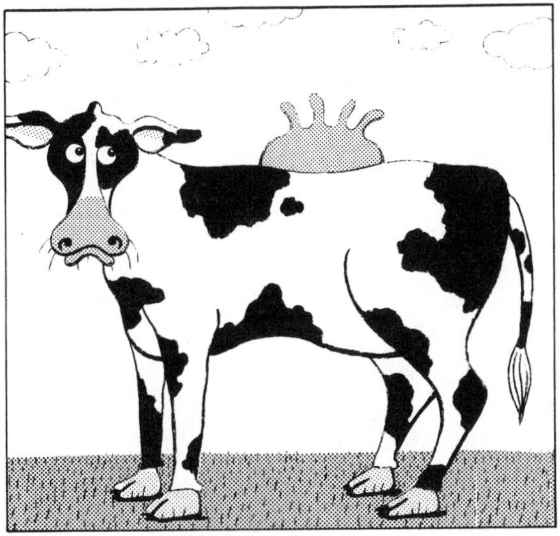

Cow with a dislocated udder

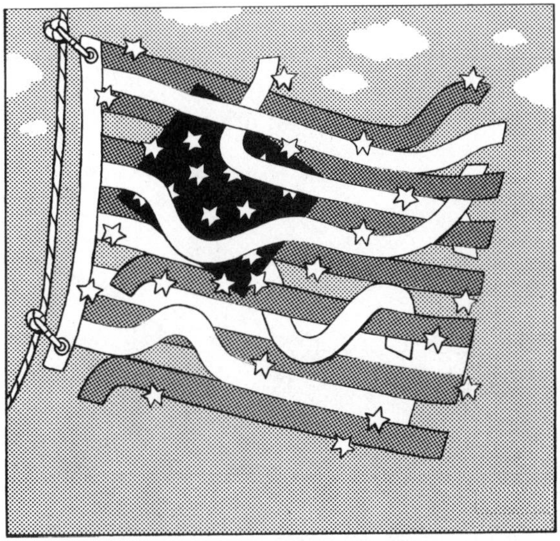

Flag after a really windy day

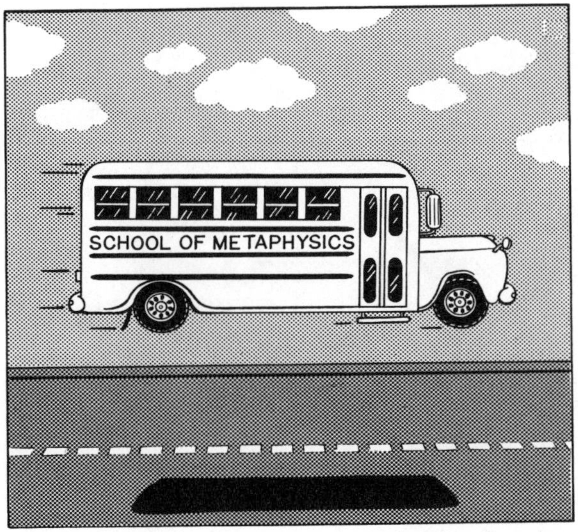
SCHOOL OF METAPHYSICS

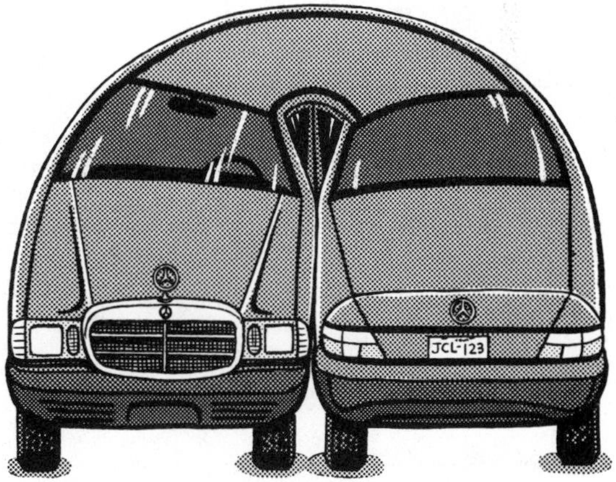
JCL-123

Mercedes bends

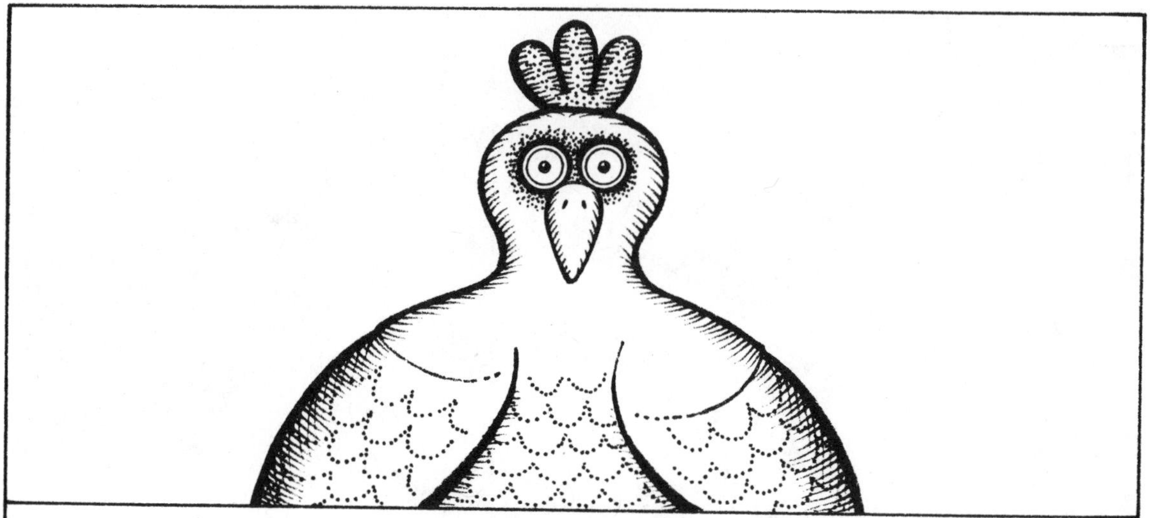

AN EGG LAYER

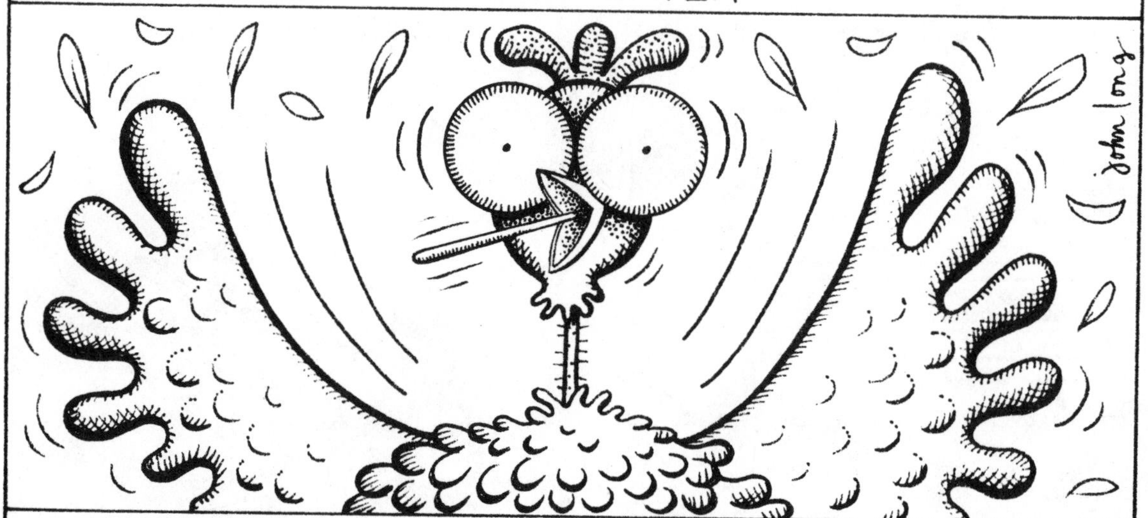
john long

A BRICK LAYER

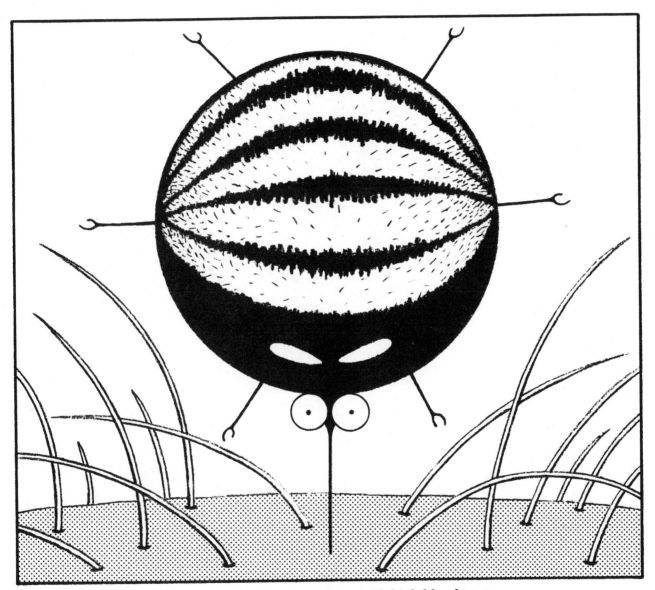

When a mosquito bites someone with high blood pressure

Off the Rack

Airplane hanger

Hangover

YOU'VE GOT TO START EXERCISING!

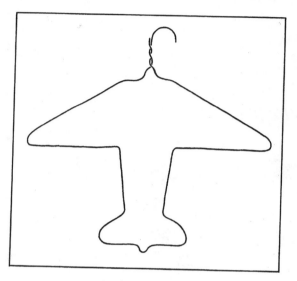

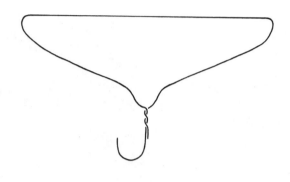

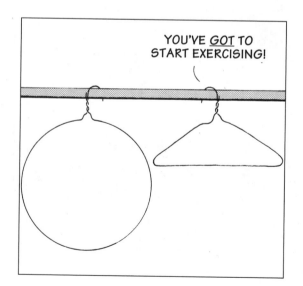

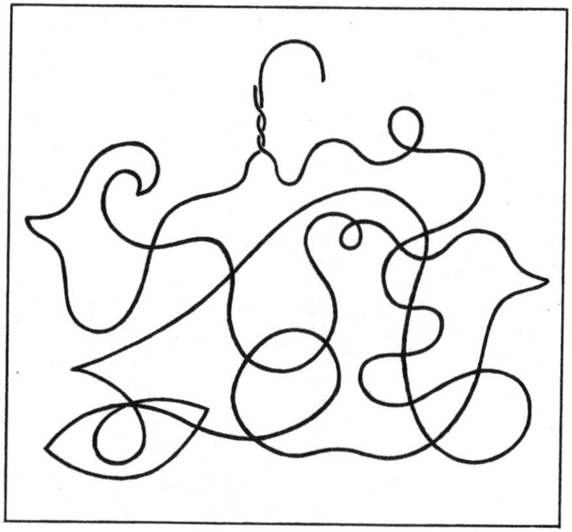

Picasso's hanger

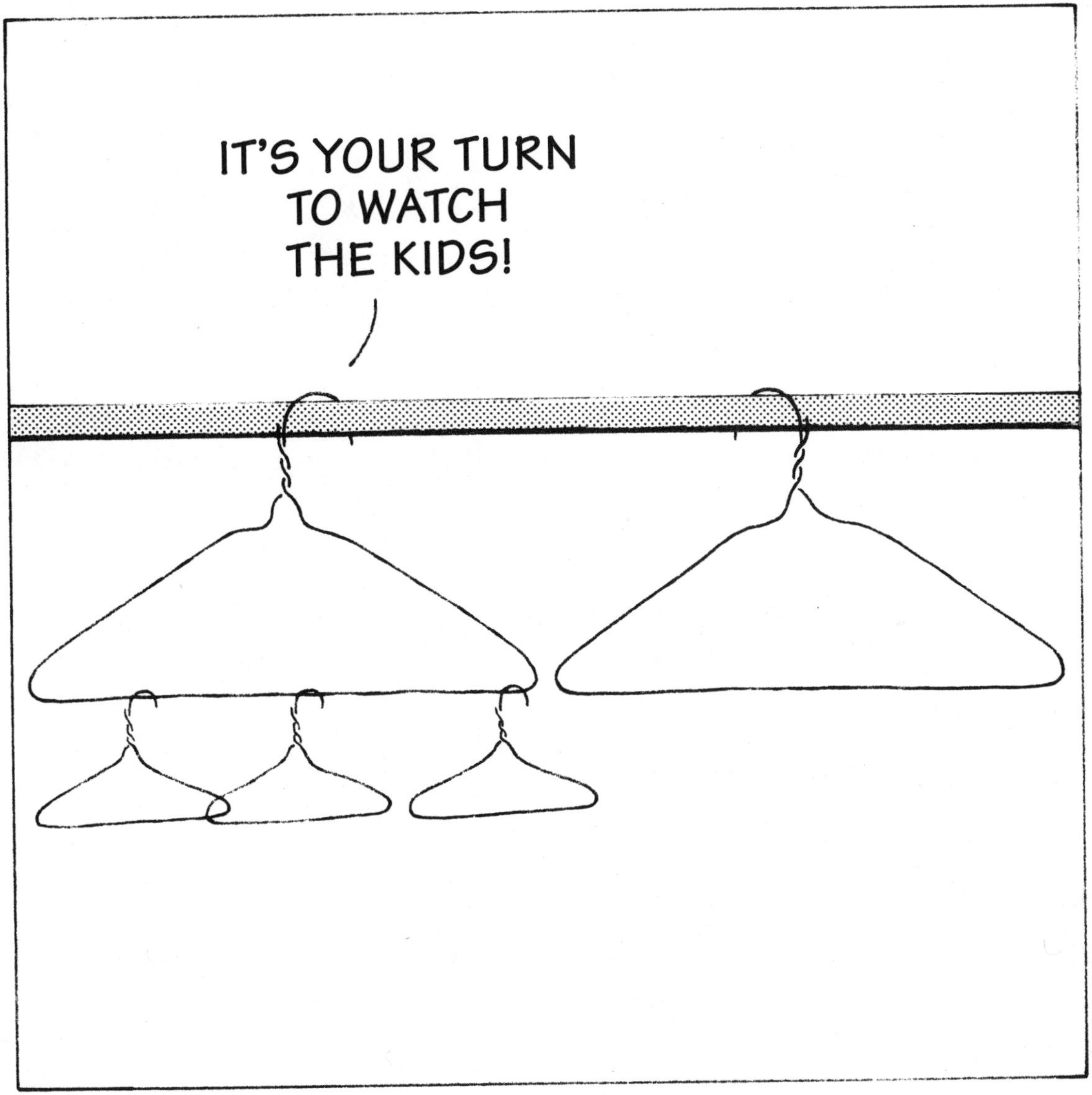
IT'S YOUR TURN TO WATCH THE KIDS!

Go Figure

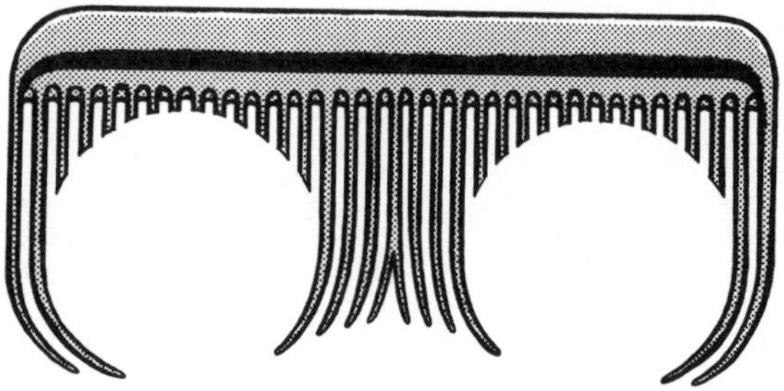

Mickey's comb

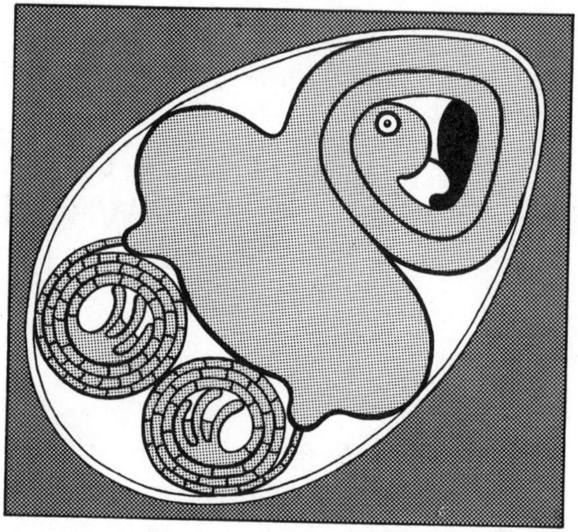

How flamingos fit inside their eggs

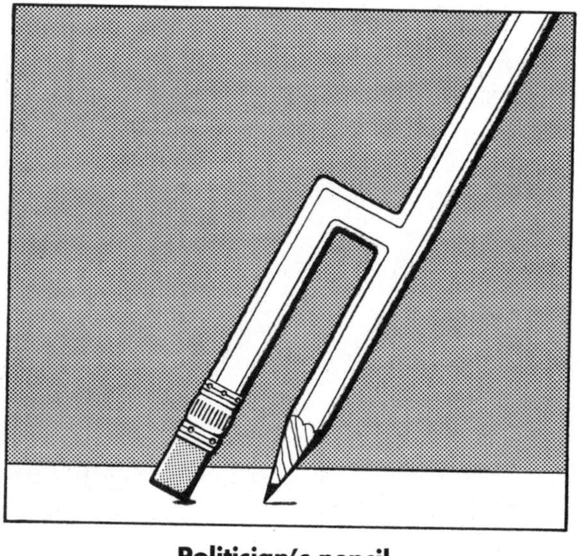

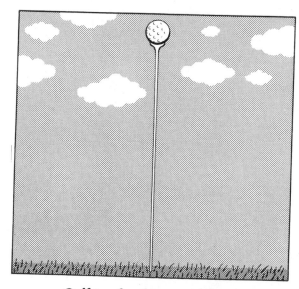

Politician's pencil

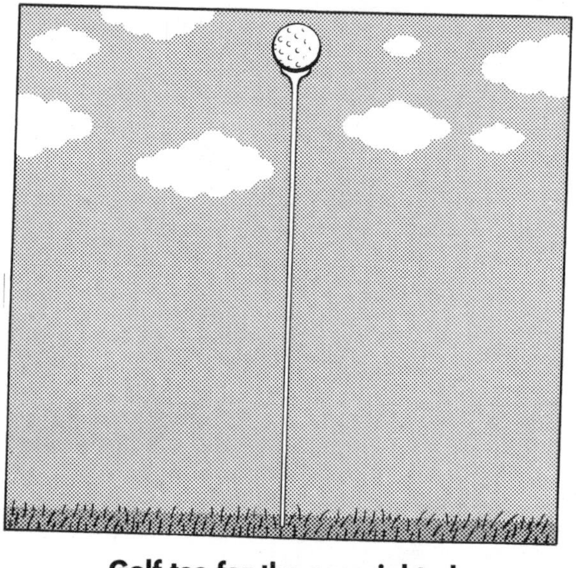

Golf tee for the nearsighted

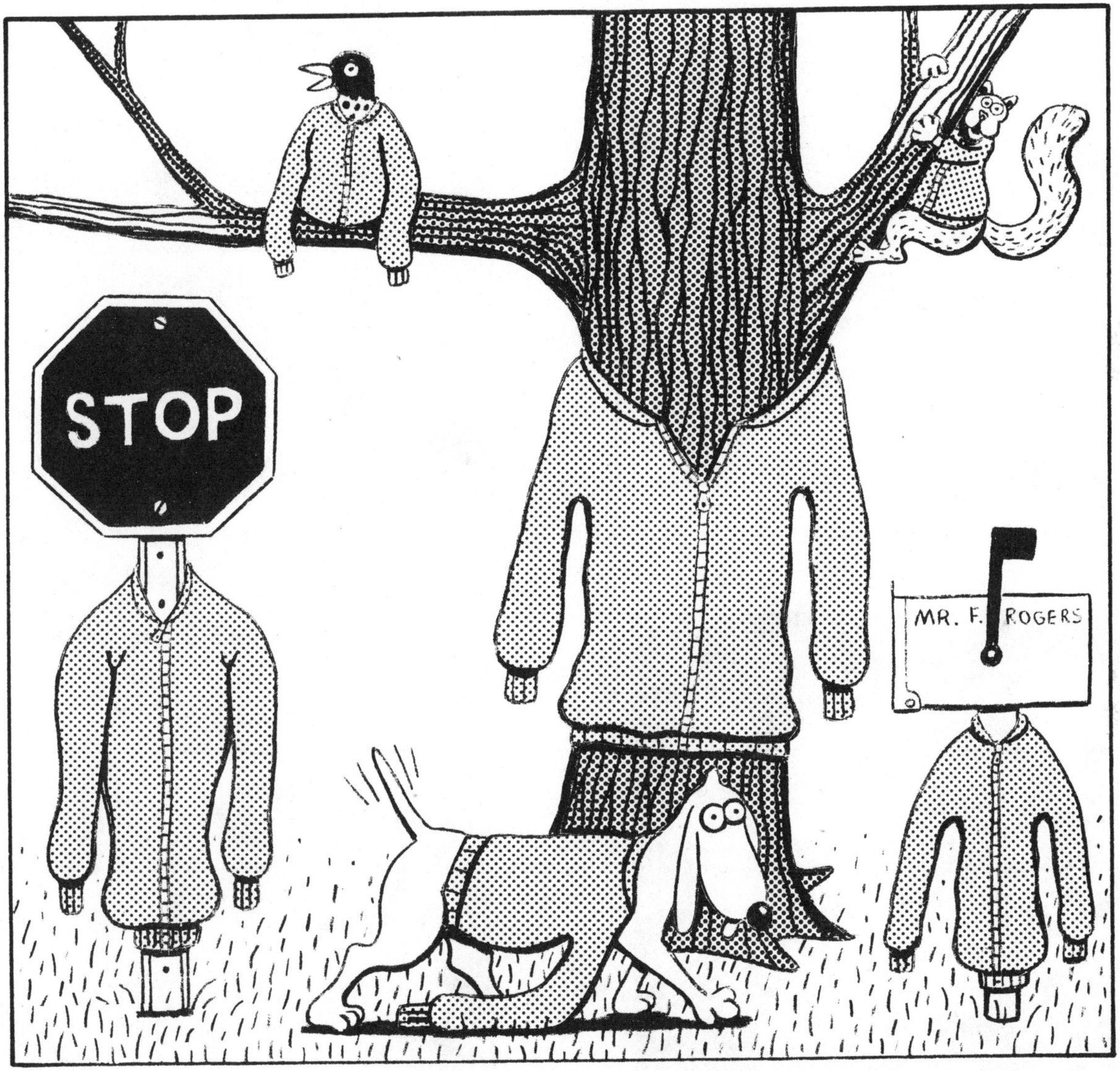
STOP
MR. F. ROGERS

Mister Rogers' neighborhood

Wrong Place, Wrong Time

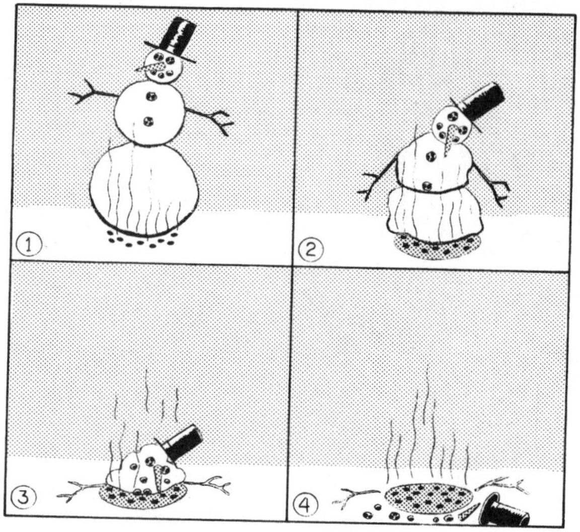

1
2
3
4

Location is everything

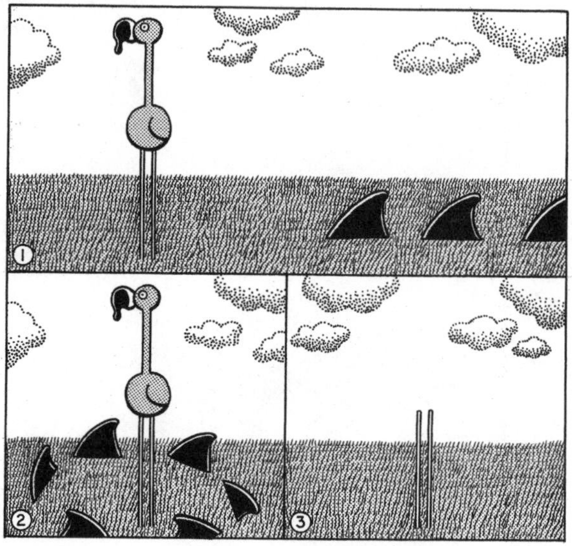

1
2
3

Lawn sharks

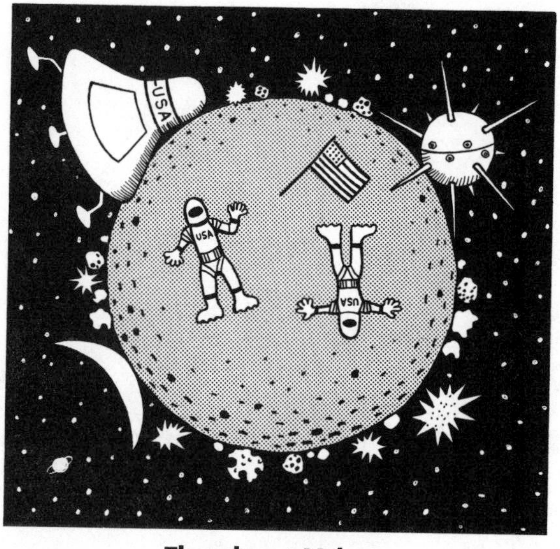

USA
USA
USA

The planet Velcro

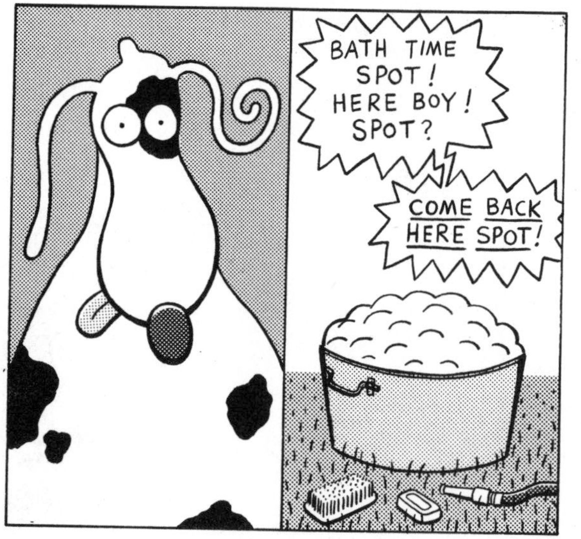

BATH TIME SPOT! HERE BOY! SPOT?
COME BACK HERE SPOT!

Spot ——— Spot remover

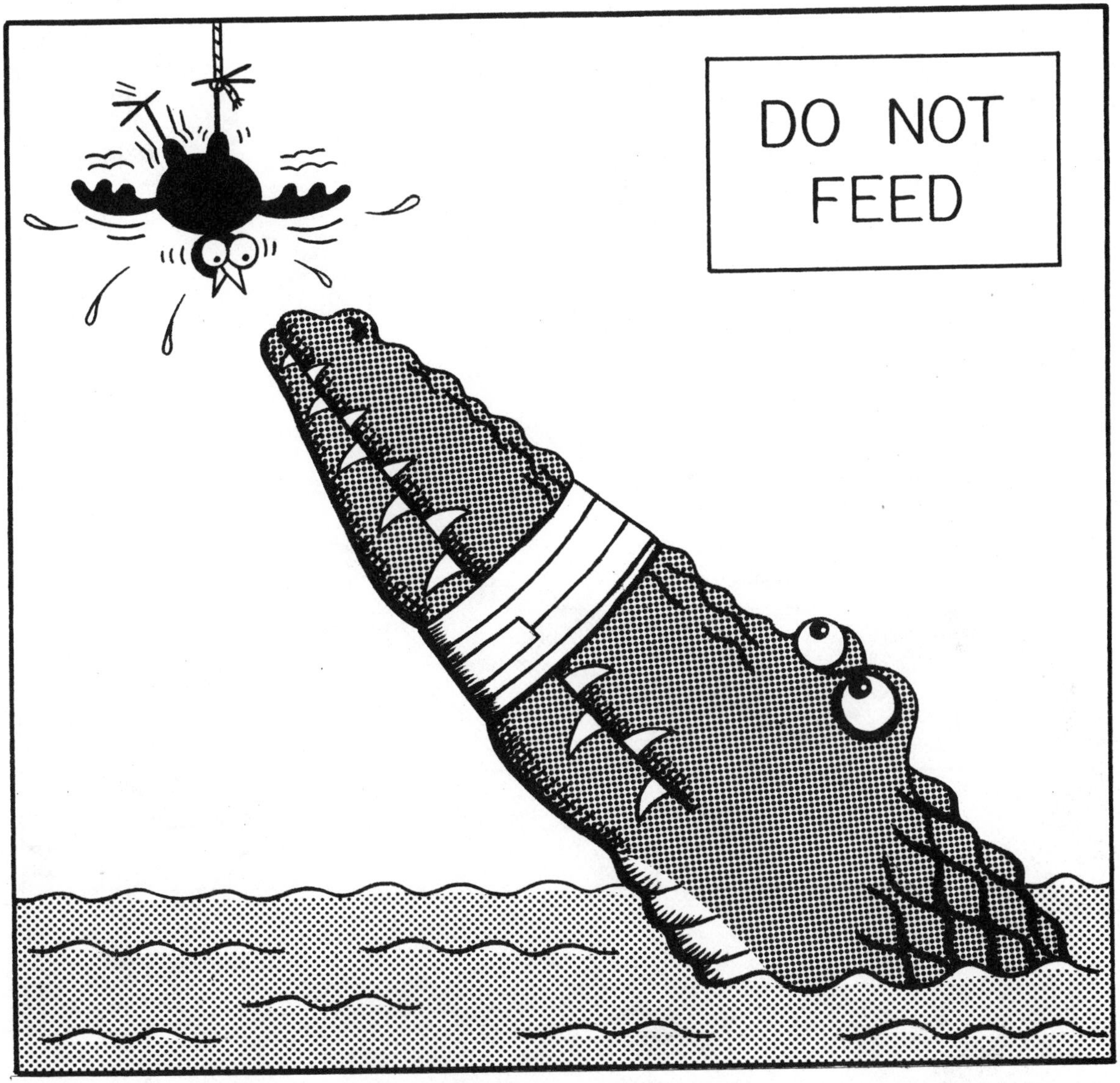
DO NOT FEED

How tape is tested

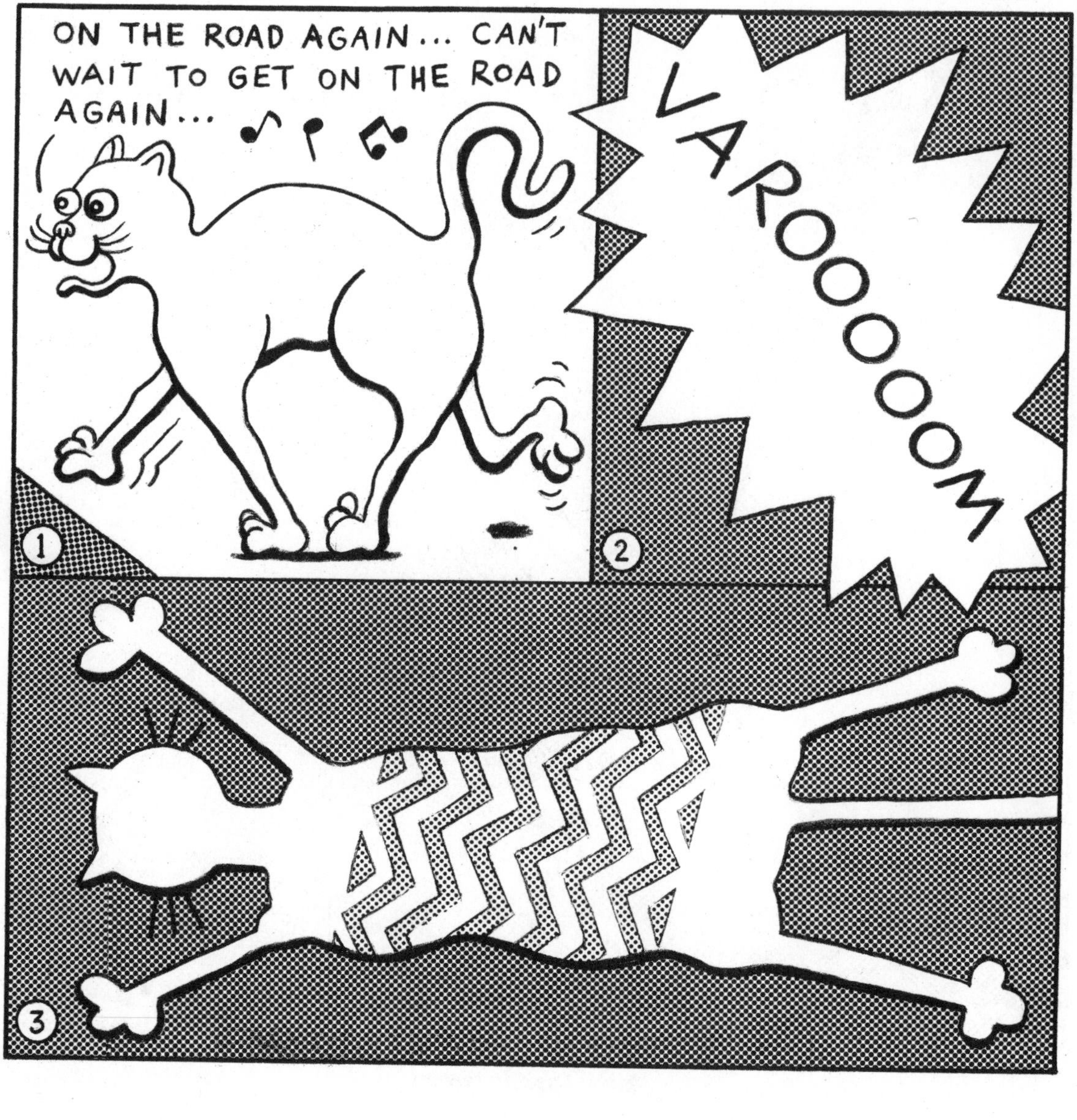
ON THE ROAD AGAIN... CAN'T WAIT TO GET ON THE ROAD AGAIN...
VAROOOOOM

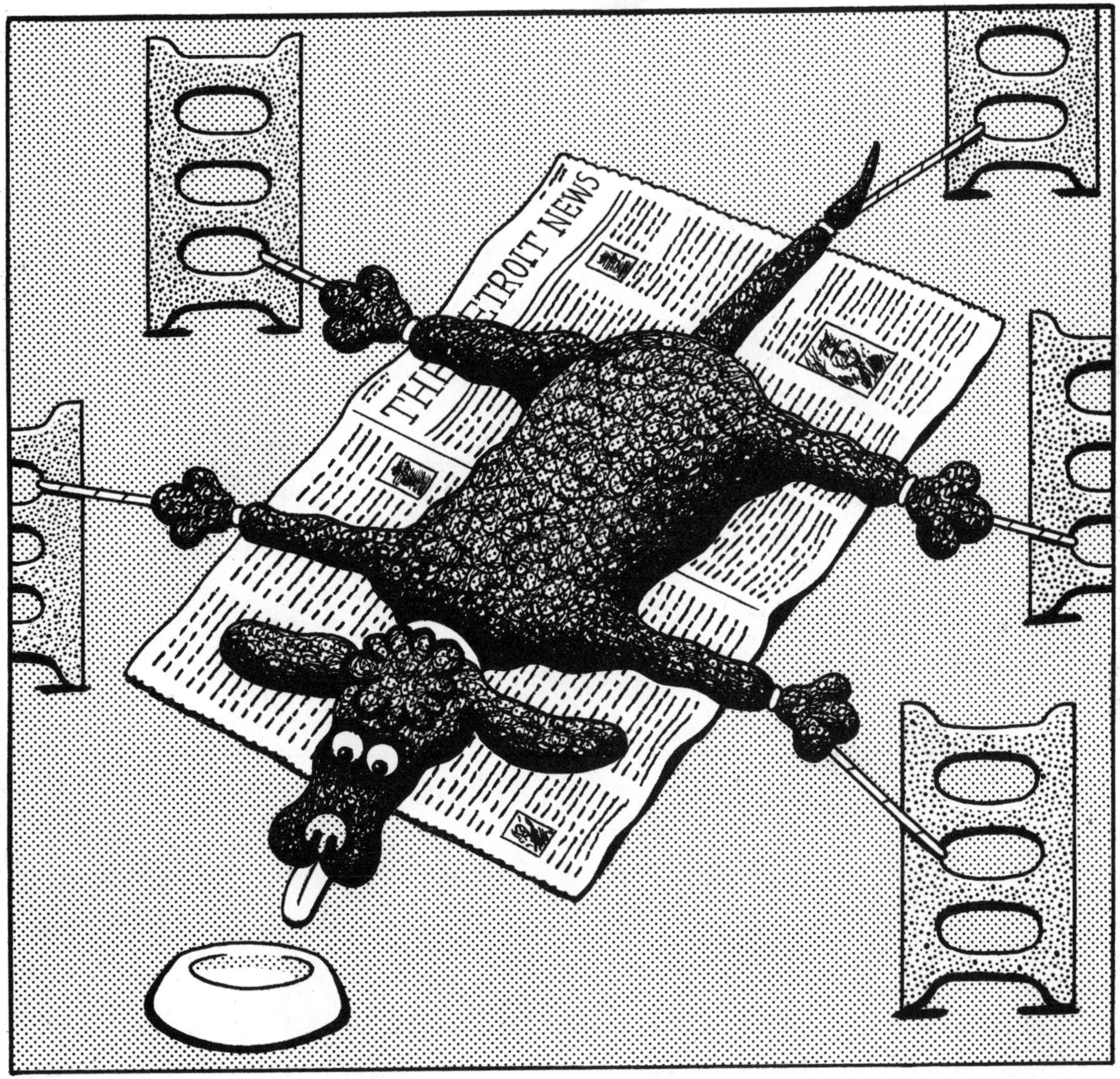
THE
ETROIT NEWS

Paper-training your dog

Untamed

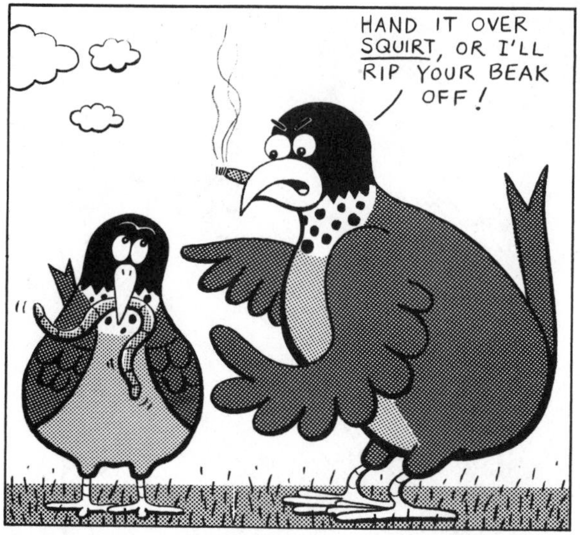
HAND IT OVER SQUIRT, OR I'LL RIP YOUR BEAK OFF!

The burly bird gets the worm

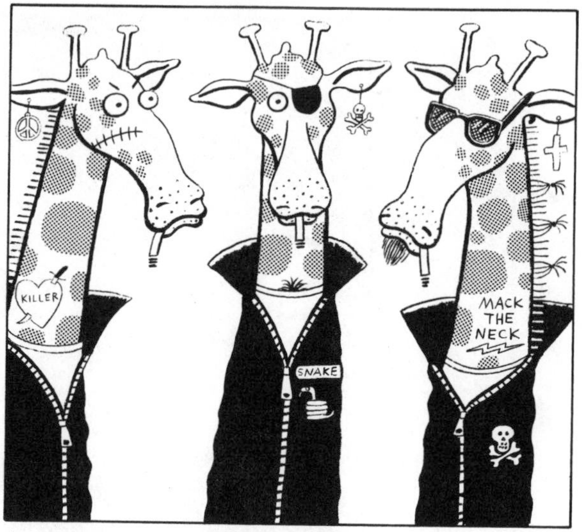
KILLER
SNAKE
MACK THE NECK

Giriffraff

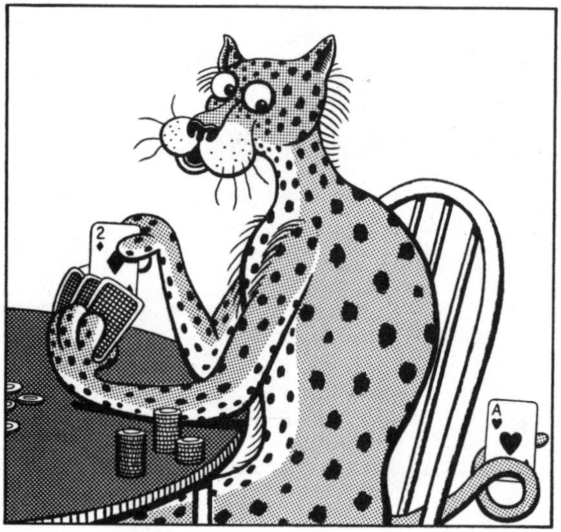

Cheetah

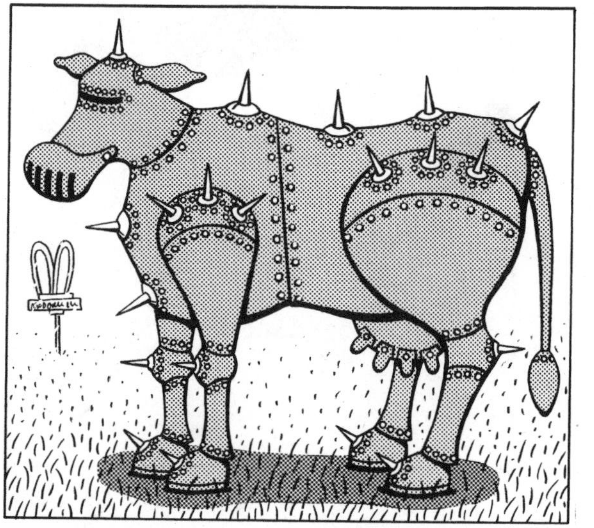

An armored cow with fast-food paranoia

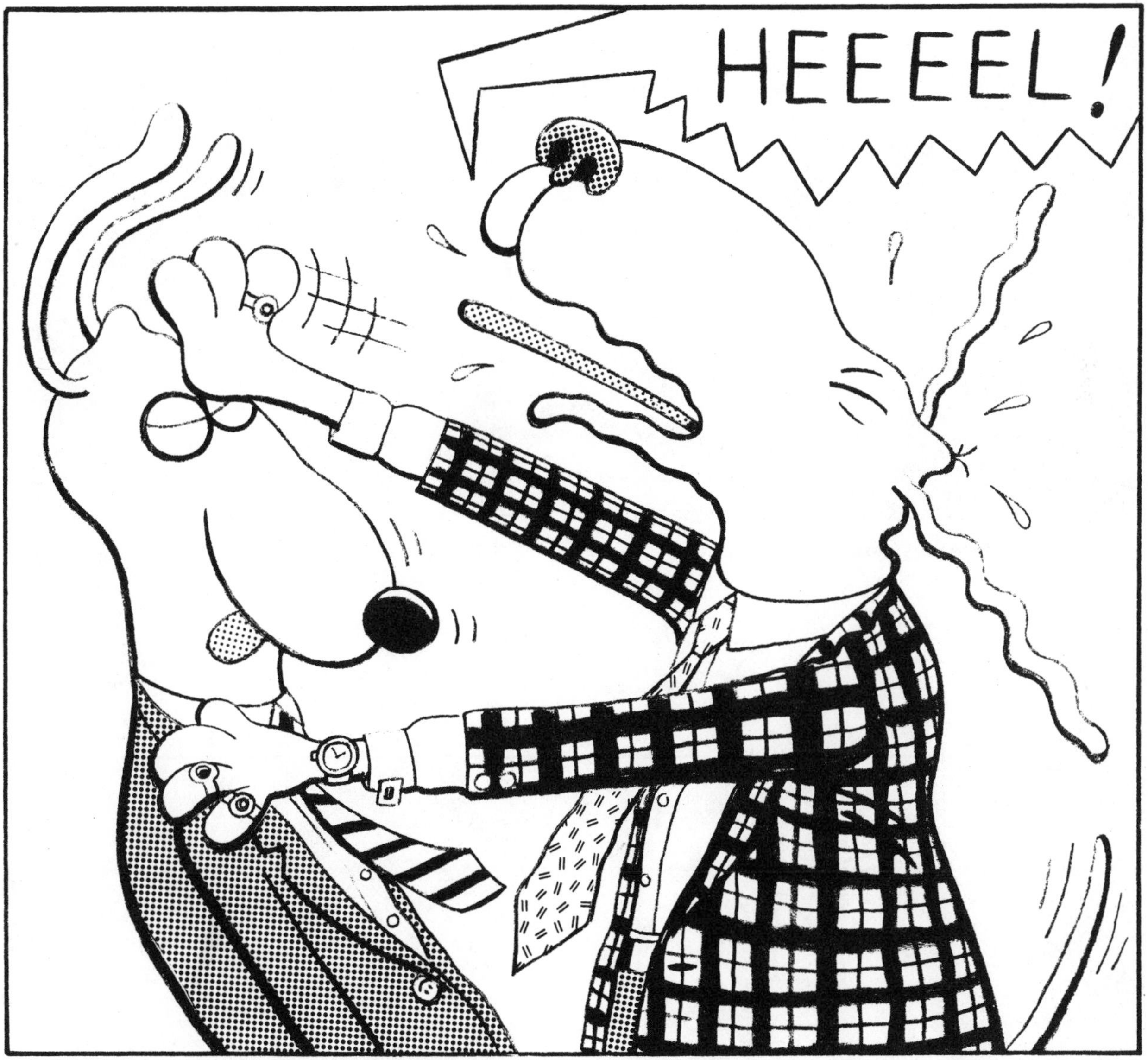
HEEEEL!

The term heel has a different meaning for Jim Bob the evangelical dog

Mornings Should be Illegal

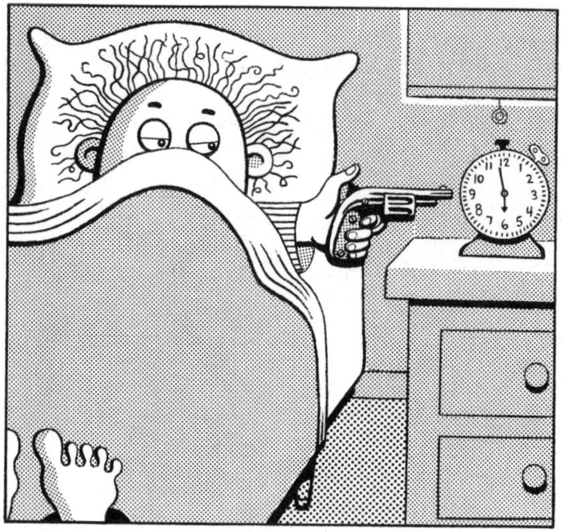

12
1
2
3
4
5
6
7
8
9
10
11

Go ahead...wake my day

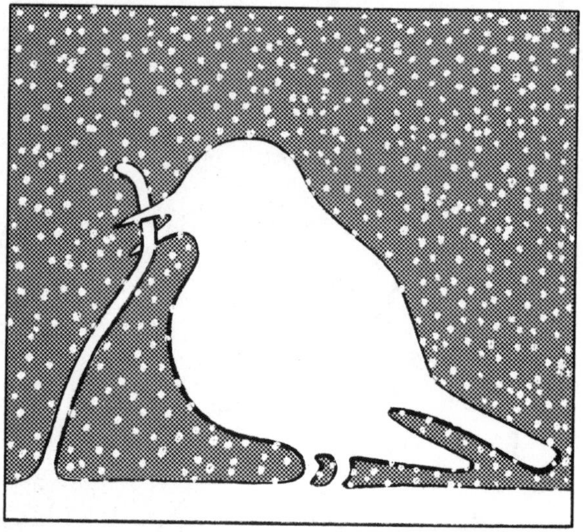

Sometimes the early bird gets frozen stiff

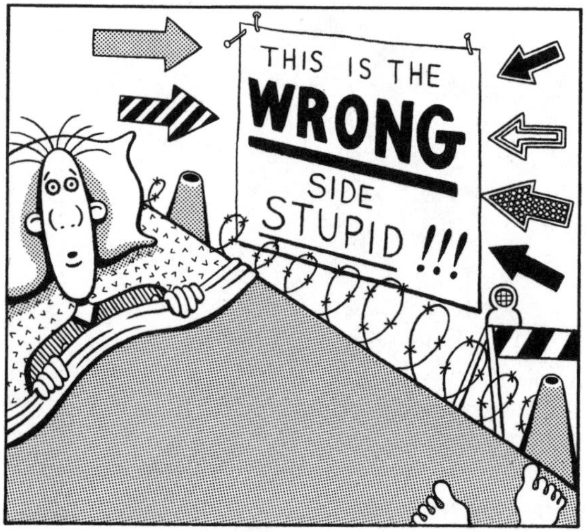

THIS IS THE WRONG SIDE STUPID !!!

Flem is determined never to get up on the wrong side of the bed again

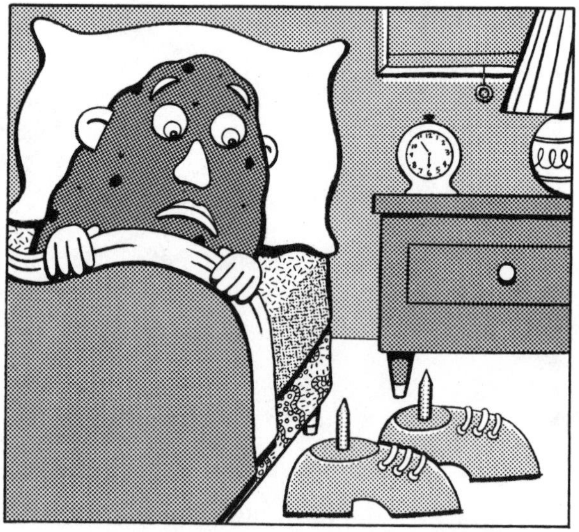

Mr. Potato Head's shoes are a real pain to put on

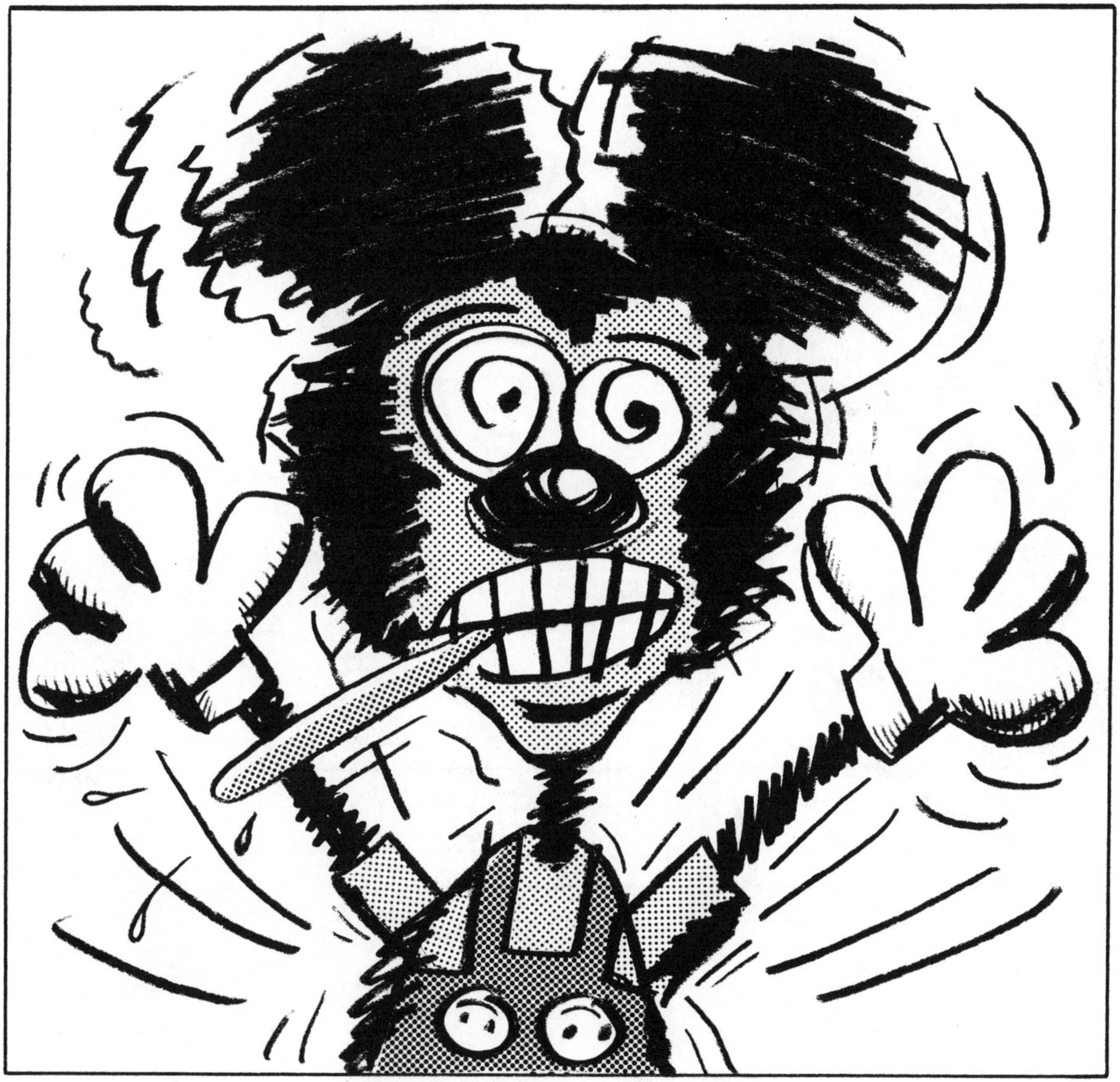

Mickey before his morning coffee

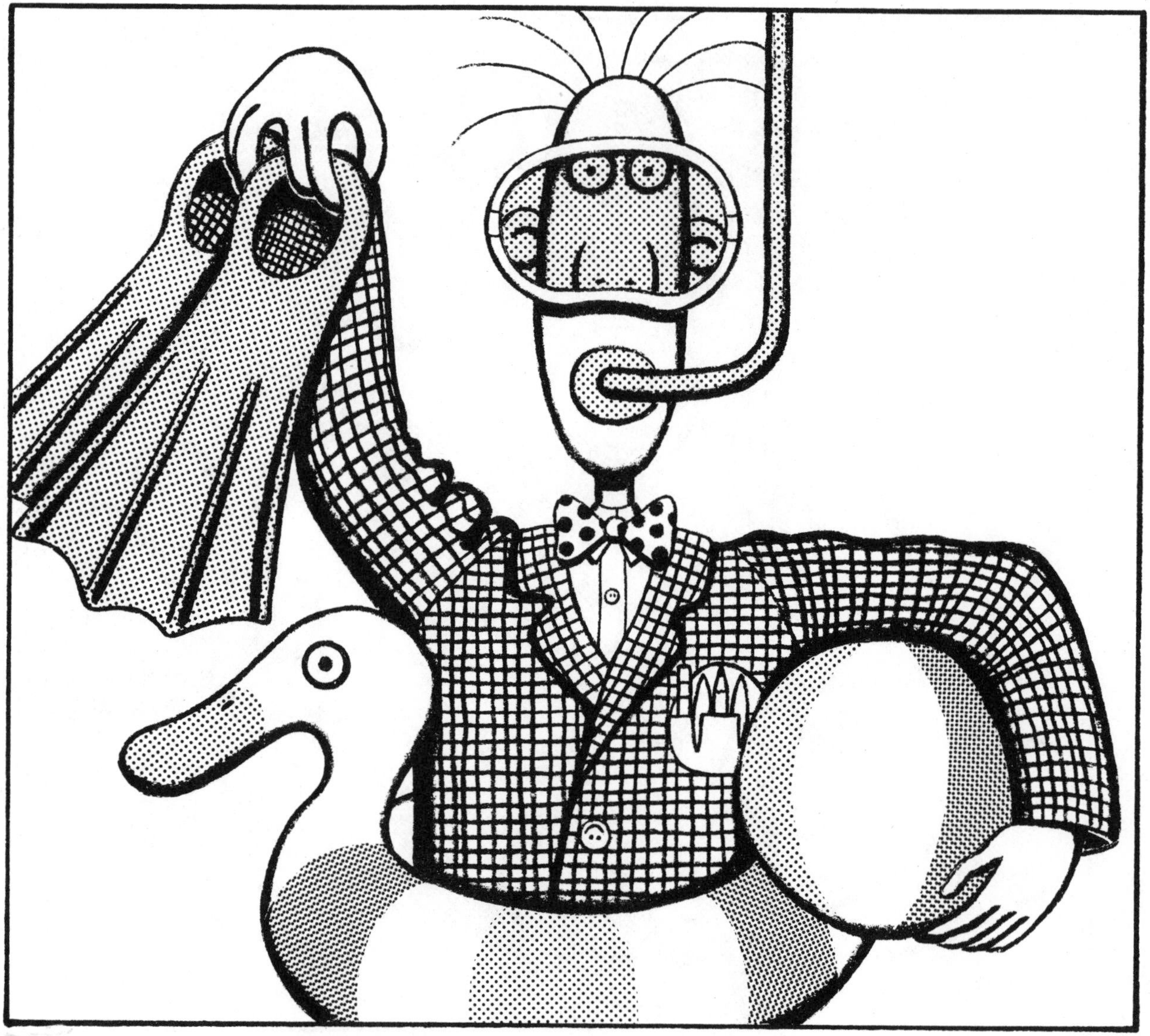

Preparing to go off the deep end

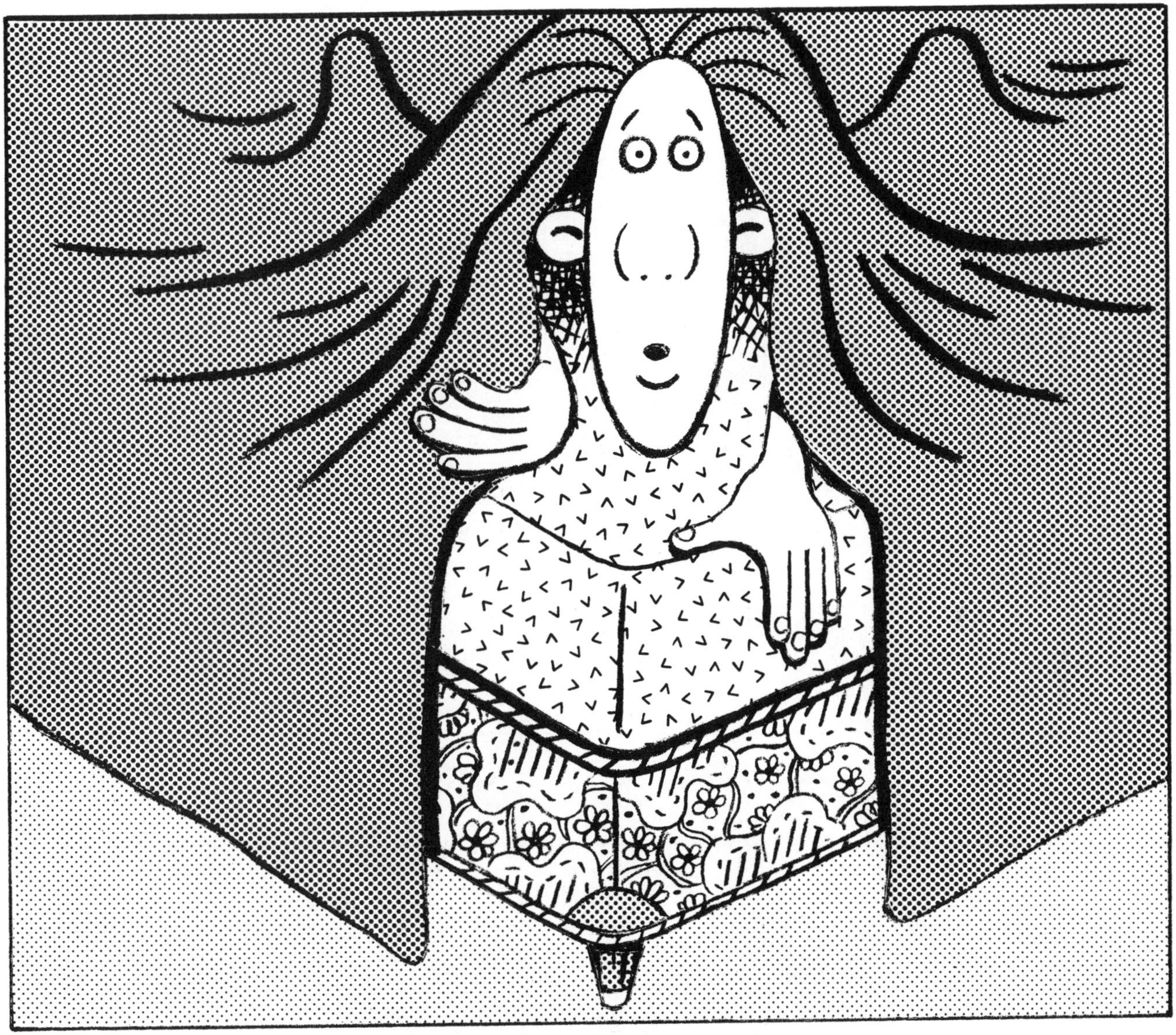

Instead of waking up on the wrong side of the bed...just sneak out of a corner

Almost Human

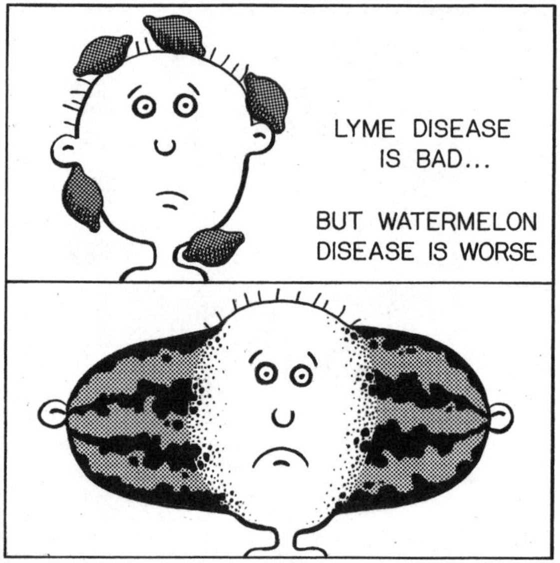
LYME DISEASE IS BAD...
BUT WATERMELON DISEASE IS WORSE

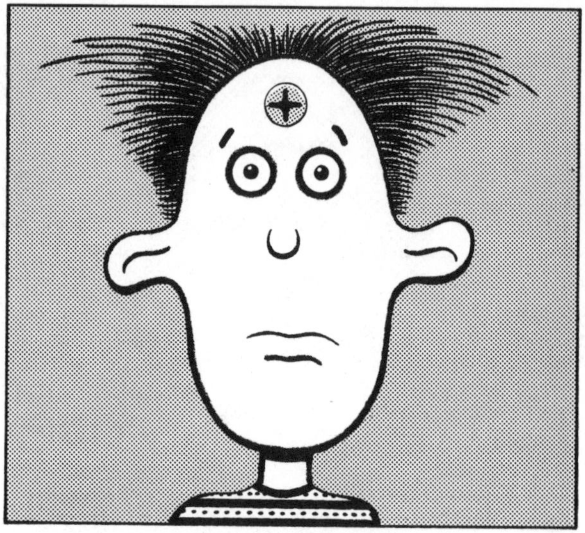

Everyone noticed Philip's screw, but no-one ever mentioned it

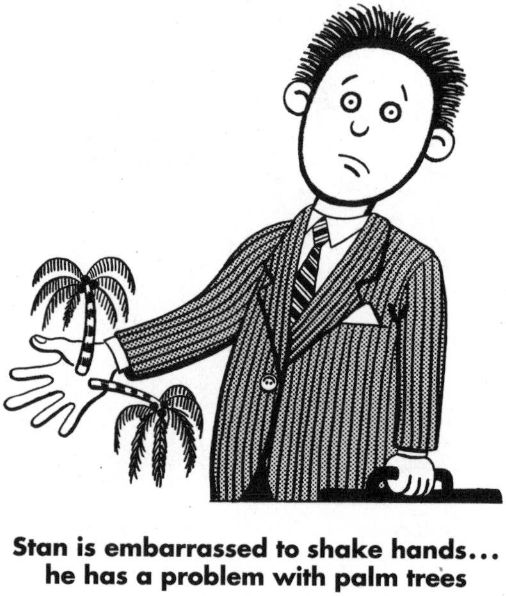

Stan is embarrassed to shake hands... he has a problem with palm trees

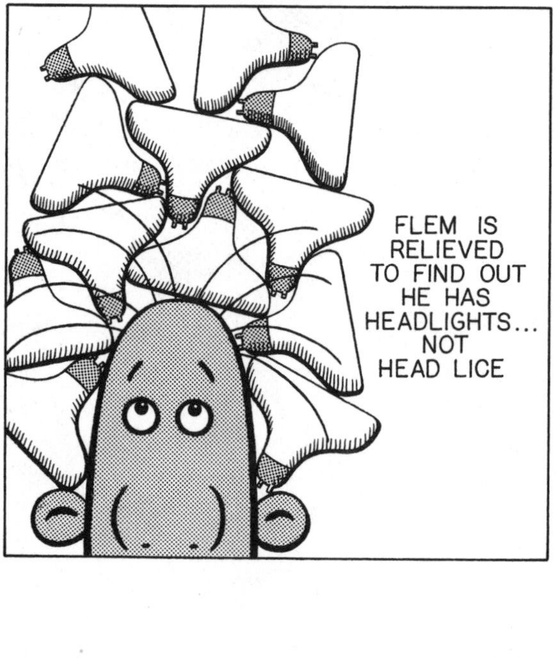
FLEM IS RELIEVED TO FIND OUT HE HAS HEADLIGHTS... NOT HEAD LICE

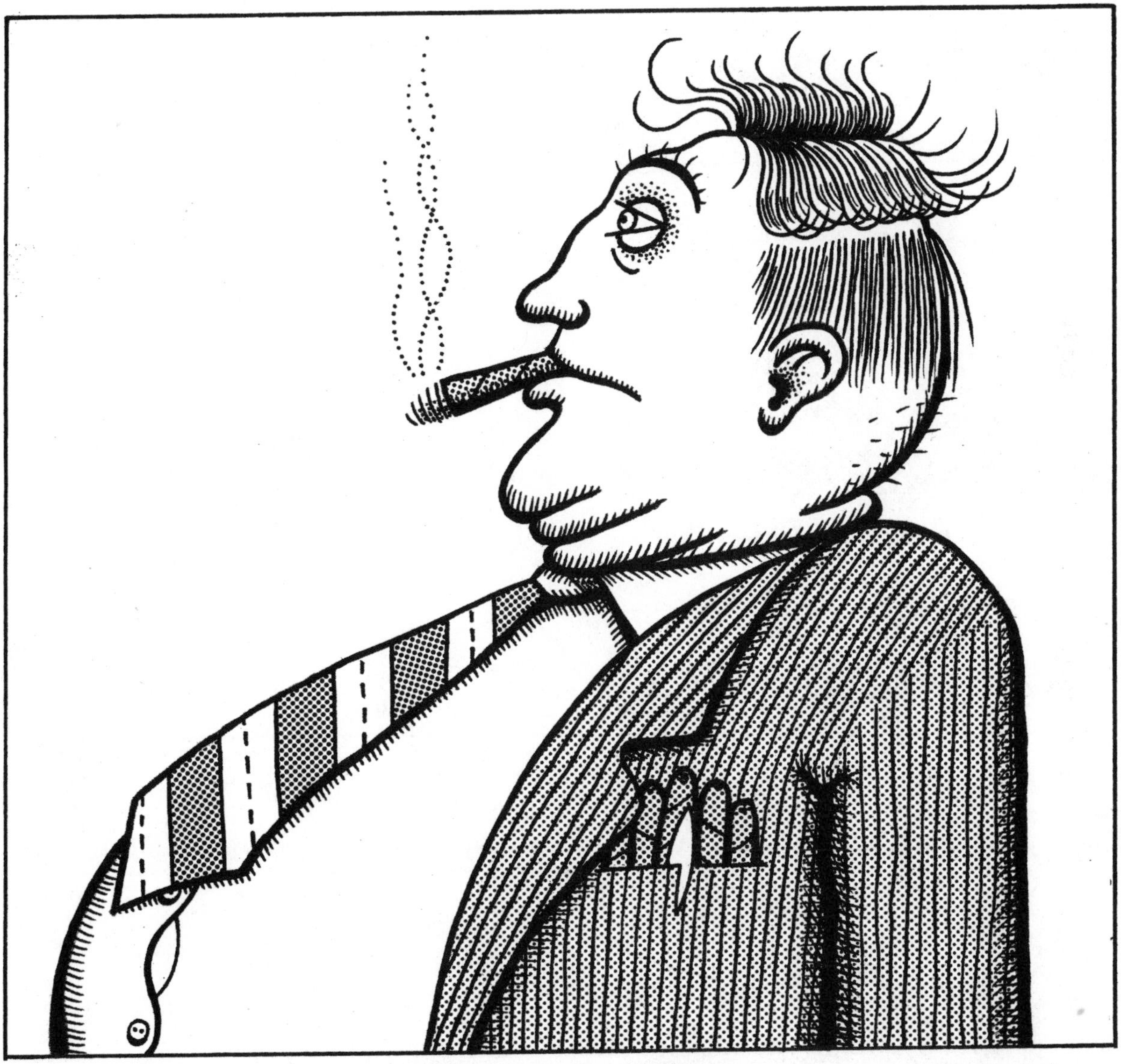

A bad toupee is just a hairy hat

Hold All Calls

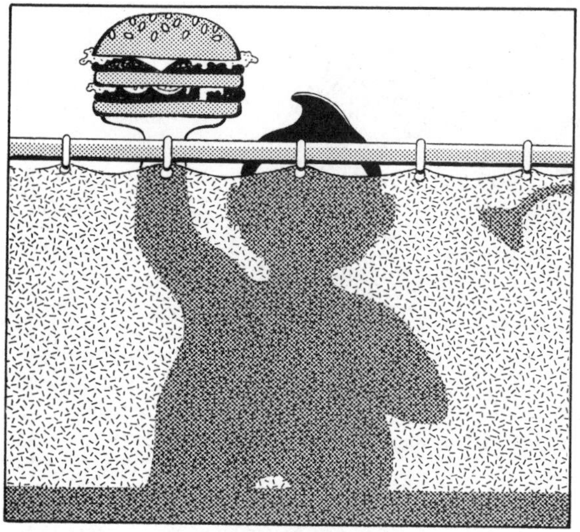

Big Boy getting ready for work

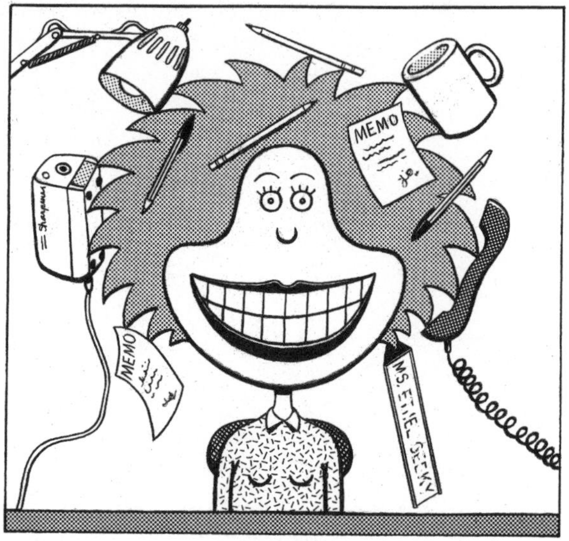
MEMO
MEMO

Too much hairspray at the office

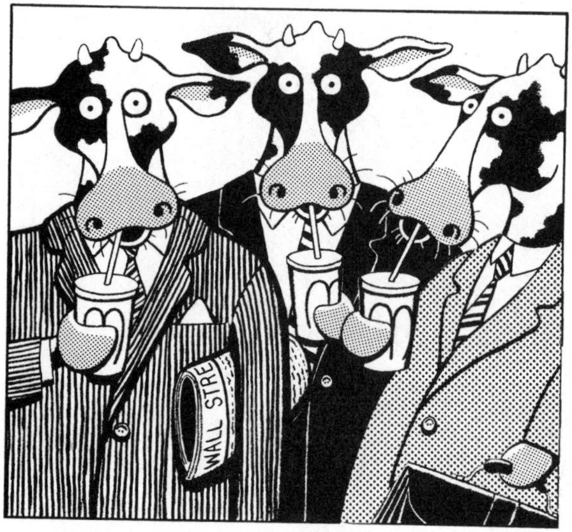
WALL STRE

Moovers and shakers

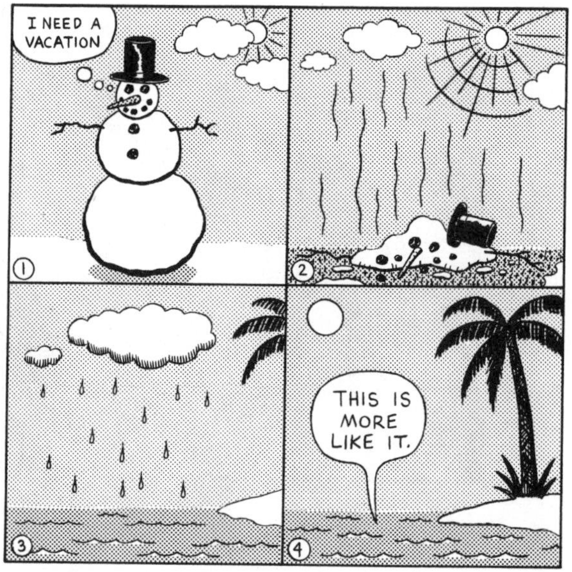
I NEED A VACATION
1
2
3
THIS IS MORE LIKE IT.
4

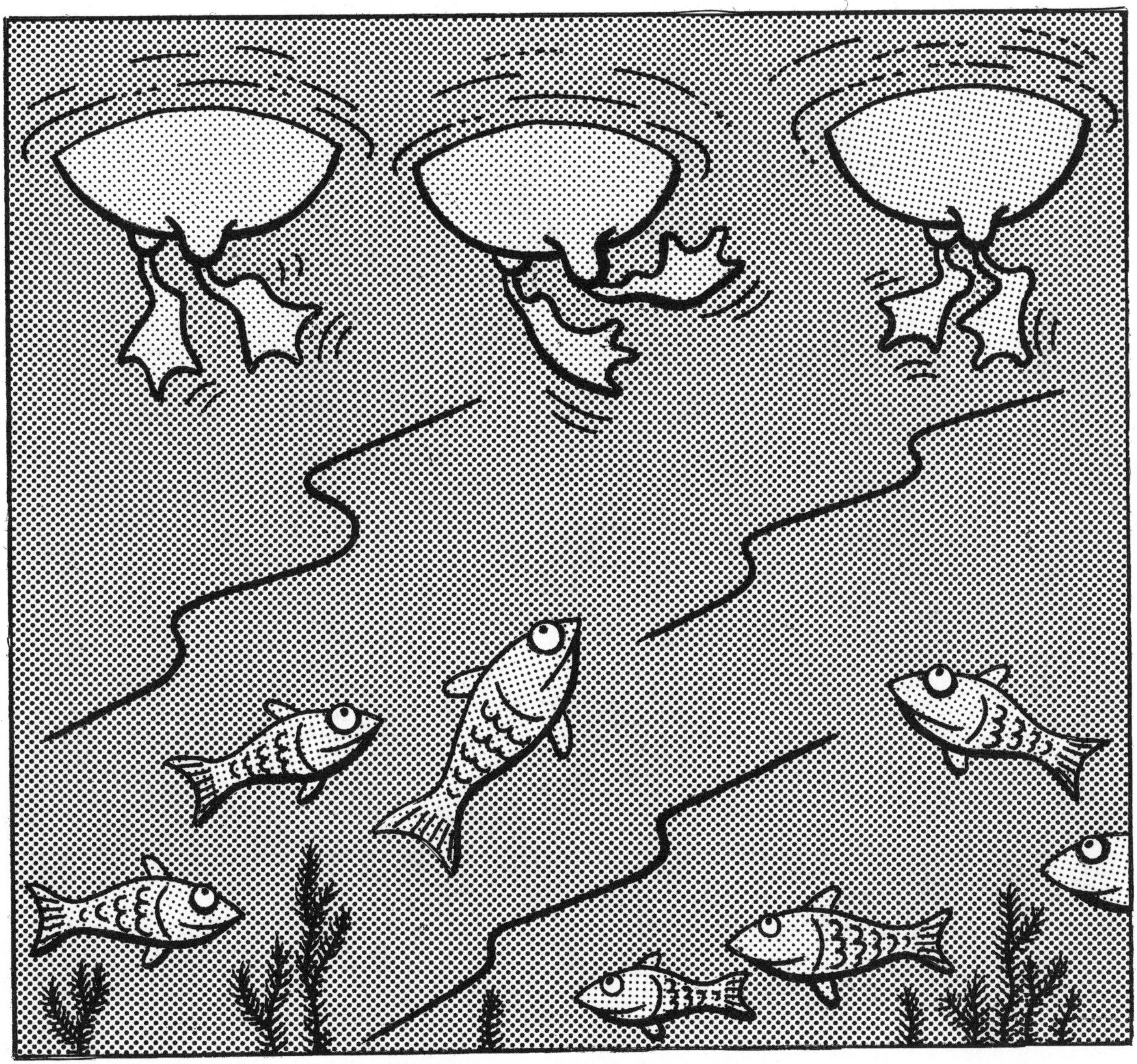

Checking out web sites

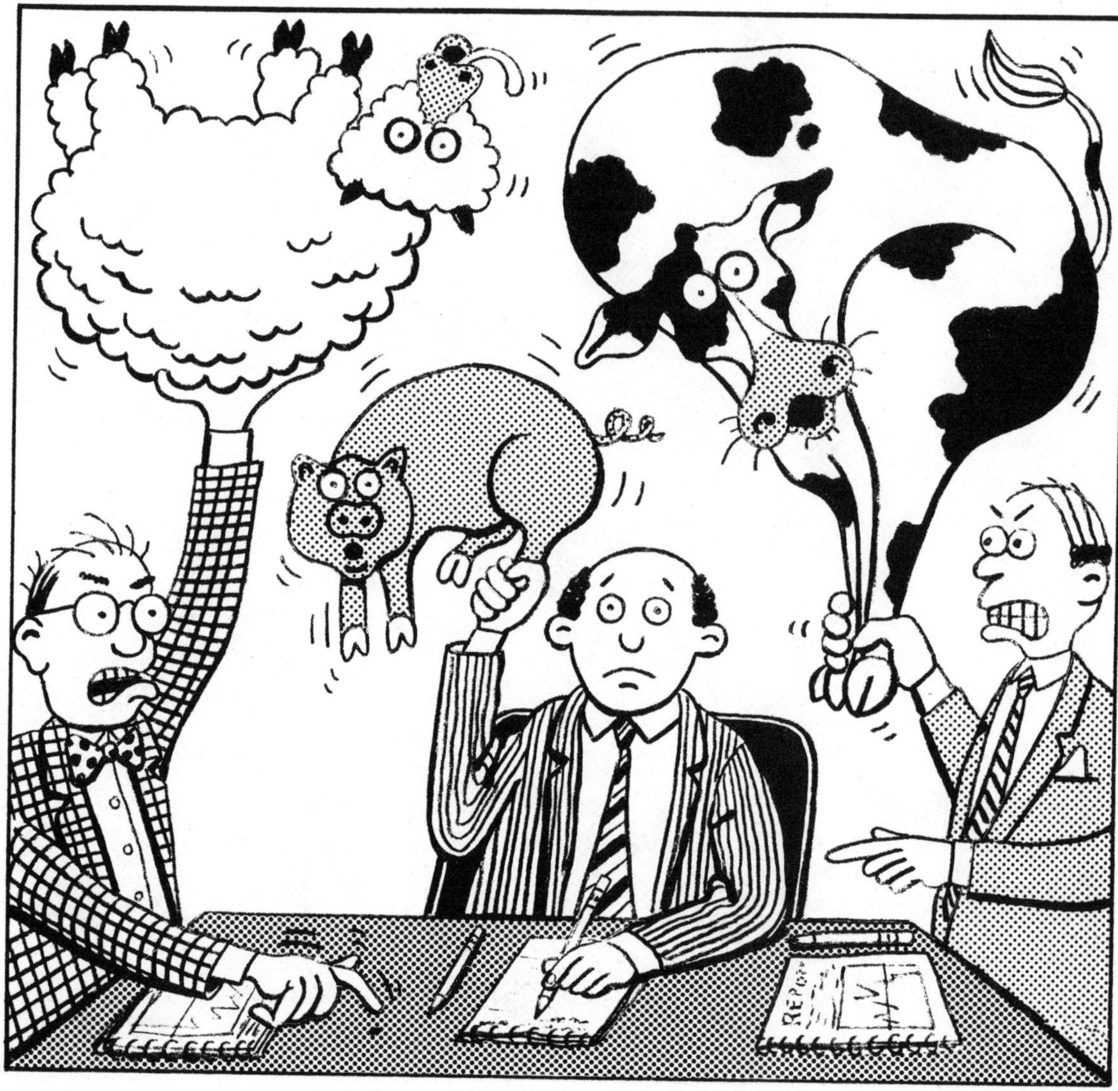

The annual stockholders meeting

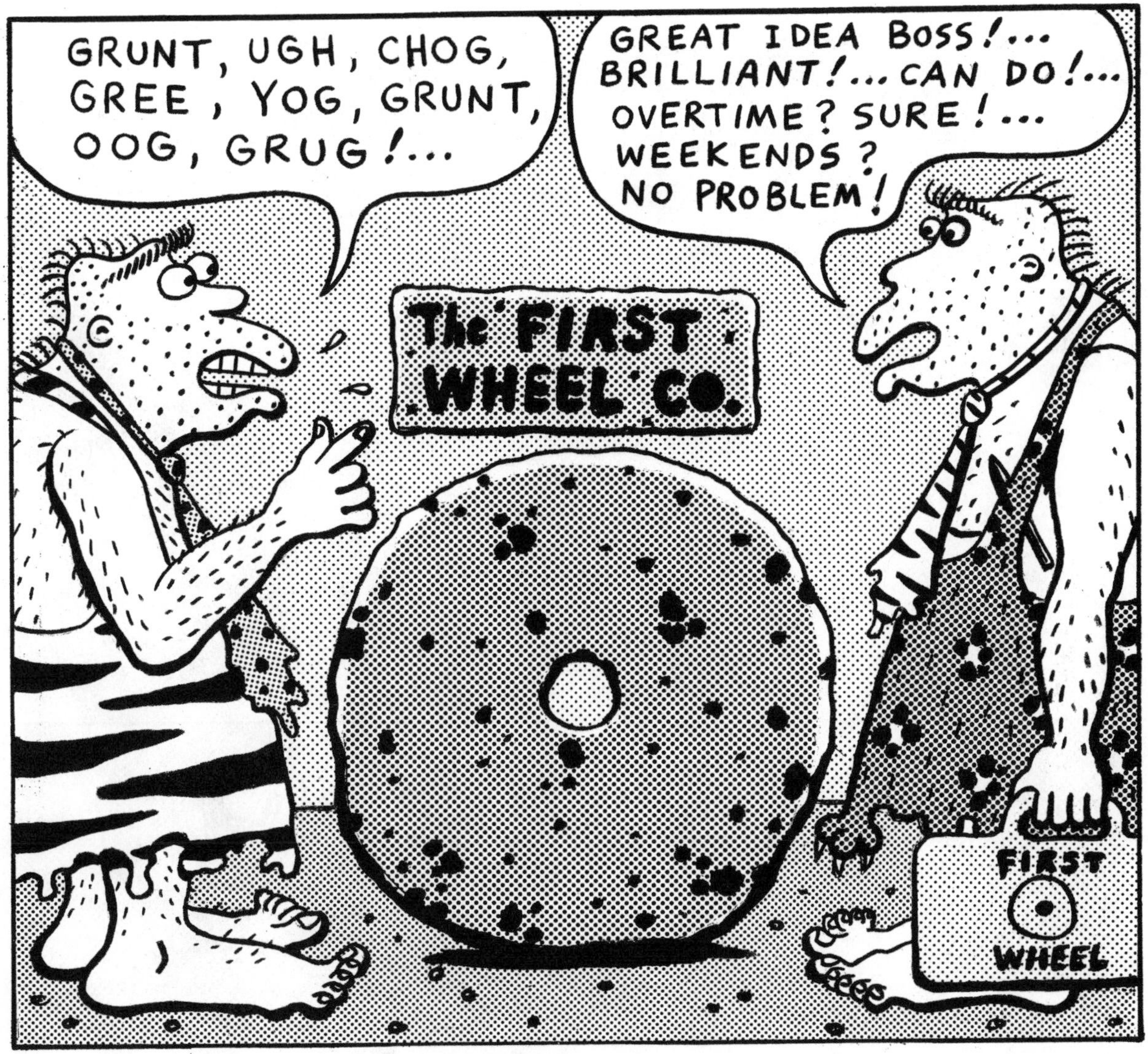
GRUNT, UGH, CHOG, GREE, YOG, GRUNT, OOG, GRUG!...
GREAT IDEA BOSS!... BRILLIANT!... CAN DO!... OVERTIME? SURE!... WEEKENDS? NO PROBLEM!
The FIRST WHEEL CO.
FIRST WHEEL

A prehistoric "yes" man

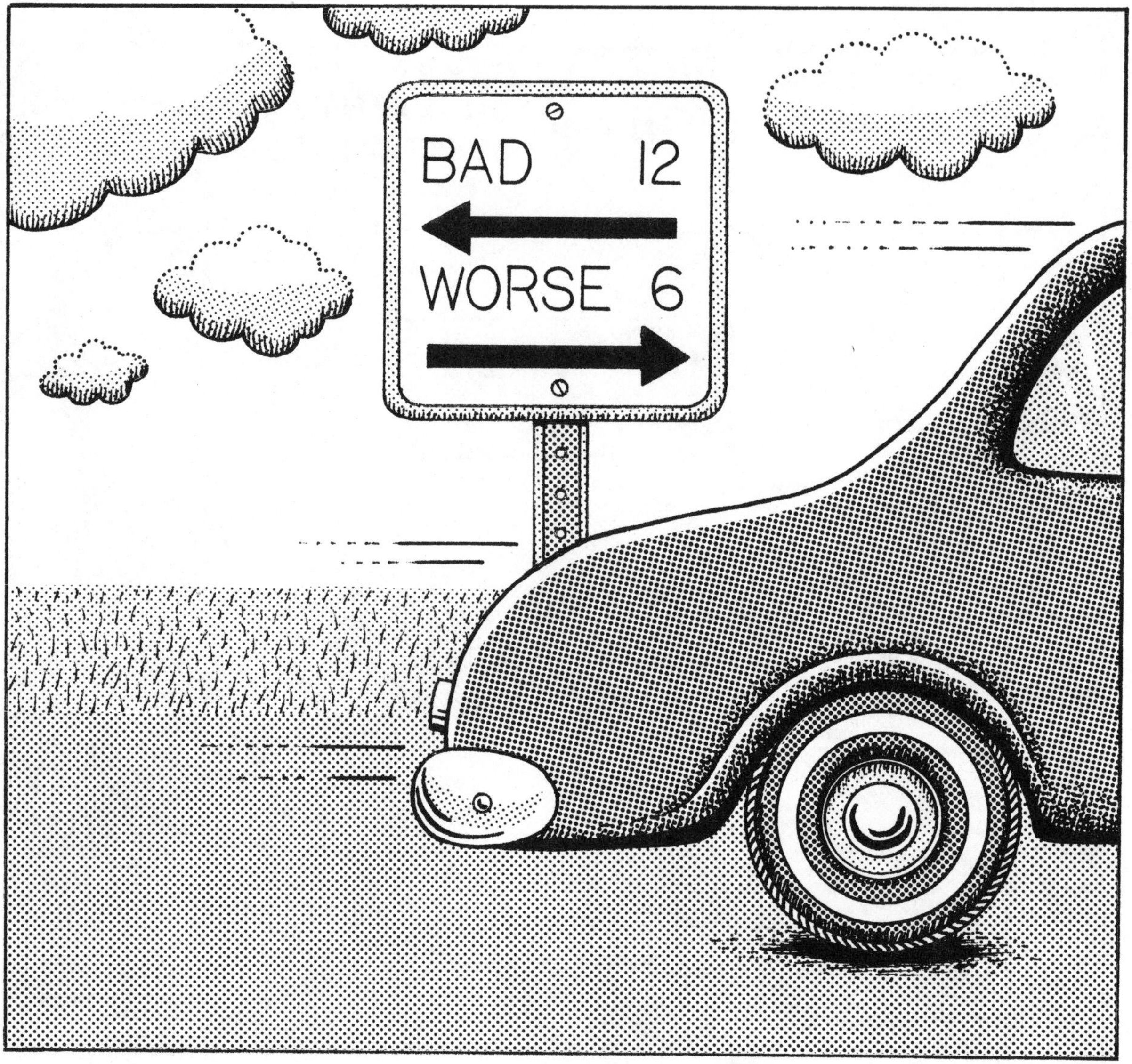
BAD 12
WORSE 6

From bad to worse

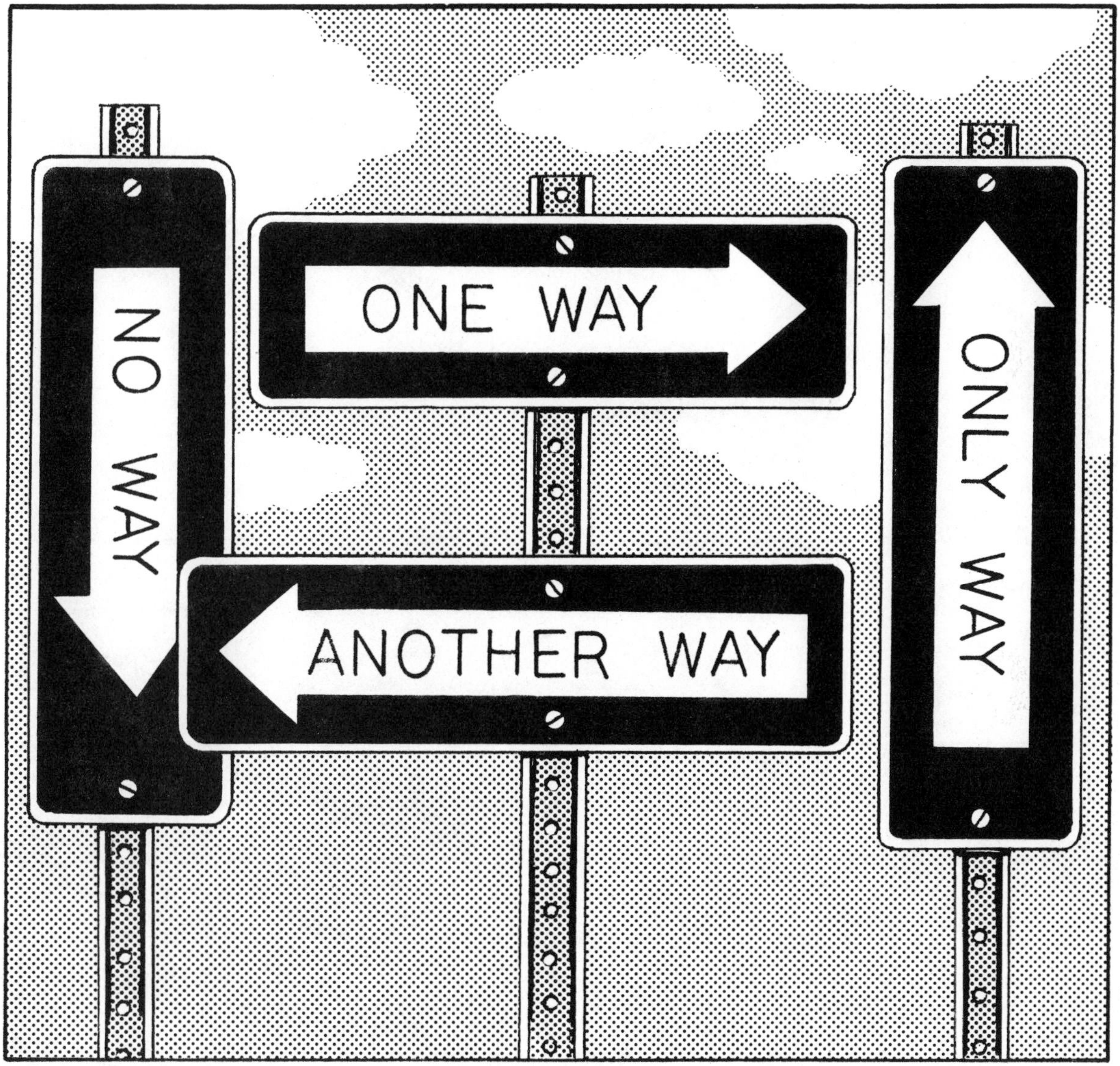
NO WAY
ONE WAY
ANOTHER WAY
ONLY WAY

Signs of confusion

It's Rough Out There

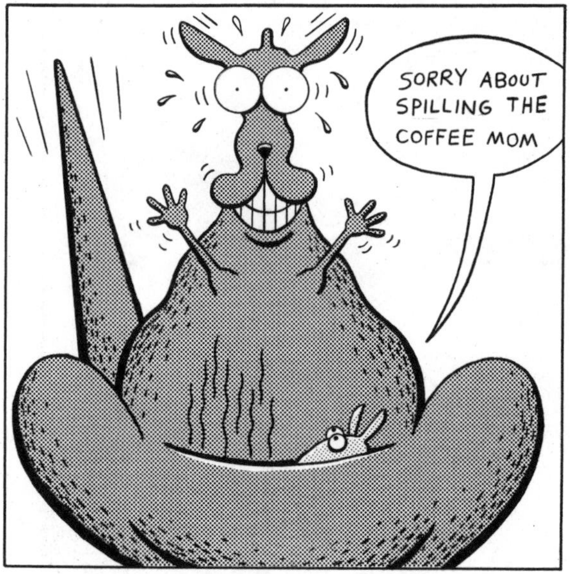
SORRY ABOUT SPILLING THE COFFEE MOM

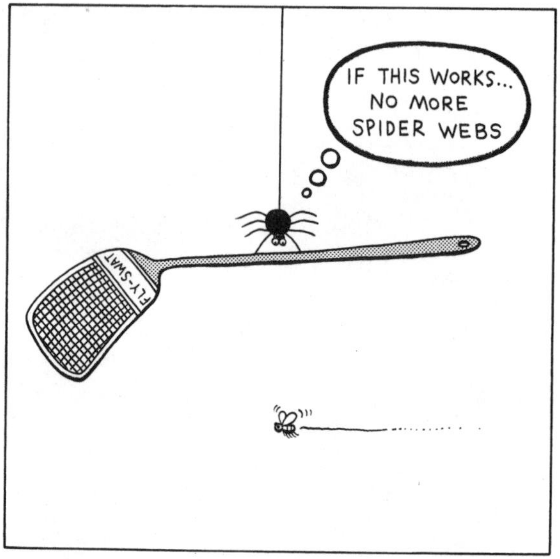
IF THIS WORKS... NO MORE SPIDER WEBS
FLY-SWAT

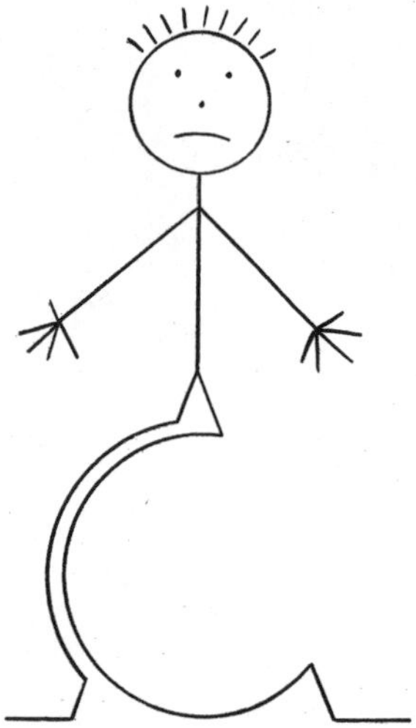

Mr. Stickfigure was hit by a bike when he was young

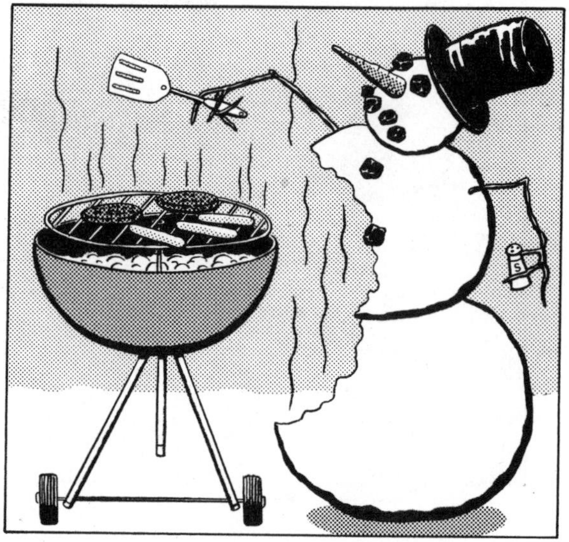

Why Mr. Snowman rarely BBQ's

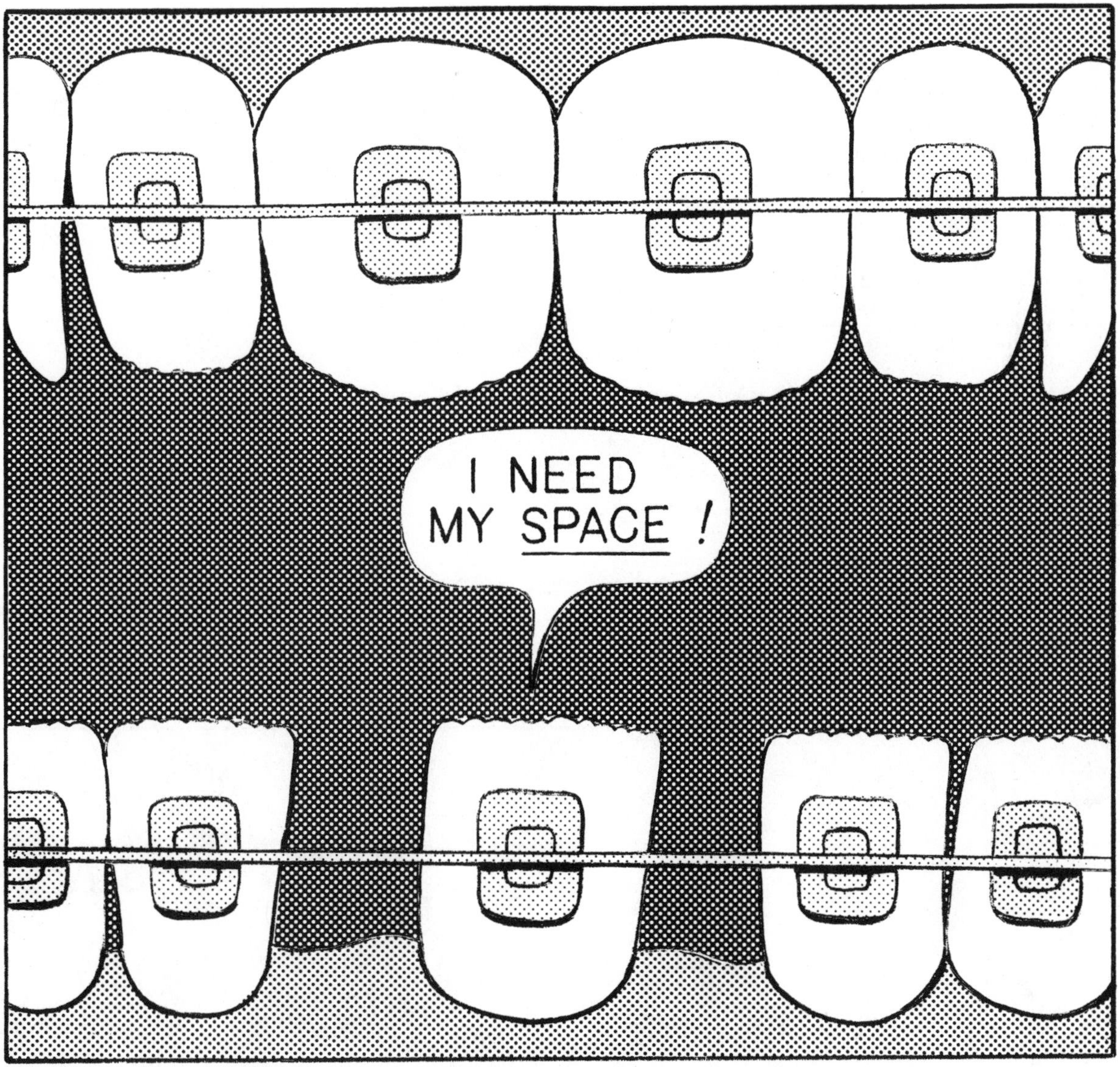
I NEED MY SPACE !

Dental anxiety

Nature's Secrets

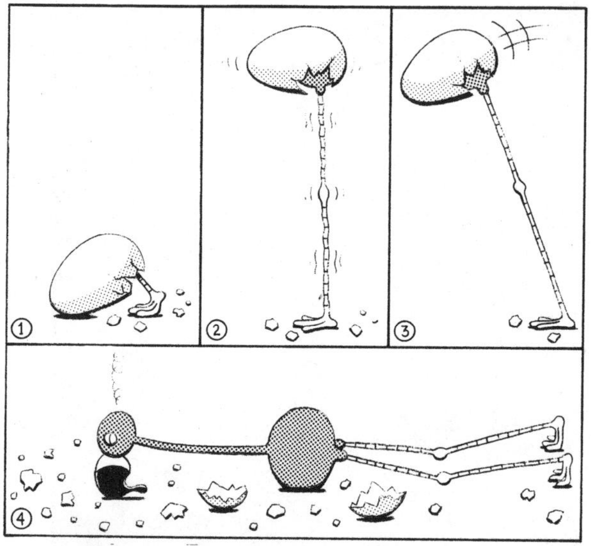

1
2
3
4

How a flamingo hatches and why it has a bent beak

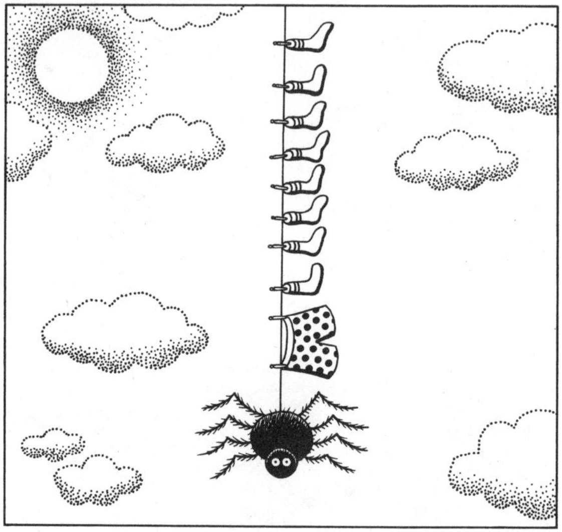

Laundry day

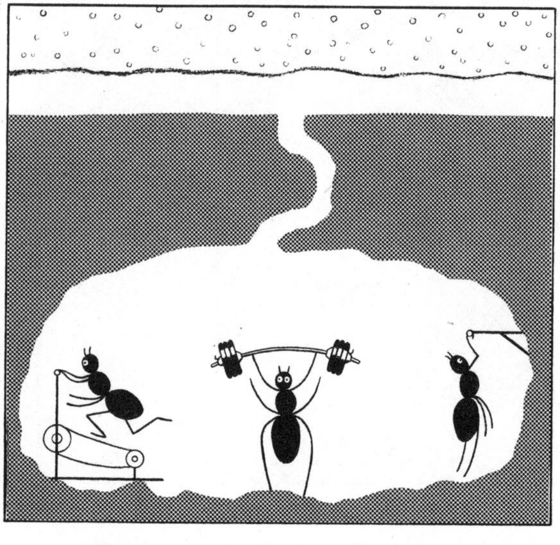

What ants do during the winter

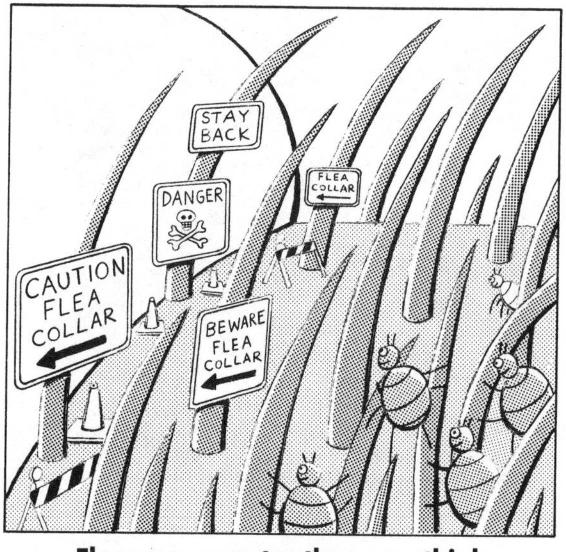

STAY BACK
DANGER
FLEA COLLAR
CAUTION FLEA COLLAR
BEWARE FLEA COLLAR

Fleas are smarter than you think

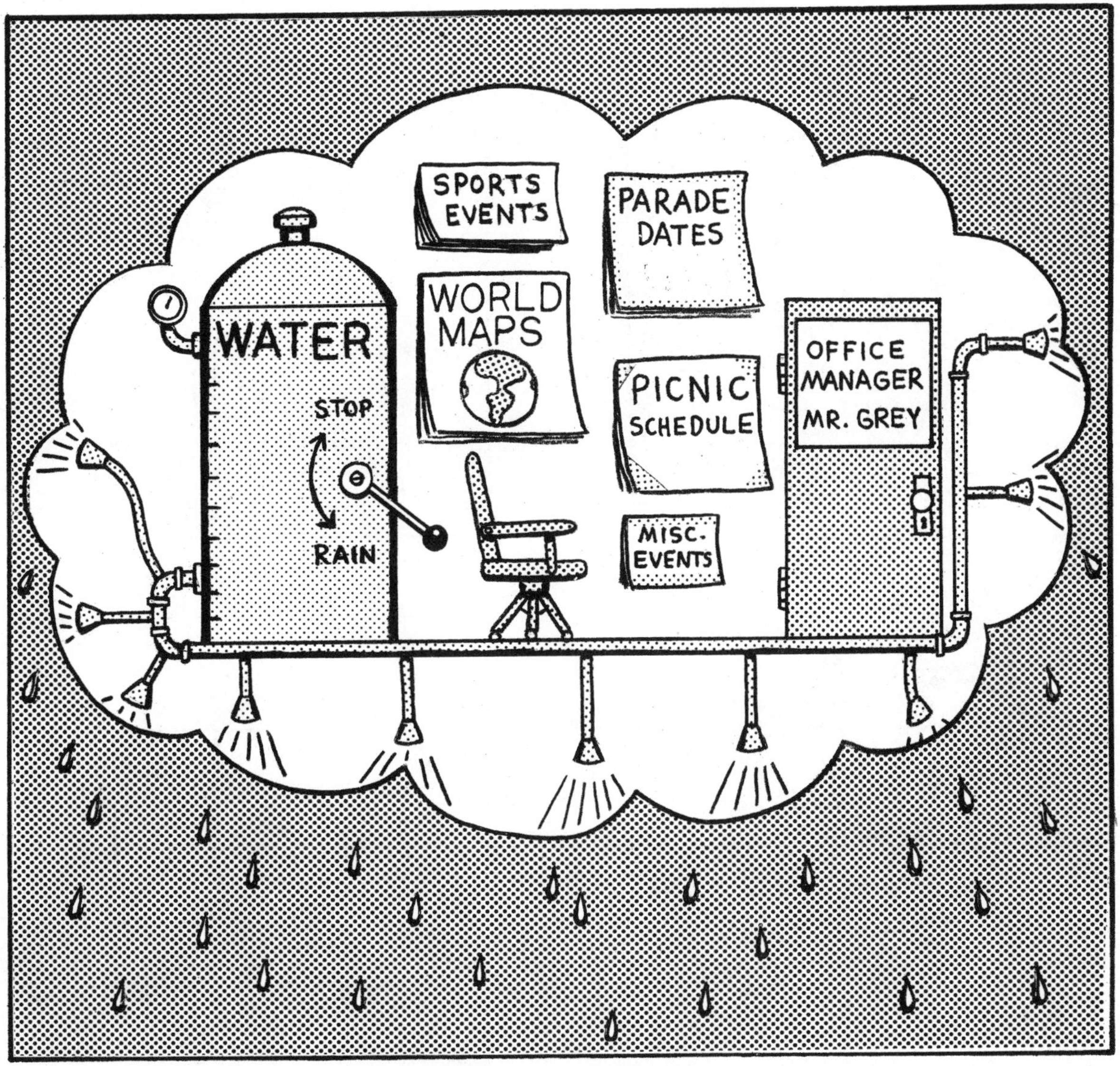
SPORTS EVENTS
PARADE DATES
WORLD MAPS
WATER
STOP
RAIN
PICNIC SCHEDULE
OFFICE MANAGER MR. GREY
MISC. EVENTS

Inside a rain cloud

Scratch-n-Sniff

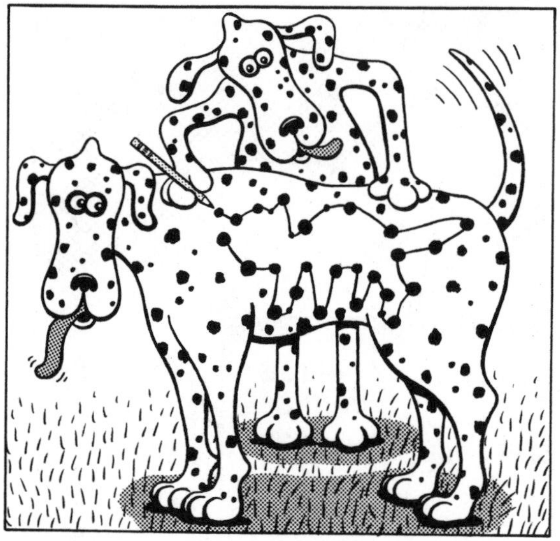

Dalmatians playing connect-a-dot

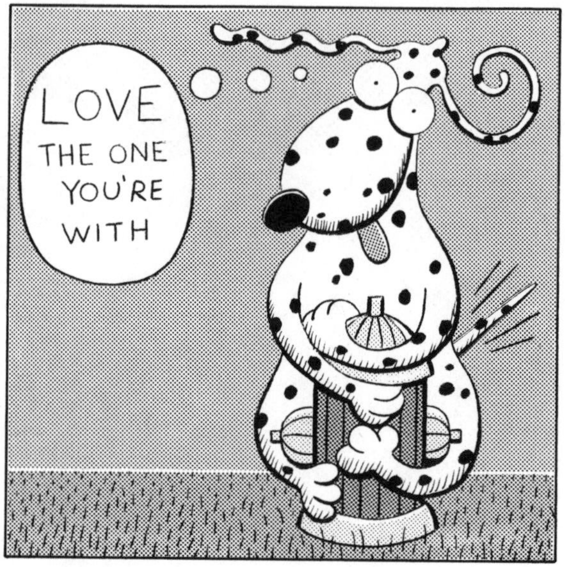
LOVE
THE ONE
YOU'RE
WITH

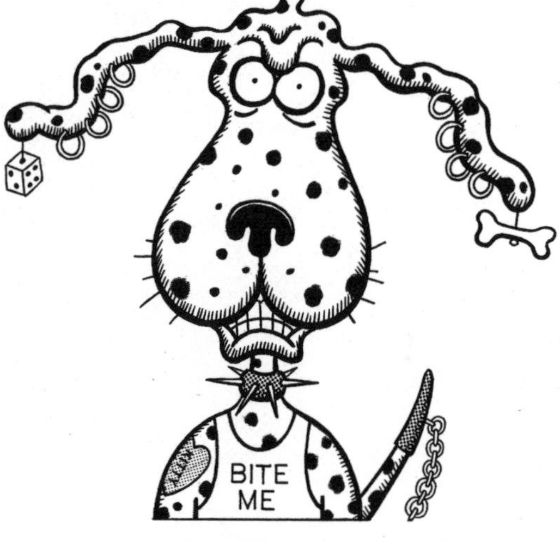
BITE
ME

Mad Dog

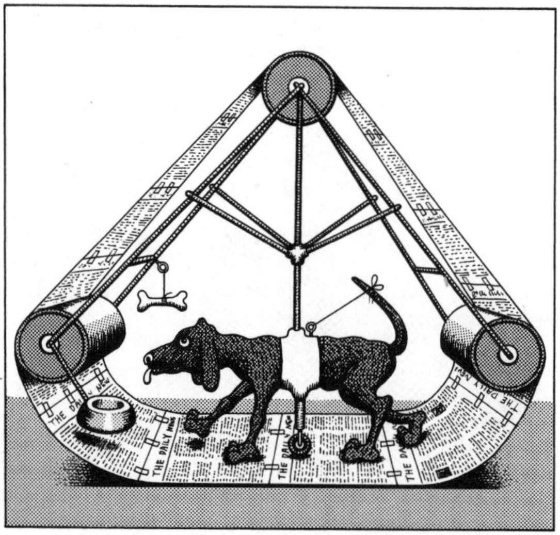

The ultimate paper-training device

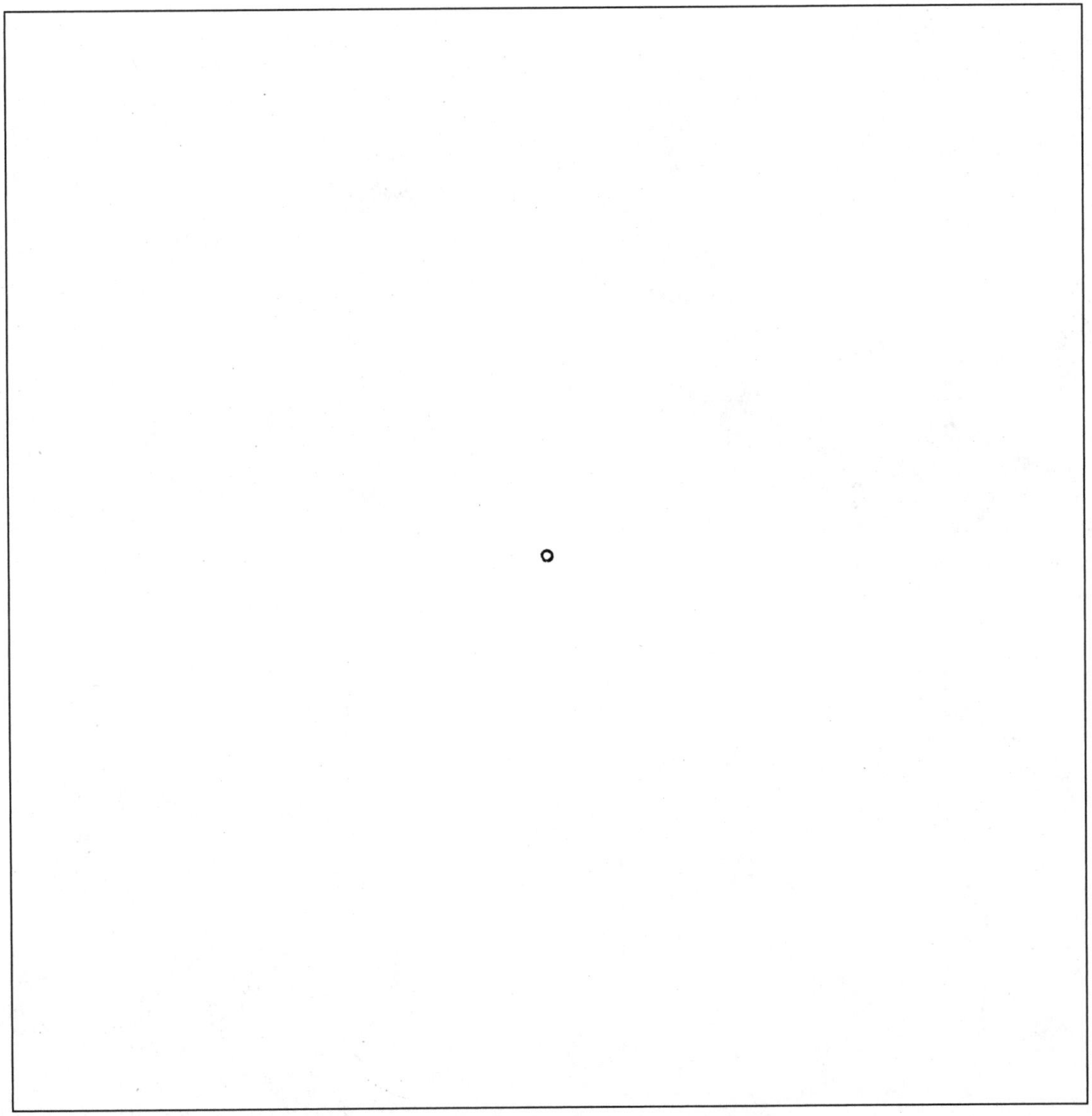

Flea collar

Less than Purrfect

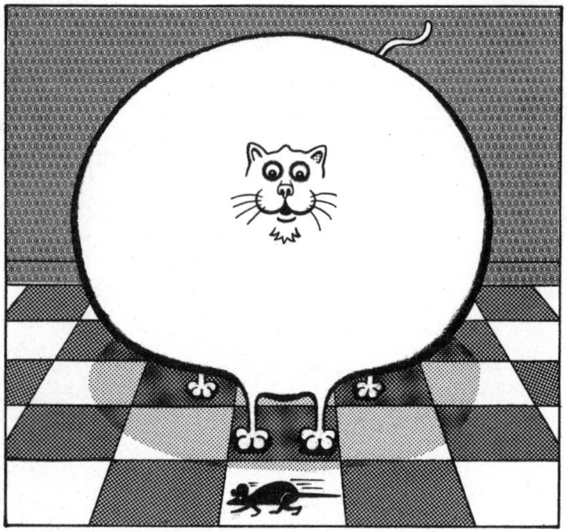

Fat chance

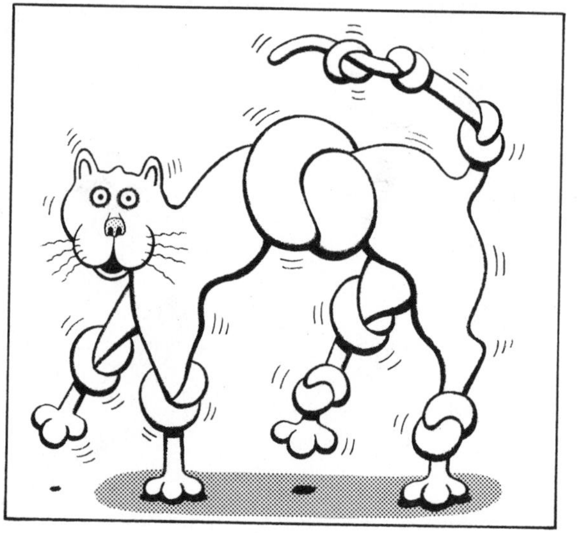

Hyperactive cat

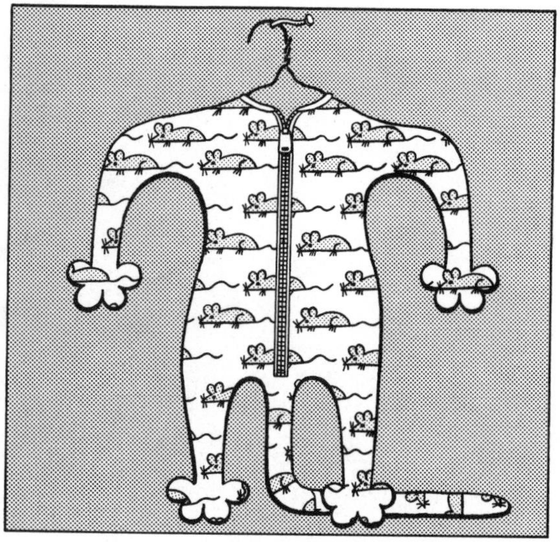

The cat's pajamas

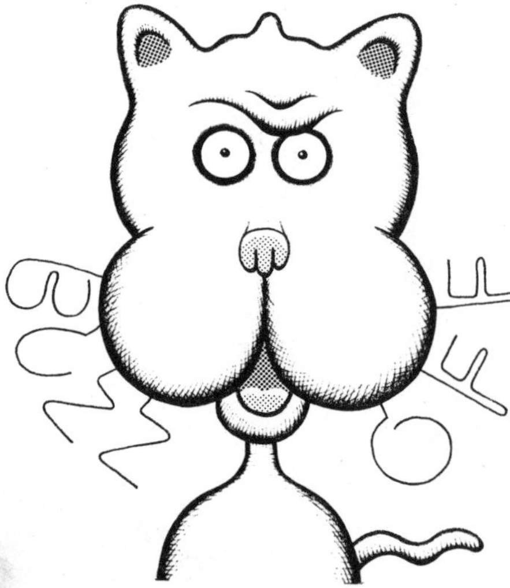

Cat with an attitude

Greetings from Idaho

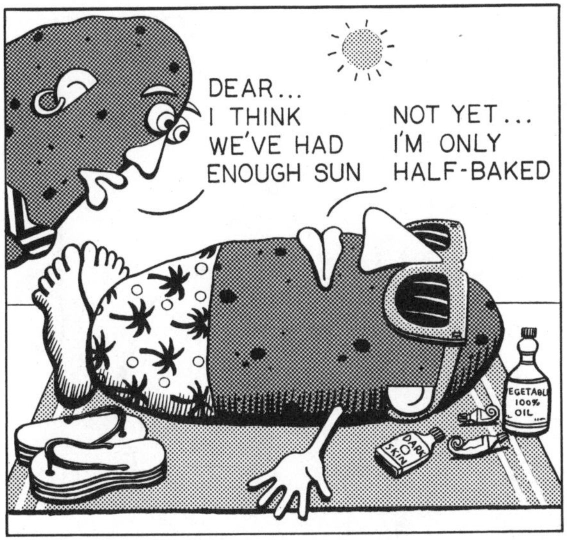
DEAR...
I THINK
WE'VE HAD
ENOUGH SUN
NOT YET...
I'M ONLY
HALF-BAKED
VEGETABLE
100%
OIL
DARK
SKIN

Born to bake

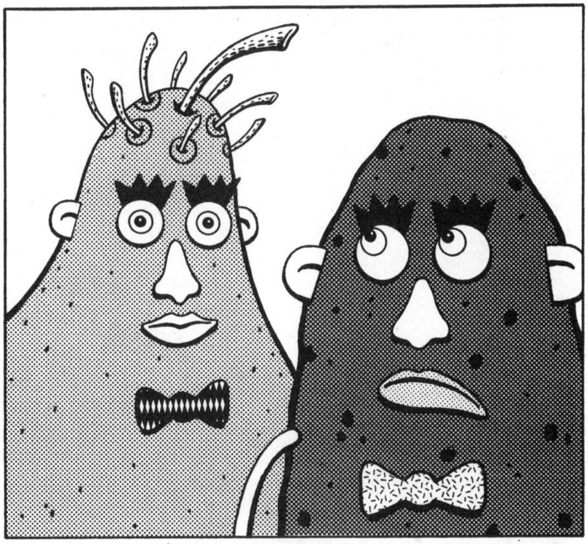

Mr. Potato Head checks out Mr. Pear's new stem transplants

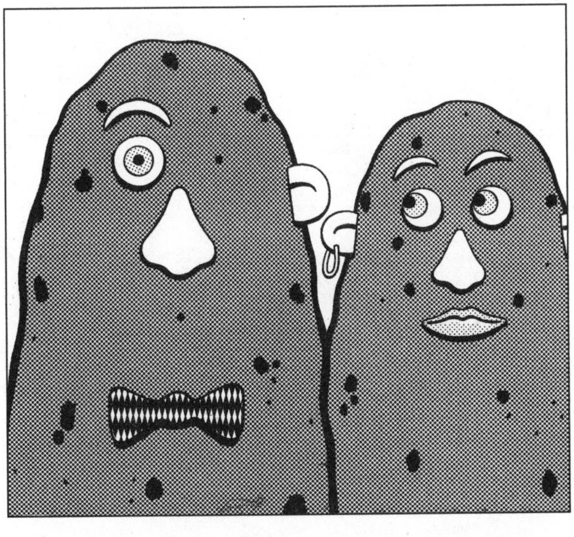

Mrs. Potato Head loves Mr. Potato Head even though some of his pieces are missing

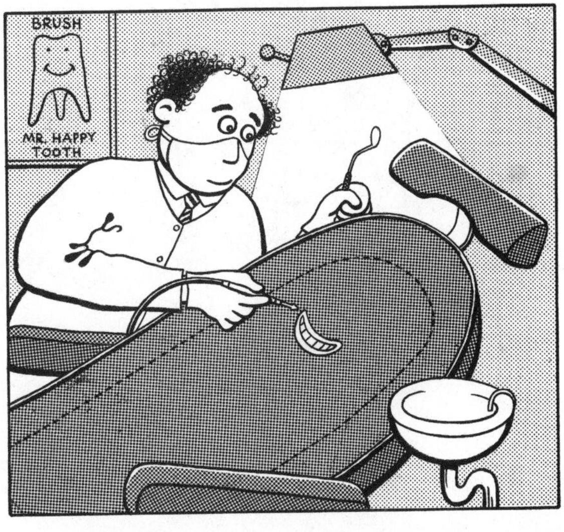
BRUSH
MR. HAPPY
TOOTH

Mr. Potato Head doesn't have to go to the dentist...he just mails in his mouth

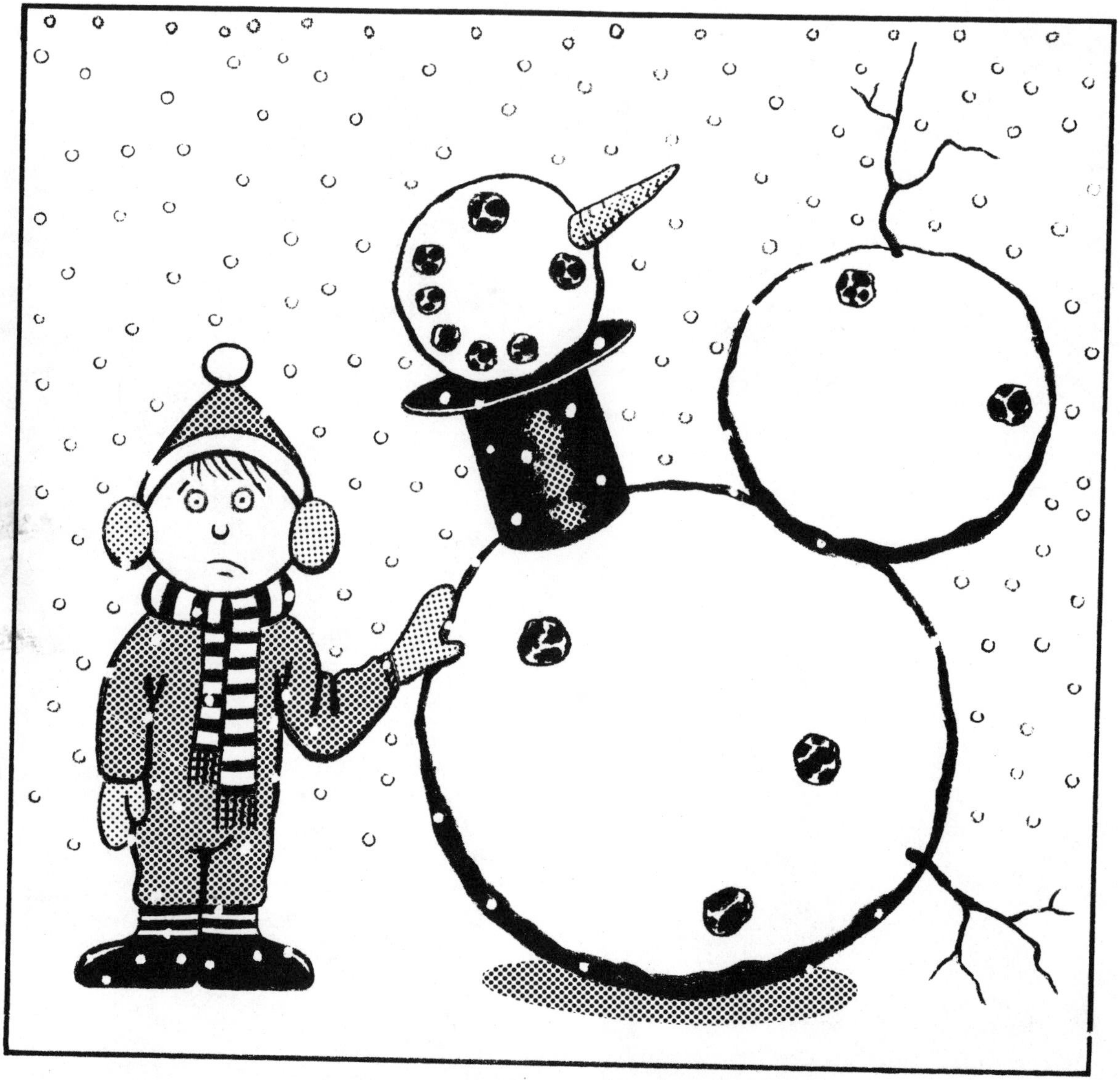

Dyslexia

Point of No Return

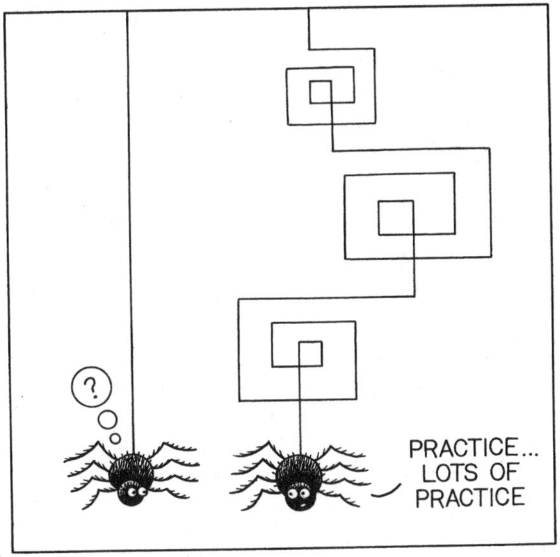
?
PRACTICE...
LOTS OF
PRACTICE

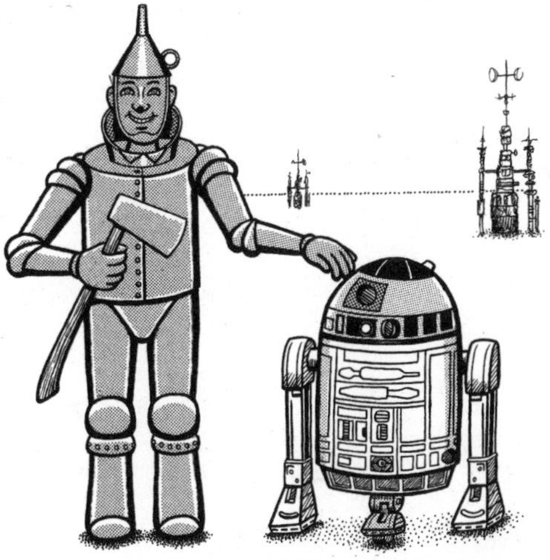

A little-known fact: The Tin Man tried out for the part of C3PO in the Star Wars movies

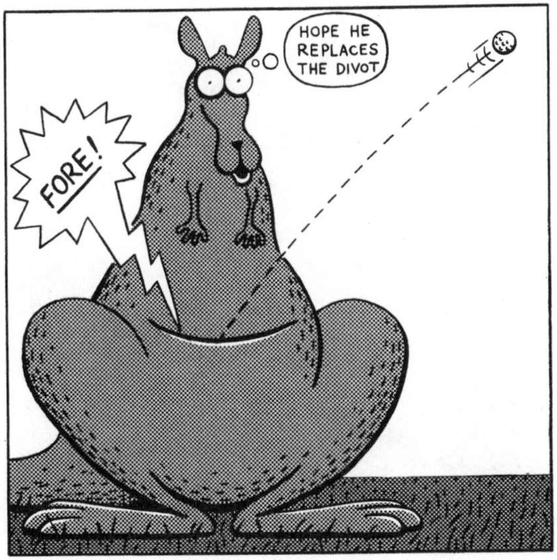
HOPE HE
REPLACES
THE DIVOT
FORE!

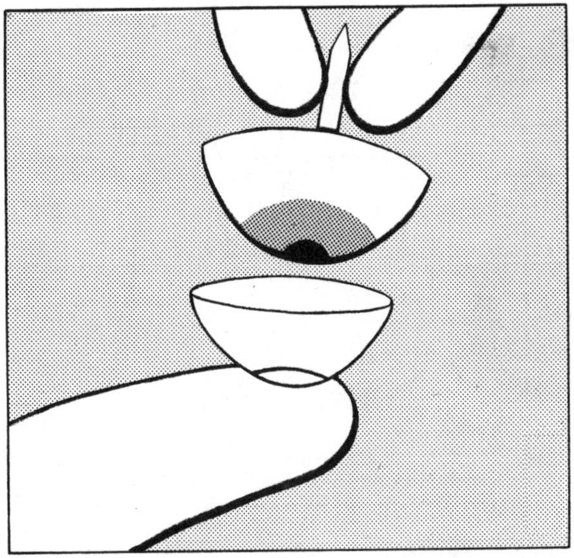

How Mr. Potato Head puts on his contact lens

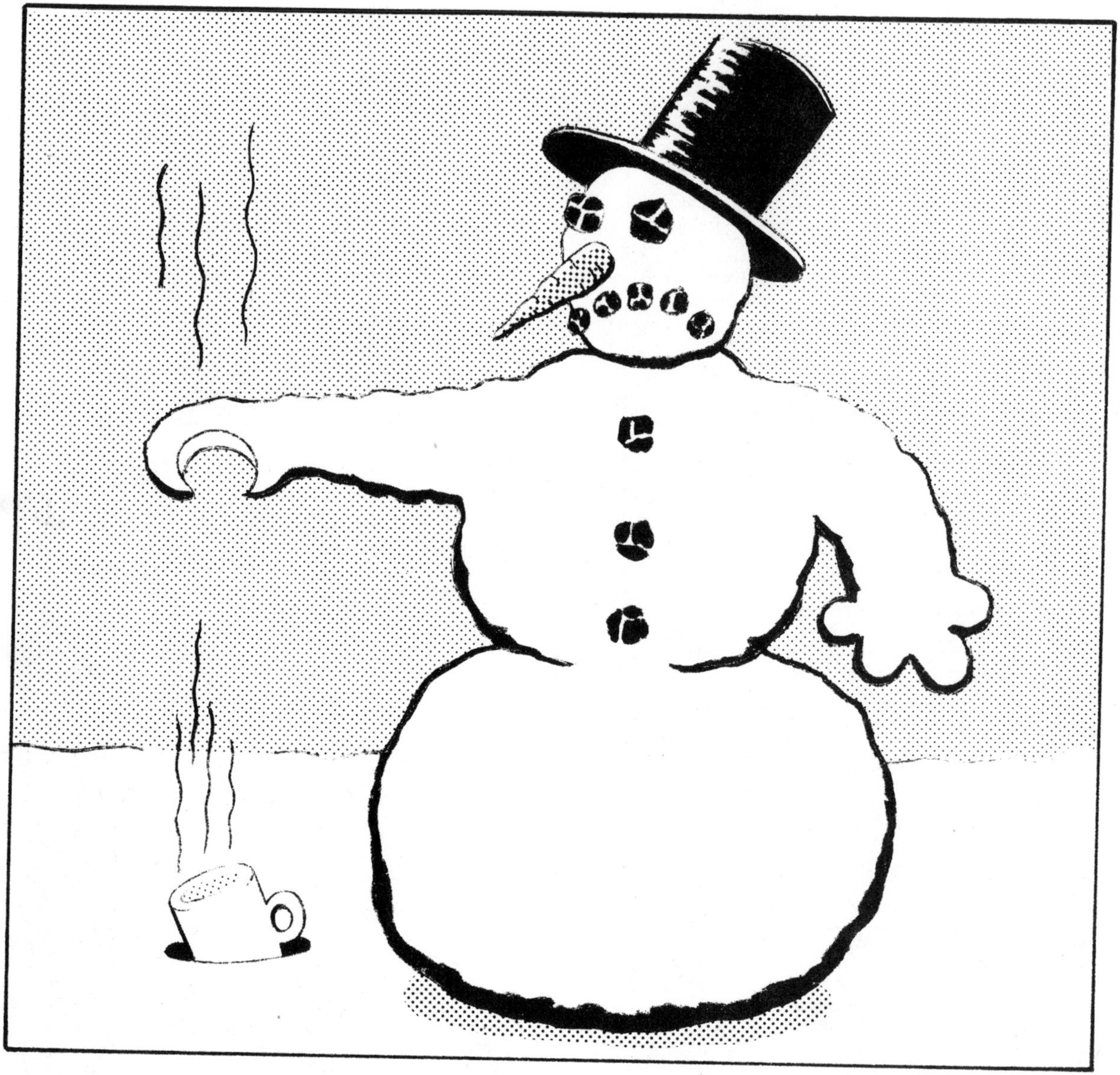

author bio

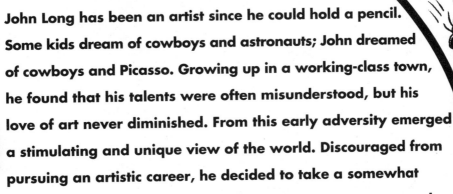

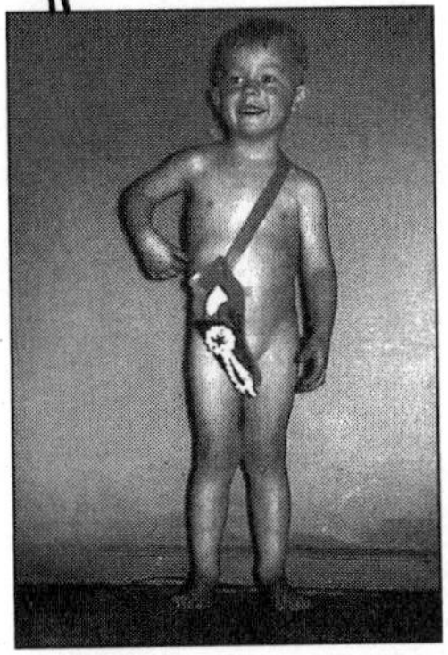

John Long has been an artist since he could hold a pencil. Some kids dream of cowboys and astronauts; John dreamed of cowboys and Picasso. Growing up in a working-class town, he found that his talents were often misunderstood, but his love of art never diminished. From this early adversity emerged a stimulating and unique view of the world. Discouraged from pursuing an artistic career, he decided to take a somewhat "safer" job as a firefighter. The strength of his artistic passion persevered, however, and he even found himself drawing between fires. Fifteen years and many fires later, John retired to become a full-time artist and now lives a life of continuous creativity—often working every day and most nights. About thirteen years ago, John's wife, Janet, also an accomplished artist, challenged him to express his humorous side. It was then that John's fine arts education met the art of cartooning—and he has never looked back.

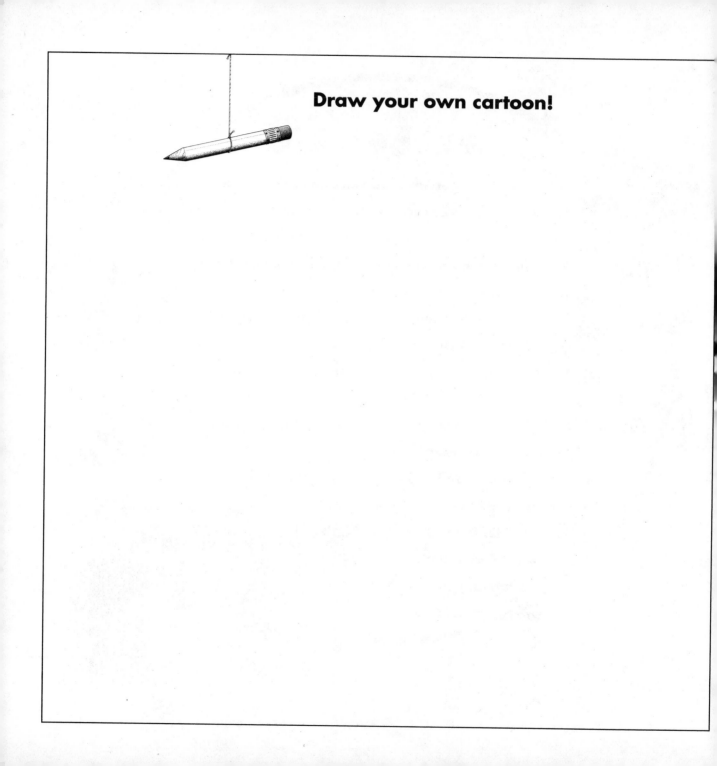

Draw your own cartoon!

COOL!

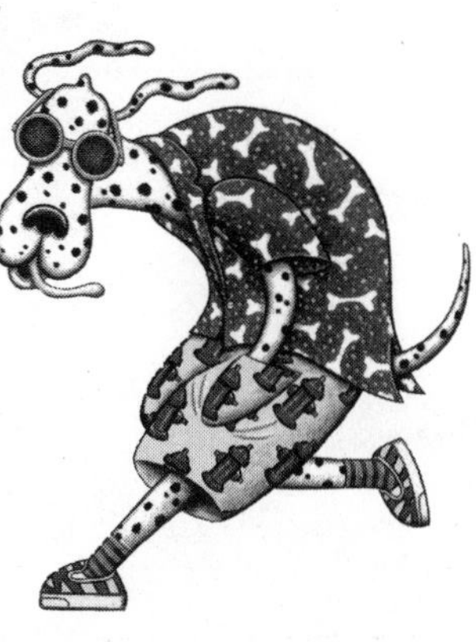

Draw on, over or around me!

Erase

Sketch

Draw

Shade

Jot

Trace

Scribble

Fill-in

Draw partner!

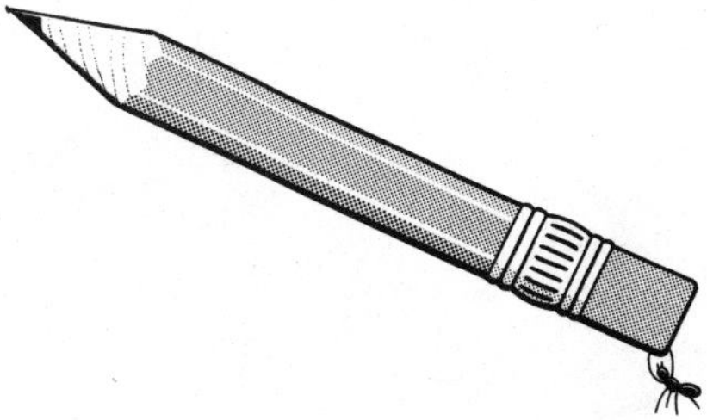